RELIGIOUS SECTS AND SOCIAL DEVELOPMENT

RELIGIOUS SECTS AND SOCIAL DEVELOPMENT

A Comparative Study of Jains, Christians and Sikhs

POORNIMA JAIN

RAWAT PUBLICATIONS
Jaipur • New Delhi • Bangalore • Hyderabad • Guwahati

ISBN 81-316-0262-1

Published by
Prem Rawat for **Rawat Publications**
Satyam Apts., Sector 3, Jawahar Nagar, Jaipur 302 004 (India)
Phone: 0141 265 1748/7006 Fax: 0141 265 1748
E-mail: info@rawatbooks.com
Website: rawatbooks.com

New Delhi Office
4858/24, Ansari Road, Daryaganj, New Delhi 110 002
Phone: 011 2326 3290

Also at Bangalore, Hyderabad and Guwahati

Typeset by Inosoft Systems, Noida
Printed at Chaman Enterprises, New Delhi

Contents

Preface

The present study examines some sociological dimensions of Religious Sects and Social Development. The choice of the subject is determined primarily by our desire to study in depth the dynamic processes that sustain and foster development. The role of religious sects (viz., Roman Catholic and Protestant of Christianity, Degambar and Swetambar of Jainism along with Sikhism respectively in general and also in a comparative way has been a relatively unexplored area of research. Although, religion and social change have been studied by a few scholars in Indian context.

So, the aim of this sociological inquiry is to establish a relationship between religious sects and social development which may in turn, remain a contribution to the fields of Sociology of Religion. This study scrutinizes the social development of the major religious sects (of minority groups) of Agra city. It presents in detail the social development of different sects at two levels, i.e., objective and subjective. Analysis of the objective indicators of their (sect's) development includes education, occupation, inter-generational occupational mobility, income per month, assets, health etc. Probe into the subjective dimensions of their development relates to the question of their attitudes towards religiosity, ritualism, sectarianism, 'conflict-harmony' and modernism.

The inspiration for the present work came from Yogendra Singh who is a unique combination of knowledge and person. His unique direction has been my shield against many deviations in this research. For this, I am greatly indebted to him. I must pay my deepest thanks to the leaders and members of different religious sects of Agra city for their enormous cooperation in our work. I must also express my gratitude to Sudipto Kaviraj for useful discussions.

I am also thankful to my teachers T.K. Oommen, R.K. Jain, M.N. Panini and Ehsanul Haq for giving me valuable suggestions.

I am specially thankful to K.L. Sharma, Ex-Vice Chancellor Rajasthan University, Jaipur, and Pro-Vice Chancellor, JNU, New

Delhi, who has rendered his valuable help both by words and deeds which has helped in revitalizing my morals and catalyzing my work. I shall remain indebted to him throughout my life.

I am also grateful to my friend Kameshwar Choudhary for giving indispensable suggestions.

Further, I must acknowledge my supreme debt of gratitude to my husband, Rajesh Sharma, my parents-in-law, Gopi Chand Sharma and Sarla Sharma, my daughter Ishita Sharma and son Gaurav Sharma for their invaluable cooperation throughout my research period. I am also thankful to my niece, Nidhi Jain who helped me in establishing rapport with most of the Sikh families who formed a part of the sample of study.

I am thankful to library staff of Jawaharlal Nehru University, New Delhi, Nehru Memorial Library, New Delhi, Sapru House, New Delhi, ICSSR, New Delhi, National Archives, New Delhi, IIPA, New Delhi, Max Mueller Bhawan, New Delhi, Agra University, Agra, Collectorate, Agra, The Cathedral, Agra and Institute of Social Sciences, Agra.

Over and above all I am greatly thankful to The Supreme Father without whose mercy and grace this work could not have been accomplished.

Poornima Jain

1 Introduction

The Problem

Social development has been one of the important goals of every Third World country. Each such society has set up its goals according to its need. Our government, since launching of the First Five-Year Plan (1951), initiated a process of development aimed not only at raising the standard of living of the people but also opening out to them new avenues for a better life. Since then, the Indian government has consistently been laying emphasis upon the development of our country, Eighth Plan recognizes 'human resource development' as the core of all developmental effort. It says:

> It is only healthy and educated people who can contribute to economic growth and this growth, in turn, will contribute to the human well-being. The priority sectors to be included in the development programme are health, education, literacy and basic needs including drinking water, housing and welfare programmes for the weaker sections.

It also recognizes the basic need to initiate people's participation in the process of development. The attitude of passive observance and total dependence on the government for development activities has become infutile. It required peoples' positive attitude in taking initiative themselves.

It has been observed that the pace of development is comparatively slower in India as compared to the western countries. Reason assigned for is value system which to a greater extent is determined by the religious values. Recently, there has been a lot of discussion upon the "role of religion in socio-economic development". It is generally agreed that religion, whatever its ultimate orientation, is very much bound up with the totality of the social process and the concreteness of the individual existence, especially in Asia, where religion largely shapes the traditional forms of culture and being so deeply involved in social and personal life, inevitably it is felt, religion often has profound implications for the course of historical development, encouraging or inhibiting economic, political and social modernization (Dube, 1965).

Interplay between religion and economic development has aroused intense controversies. First, it is held that economic development (capitalism) causes religion (Marx, 1976; Tawney, 1926; Schoffeleers and Meizers, 1978). Second school of thought, whose main profounder is Max Weber asserts that religion caused capitalistic development especially Protestantism (Runciman, 1985; Kariyil, 1988), on the one hand, and Hinduism and its associated value system and institutions (traditional Indian) such as the doctrine of *karma*, caste system, joint family etc., hinder economic development. Later, thesis of Weber attracted several supporters (Kapp, 1963; Misra, 1962; Myrdal, 1986; Andreski, 1983; Sorenson, 1988; Saran, 1963) and it has been felt that cultural factors retard development. As a reaction to this, it has been established that "Hinduism and other Indian religions do not serve as a barrier in economic development" (Singh, 1989; Dube, 1965; Timberg, 1978; Nevaskar, 1971; Narayan Swami, 1988; Chandra, 1964; Singer, 1972; Srinivas, 1966; Karve, 1968; Kusumakar, 1982; Majumdar, 1965; Bose, 1975; Vidyarthi, 1970; Sinha, 1977; Saberwal, 1971). Siayigh doubts that religion determines positively or negatively economic development. Fifth school of thought believes that factors other than religion are responsible for development (Hagen, 1962; Schumpeter, 1949; Aron, 1967). The above controversies indicate that the relationship between religion/sect and socio-economic development is a complex one. In most of the studies religion and sect are used interchangeably. In the present study, sect is used to refer more crystallized code of conduct.

For fulfilling the goal of development, people's participation in the development programmes is necessary and to achieve this their attitudes towards development need to be changed. These attitudes to a large extent are shaped by an individual's affiliation to a particular sect/religion. So, the problem selected here, for study is to examine the role of sect affiliation in forming the attitudes of an individual towards factors that may have significant implications upon development process.

Social development has been viewed differently as stated above. Broadly speaking, it is the overall progression of the society (Pimpley et al., 1989). It is a process of social and economic transformation of the society.

Former includes social-attitudinal change pertaining to the desired goals.

In the present analysis social development implies level of education, type of occupation and occupational mobility, participation in social activities (as pointed out by Lerner as two of the three indicators, besides empathy; of modernization, which is used synonymously with development; quoted by Dube, 1988:17) such as "club membership, office held, health, income, property and assets owned". Attitudinal change is measured on five scales constructed "by the researcher on religiosity, ritualism, sectarianism, conflict and harmony and modernization, also their attitudes toward selection of their children's education, women's education, women's participation in jobs and scientific outlook, as the process of development is impeded without emergence of mobile personalities" (Lerner, quoted by Dube, 1988: 19). The present study deals with changes in the social-institutional and the value-attitudinal dimension. Our society has been suffering from a long period with the evil institutions and practices of caste, joint family, purdah system, communal riots, ritualism, illiteracy, lower status of women, social activism (measured in terms of active participation in various organizations), religious orthodoxy, sectarianism and traditionalism.

In the present study, an attempt has been made to analyse the relationship of Jain, Christian and Sikh sects with social development measured in terms of attitudinal changes in the above mentioned dimensions in Agra city. On the basis of available literature, experiences and observations, following indicators for analysing social development have been taken into account, viz., religiosity, ritualism, sectarianism, modernization and conflict and harmony.

The focus is on the attitudes of members of Christian (Roman Catholic and Protestant), Jain (Degambar and Swetambar) and Sikh sects regarding education, employment, medical aid rendered to the sect people and to society at large, charity to religious organizations along with the above-mentioned indicators.

It is assumed that lesser the degree of religiosity more developed a sect is, similarly, lesser the feeling of sectarianism (i.e., more liberal attitude) more developed a sect is, lesser the degree of conflict but higher the degree of harmony (measured in terms of inter-/intra-sectoral and inter-religion interaction) more is the degree of development. Likewise, more modern (seen in terms of rational attitudes towards various traditional institutions and practices) is considered more developed. A sect's degree of development is also measured in terms of some objective indicators such as education, occupational mobility, health, family structure, income, assets etc.

The present study deals with the nature and functioning of the religious sects of the Jain, Christian and Sikh in Agra city in the light of above sociological propositions. Agra has been one of the oldest and important settlers of the three religious communities/sects. Christians comprise the Roman Catholics and Protestants, former being predominantly Anglo-Indians and latter purely Indian converts. Among Jains, Degambars are mostly natives of Agra whereas Swetambars have mostly immigrated from Pakistan/Punjab during partition of India in 1947. Sikhs are also migrants from Pakistan and Punjab after 1947 and 1984 respectively. Besides differences in the origin and growth of these sects, variation is seen in their attitudes towards religion, social and economic activities.

The present study also deals with the impact of religious sects on social development of the individual. Since the advent of humanity, religion has been at the very roots of man's development in all spheres of life, but in the present time the role of religion/sect in man's social development is questioned. Therefore, the study examines following specific problems:

1. What is the relationship of religious sect with social and cultural life of its members?
2. What changes have been taking place in the attitudes of Jain, Christian and Sikh sects in the ritual performances?
3. What is the relationship between religiosity, ritualism, sectarianism, conflict and harmony and modernism, and how are these influenced by age, sect-affiliation, education, occupation and income of an individual?
4. What is the interplay between sect and society: how does sect shape the society and vice versa?
5. What are the differential effects of religious sects on the social development of individuals in particular and society in general?

Rationale for the Study

Most studies conducted so far on the relationship of religion/sect and socio-economic development has revealed that religion has not proved a hindrance in development. But no comparative study of socio-economic development vis-a-vis sect of different religions has been made so far. This inspired the researcher to take up this study. All the three religions constitute the minority groupings in Indian society. Their ratio in the total population of India is: Christians 2.4%, Sikhs 2% and Jains 0.5% (*India*, 1991). Nevertheless, some are more developed as compared with others. The relevance of this study also lies in developing a perspective useful for the overall development of our society. From the subject's point of view it is important to study such problems because in the 'sociology of religion', study of sect forms an important and specialized area. Its significance also lies in studying the relationship of sect with social development on one hand, and structural and ideological differentiation within the religious system itself on the other. In this sense, religious sects constitute both indicators of causative elements in the process of social transformation and vice versa. A sect has been defined as a group of people following some leader, whether his influence be permanent and worldwide, e.g., Calvin or local and temporary, e.g., Antoinett Bourignon. The group may maintain its footing within an organized communion, like the Clapham sect; it may actively or passively take up separate existence like the Jansenists (James: 315).

Methodology

The Sample

From the records of the Municipal Corporation of Agra, five wards (Hariparwat for Roman Catholics, Shahganj for Protestants, Rakabganj for Degambars, Lohamandi for Swetambars and Sadar for Sikhs) having maximum concentration of the five sects were selected for the present study. Afterwards, a census of all the five wards of the respective sects was conducted for knowing the background data of each sect. This was followed by a pilot survey carried on ten units from each sect selected randomly. Then, the major survey was conducted.

Households for survey were randomly (lottery method) selected from each ward. From Hariparwat ward 50 household of Roman Catholics, from Shahganj ward 50 household of Protestants, 50 each from Rakabganj and Lohamandi wards of Degambars and Swetambars respectively, and 100 households of Sikh from Sadar ward. Sects among Sikhs could not be identified because of the unavoidable socio-political situation prevailing in the country. Thus, total sample comprises three hundred households.

Two sample t-test was used for the testing of the hypothesis of the equality of population mean. Suppose we have two random samples of sizes n_1 and n_2 having values X_1, ... X_n and Y_1, Y_2, ... Y_n drawn from two different normal population having different mean.

We wish to test the hypothesis :

$H_0 = u_1 = u_2$

On the basis of the selected samples, we used the following test statistics for testing this hypothesis:

X–Y

t= ....

1 1

s....... + ...

n_1 n_2

where X = mean of the first sample

Y = mean of the second sample

and $s^1{}_2$ is known as pooled variance and is defined as:

$(n_1–1)\ s_1^2 + (n_2–1)\ s_2^2$

s_2 = ...

$n_1+n_2–2$

where

s_1^2 = variance of the first sample

s_2^2 = variance of the second sample.

In our case sample sizes are very large, so we used normal approximation, etc.

if t calculated < 1.96 accept H_O

and if t calculated > 1.96 reject H_O

where 1.96 is the tabulated value of N (0, 1) at 5% level of significance.

Methodology

Methods used in the study are historical and comparative. The study has been focused on the variation in social, cultural-attitudinal aspects of different sects that have shaped their present state of social development. This difference and the causes of social development of particular sect have to be understood historically, and therefore, it becomes necessary to trace the social origin and development of various sects in relation to their involvement in various activities of life. In addition, comparative method is employed to analyse the difference in the social background and development of different sects within one religious community and various communities.

Techniques of Data Collection

Observation

For the purpose of present study, survey research technique has been used. Both participant and non-participant observation techniques have been used. Participant observation has been used in studying social and ritual practices of the sects.

Interview Schedule

The interview schedule is divided into seven major sections viz., background information, religiosity, ritualism, sect and society, conflict and harmony, modernism, and development.

Focused Interview

Nature of our study demanded focused interview for in-depth attitudinal investigation. This technique was used for collecting information from the leaders (social or religious) of the various sects.

Notes were not taken at the time of interview with the exception of some information recorded in praise of the respondents. As soon as the interview was over, the recorded points were elaborated. Field-work was supported by memory aids which proved of utmost value.

Even though, we covered a variety of issues in the interviews, some of the main items investigated could be identified as follows:

(i) Attitudes of the sect leaders (both religious and social) towards members of the other sects within the same religious group.
(ii) Role of a sect in providing medical services to its members and society at large.
(iii) Attitude of sect leaders in providing employment in their educational institutions to their sect members.
(iv) Issues related to role of sect organization in promoting development.

In all we covered five leaders, one from each sect. Subjects selected for interviews were those who were recommended by most of their sect fellows. On an average, one interview lasted for one and a half hour.

Attitude Measurement

For the analysis of sect's role in social development attitudinal scales on religiosity, ritualism, sectarianism, conflict and harmony and modernism have been constructed.

Verbal Method

Relevant information was gathered through verbal method from the elderly members of the sects, mainly regarding history of the sects.

Building Rapport

Even though the author herself belonged to the same city and to one of the sects (i.e., Degambar) under study, it was not enough for a free entry into three different communities. Access to Christian sects, i.e., Protestant and Roman Catholic, was made possible with the help of Pastors and Archbishop of the churches and of the cathedral who introduced the respondent with the church and the clergy. Problem of rapport building was not much with the sects of Christianity because, first, they formed the highly qualified community and second, most of the respondents felt that the respondent, an educated person, also belonged to their own category. With Jains, reference of the researcher as Jain helped much in making closer links with the community. Rappert with the Sikhs was established by participating in religious ceremonies in Gurudwaras and also with the help of known persons of the community. Those who were not known were given reference of the Granthiji of the gurudwara and other Sikhs who were already interviewed.

Roman Catholic community was found to be more orthodox as compared to other communities. Most of the respondents showed their reluctance in giving information, a few outrightly refused to answer and one respondent after giving first four information snatched the schedule from the interviewer's hand and struck of all the information given and finally tore away the first page of the schedule and started arguing with the researcher. Most of the respondents cooperated with the researcher.

Maximum cooperation was received from Protestants. They showed a positive attitude towards the research work. Data collection was most easy from this community.

Degambars were also orthodox. In the beginning, data collection was comparatively easier, but later on as they came to know about the researcher's marital status (inter-caste marriage) they withdrew from giving the information. After much persuasion it was made possible to receive the information. On the whole, researcher got cooperation.

Swetambars were found more liberal in their attitudes. More extrovert than their counterparts, they easily rendered all the information excepting that of income which was not openly given by any member of any sect especially those belonging to business class.

Among Sikhs there were two types of respondents. One who had been staying at Agra since a long period easily gave the information (although after establishing rapport) and others who had migrated to Agra in 1984 formed a very orthodox group and were reluctant even in talking to the researcher. On the whole the entire Sikh community was found feeling very insecure, but with the help of some known persons, respondents were taken into confidence. Overall, they gave their cooperation.

After careful selection of the sample from the respective sects of Jain, Christian, and Sikh religions, data collection was started. The researcher personally visited each household on an average of three times and gathered information about their background. Scales were constructed on social and religious practices, ritualism, sectarianism, conflict and harmony, and modernism. The interview schedule constructed for the present study was used to get the required data from head of every household (as they are the decision makers in most of family matters and act as agent of change) selected in the sample. Responses recorded were carefully analysed themewise. This analysis is presented in the succeeding chapters.

Reliability of Data

To a large extent some of the oral responses and reports by the different sect members could easily be matched with actual observation and by asking from their fellow sect members and other neighbours. Most of the information was verified from others. An attempt has been made to obtain verification of some of the less obvious aspects such as income, participation in various activities, inter-sect participation etc.

Secondary Sources of Data Collection

We have also used secondary sources for collecting empirical data, both qualitative and quantitative. We gathered relevant data on various organizations and their role in social development, number of baptisms, matrimonies, burials, number of various sect fellows in Agra from very beginning, number of temples, gurudwaras and churches and data of their inception etc. We got these details from the church registers, gurudwara records and trusts offices of Agra as well as from the cathedral, district and national archival records, different libraries of Agra and Delhi, Agra Collectorate, census reports, especially, District Census Handbook of Agra, Agra District Gazetteers, manuscripts, Catholic directories etc. We also looked through several writings on the sociology of religion, history of the sects, religion and development, religion and change and also some selective writings on Indian religions and the theories of economic development.

Chapterization

Chapter first focuses on discussion of the problem of study and the methodology used for the same. Second chapter deals with the review of related literature on Weber's "Protestant ethic and the spirit of capitalism" thesis both in Western and Indian contexts, religion and development and specific studies pertaining to Christian, Jain and Sikh religious communities. Third chapter relates to the history of Jain, Christian and Sikh communities in Agra. Chapter four deals with the social and religious practices of the different sects and effect of age, sect, education, occupation and income upon religiosity and ritualism and attitudinal changes in ritual and ceremonial performance in various sects. Chapter five examines the relationship between sect and society that is to see whether sect affiliation shapes social relations or vice versa. Sixth chapter focuses on the conflict and harmony within the sect and among the different sects and how conflict and harmony is affected by age, sect affiliation, education, occupation and income of an individual. Seventh chapter centres on sect and modernism. Chapter eighth discusses sect and development and forms the last substantive chapter and ninth gives the major findings and methodological and substantive gains of the study.

References

Andreski, S. (ed.) (1983), *Max Weber on Capitalism, Bureaucracy and Religion*, George Allen and Unwin, London.

Aron, R. (1967), *Industrial Society: Three Essays on Ideology and Development*, Praeger, New York.

Bose, N.K. (1975), *Structure of Hindu Society*, (Trans.) from Bengali by Andre Beteille, Orient Longman, New Delhi.

Chandra, B. (1964), "The Problems of Poverty and Indian National Leadership", *Enquiry*, 2 (54–106).

Dube, S.C. (1965), "Cultural Problems in the Economic Development of India", in *Religion and Progress in Modern Asia*, R.N. Bellah (ed.), The Free Press, New York.

——— (1988), *Modernization and Development*, Vistaar Publication, New Delhi.

First Five-Year Plan (1951), Planning Commission, Government of India, New Delhi.

Eighth Five-Year Plan (1992), Planning Commission, Government of India, New Delhi.

Hagen, E.E. (1962), *On the Theory of Social Change: How Economic Growth Begins*, The Dorsey Press Inc. Homewood, Illinois.

India (1991), A Reference Annual, Publication Division, Ministry of Information and Broadcasting, Government. of India, New Delhi.

James, E.O., *Encyclopaedia of Religion and Ethics*, p. 315.

Kapp, W.K. (1963), *Hindu Culture. Economic Development and Economic Planning in India*, Asia Publishing House, Bombay

Kariyil, A. (1988), "Religion and Material Development", *Journal of Dharma*, XIII, October–November, (312–327).

Karve, D.G. (1968), *Hindu Society: An Interpretation*, (ed.) 2, Deshmukh, Poona.

Kusumakar, H. (1982), "Colourful Re-enactment of Jain Mythology", *The Times of India*, 3 February.

Majumdar, R.C. (1965), *Swami Vivekananda: A Historical Review*, General Printers and Publishers, Calcutta.

Marx, K. (1967), *Capital*, International Publishers, New York.

Misra, V. (1962), *Hinduism and Economic Growth*, Oxford University Press, Bombay, p. 206.

Myrdal, G. (1986), *Asian Drama* (3 vols.), Pantheon Books, New York.

Narayan, Swami (1988), quoted by Antony Kariyil in *Religion and Material Development*, op. cit.

Nevaskar, B. (1971), *Capitalists without Capitalism: The Jains of India and the Ouakers of the West*, West Fort C.T. Greenwood.

Pimpley, P.N., Singh, K.P. and Mahajan, A. (eds.), (1989), *Social Development*, Rawat Publications, Jaipur, p. 4.

Runciman, W.G. (ed.), (1985), *Max Weber*, Cambridge University Press, London.

Saran, A.K. (1963), "Hinduism and Economic Development in India", *Archives de Socialogie des Religions*, 15 (87–94).

Schoffeleers, M. and Meizers, D. (1978), *Religion, Nationalism and Economic Action*, Van Garum, Assen, The Netherlands.

Schumpeter, J.A. (1949), *The Theory of Economic Development*, Cambridge, Mass.

Singh, Y. (1989), "Relevance of Max Weber for the Understanding of Indian Reality", in *Perspectives on Capitalism, Marx Keynes, Schumpeter and Weber*, Krishna Bhardwaj & Sudipto Kaviraj (Eds.), pp. 224–228.

Singer, M. (1972), *When a Great Tradition Modernizes: An Anthropological Approach to Indian Civilization*, Praeger, New York.

Sinha, S. (ed.) (1977), *Anthropology in India*, Vol. 1, *Cultural Anthropology*, Anthropological Survey of India, Calcutta.

Sorenson, G. (1988), "Internal and External Intertwined: Five Obstacles to Development in India", *Guru Nanak Journal of Sociology*, 9(1).

Srinivas, M.N. (1966), *Social Change in Modern India*, University of California Press, Berkeley.

Tawney, R.H. (1926), *Religion and the Rise of Capitalism*, The New American Library, New York.

Timberg, T.A. (1978), *The Marwaris: From Traders to Industrialists*, Vikas Publishing House, New Delhi.

Vidyarthi, L.P. (1970), "Socio-Cultural Implication of Industrialization in India: A Case Study of Tribal Bihar", Planning Commission, New Delhi.

2 Review of Literature

In the sociology of religion, relationship between religion and economic development constitutes the core. This mostly revolves around Max Weber's formulations which comprises two major theses: (a) Protestant ethic aided in the rise of the spirit of capitalism (16th–17th century Europe), and (b) that the ethic of the major Oriental religions was not conducive to capitalistic development in Asia. These theses and their antitheses have contributed significantly to the development of research work in this area. These formulations have been analysed both in Western and Indian contexts and more in case of India.

Firstly, we shall discuss briefly Weber's first thesis which has given a new dimension to Marx's thesis, 'capitalism causing religion'. Weber believed that Calvinism had the greatest effect upon capitalism. He emphasized on the doctrine of predestination (i.e., everything in man's life is predetermined), and calling. He believed that religious beliefs can be a major influence on economic behaviour. He argues that the capitalist enterprises are organized on rational and systematic lines. This is based on the 'spirit of capitalism', a set of ideas, ethics and values which implies that 'time is money, credit is money'. A businessman should behave with industry and frugality and punctuality and justice in all his dealings. This 'spirit of capitalism' is not a way of making money, but a way of life which has ethics, duties and obligations. Thus, the rise of 'ascetic protestantism' preceded the development of western capitalism. John Wesley writes, "Religion must produce industry and frugality. These can produce riches. These riches must not be spent on luxuries, fine clothes, lavish houses, frivolous entertainment but in the Glory of God. That is reinvesting in business. A vegetable diet and cold baths are recommended". These theses are both theoretically and empirically tested in Western and Indian contexts.

Western Context

Runciman (1978) argues that Weber did not claim that protestantism as such caused the development of industrial capitalism. Rather, he establishes a particular affinity between certain doctrines of protestantism implying a conception of salvation through the pursuit of a secular calling and the style of life necessary for the successful accumulation of capital through commercial activity. In his view, the ideal of 'Christian asceticism' is basically different from that of asceticism as conceived by any of the other great religions; as a result, it alone played a decisive role in the development of a 'rationalized' work ethic without which capitalism would not have developed in its present form. Aron (1967) posits the view that "protestantism is not the cause, but one of the causes of certain aspects of capitalism".

Troeltsch has established the fact that social reality is significantly influenced by religion. He has sought to adopt the ethical content of Christianity to modern social problems, faced with disintegrative consequences of capitalistic modernization, the social role of religion was rendered effective in shaping of human society. The author distinguishes two major functions of religion in modern societies: (i) of generating religious consciousness, and (ii) social function of religion. Objective religion in particular, i.e., the cultural institutions of religion (religious activities within the community worship etc.) furnishes a potential for social integration.

Collins (1986a) supports Weber's theory as the only comprehensive theory of the origins of capitalism. It is alone in accounting for the emergence of the full range of institutional and motivational conditions for large-scale world transforming capitalism. He feels that this theory needs to be supported by a theory of the operation of mature capitalism.

Munch (1988) argues that the features of ascetic protestantism are that communal association tend the universal with the individual being inwardly committed to the community's norms, and that it joins together economic action and a general system of meaning and values; neither of these features has been examined to a comparative extent under other religions.

Weber's thesis have aroused a great deal of controversy in Western as well as in Indian context. Some of the major critiques are Samuelson, Tawney, Schumpeter, Rachfahl and Brentano, Poggi etc.

Rachfahl and Brentano stressed that the spirit of capitalism originated even before the reformation. Tawney (1926) points to the socio-structural factors that determined entrepreneurship in post-reformation Europe. He argues that "capitalism caused the present day form of Protestantism" rather than vice versa. He admits that capitalism had existed in medieval Italy and Flanders (both Catholic dominated areas) and that the capitalistic spirit was "only too familiar to the saints and sages of the middle ages". Further, he asserts that the social situation of Calvinist rather than their ethics encouraged them to take up capitalistic tasks. He also believes that new religion (Puritan) has given way to capitalistic development.

Another view held by some is that there is no relation between religion and economic action. Samuelson (1961), on the basis of his studies on rise of capitalism in Europe and America, inferred that factors other than religion were involved in the promotion of trade, industry and capital formation.

Hagen (1962) illustrates that presence of one or another religious dogma is in no sense a necessary accompaniment of economic growth; it is not a cause. To him, increase in the scale of the society, the appearance of cities, literacy and modern means of communications, are all steps in the transition to economic growth rather than causes, same applies to change in religious ethics. Like Tawney, Gerth and Mills argue that capitalism existed in its infancy in Babylonian, Roman, Chinese and Indian societies, but nowhere did these elements lead to rationalization which characterizes the development of modern capitalism.

Shils (1987) observes some developments in a reverse direction. In the West, a more conservative body of political philosophers and publicists has emerged and more conservative parties have acceded to power. They wish to restore greater opportunity to private business and to make it possible for the initiatives of private enterprise to be successful; they wish their societies to rely upon the market. They are more attended with traditional religious beliefs, and are more inclined to affirm the virtues of traditional family life, and the responsibility of parents for their children.

Shils talks of two outlooks: (i) religious dispositions, and (ii) a naturalistic outlook, a partial product of scientific rationalization of the world, partly a product of religious insensitivity and of the experience of coping with the biological and ecological needs of the individuals.

Marshall (1987) has tried to explore (i) the manner in which Protestants came to adopt a new and revolutionary attitude towards everyday activities, and (ii) how did the Protestants come to conclude that they must practice a methodical, systematic, 'modern capitalistic' manner of life? He has also investigated the activities of the pre- and post-reformation business classes in order to determine whether or not Weber's hypotheses about the practical consequences of protestant teaching can be corroborated by empirical data.

The author argues that prior to reformation it was not possible to detect such beliefs and practices among the business classes in any part of the globe. Rather, economic traditionalism would be the norm both as an ideal and practice.

Marshall (1982) also found an association between ascetic protestantism and rational systematic pursuit of honest profits by means of diligence in a vocation. Further, he explains that (i) it is the capitalistic ethic that explains the origins and development of Calvinist beliefs, rather than vice versa, and (ii) the origins of the capitalistic mentality and capitalistic conduct are ultimately economic.

Schumpeter (1987) explains his theory of economic development in terms of a state of equilibrium which is upset by individuals who take on the function of an entrepreneur; they 'innovate' by bringing given economic resources together into new combinations (e.g., technologies, marketing strategies, forms of business organization and by actually translating these combinations into reality). Since the entrepreneur is not an owner of capital, new combinations can only be realized and development can only take place if he is given credit. His theory does not contain non-economic assumptions in order to explain the basic mechanism of growth. Individual motivation, social conditions of action, class structures, belief systems, anthropological presuppositions and historical contexts do not enter into the model.

He writes (1949), "Technological progress had already become the result of systematically conducted scientific research, it occurred almost automatically, and was no longer dependent on the bold action of imaginative individuals."

Poggie (1983) widens the scope of the applicability of the concept of calling not only to the gainful activities performed on the market, but to characterize other pursuits such as priests, the soldier, the physician and the bureaucrat. He raises two questions about the logical status of the spirit of capitalism:

1. Did Weber simply intend to put forward a credible construct of the spirit of capitalism or did he also intend to prove that that spirit had dwelled in the minds of the early capitalist entrepreneurs?
2. Does the Protestant ethic prove that this made a significant difference to the larger story; that the spirit of capitalism was an essential condition for the genesis of modern capitalism?

Poggi believes it impossible to offer conclusive proof to that effect. For him relationship between spirit of capitalism and modern capitalism is indirect.

He claims that the Protestant ethic does not reconstruct the activities of concrete historical groups and does not depict the selection processes through which entrepreneurial groups activated by the spirit of capitalism emerged and set about conducting business in a new way. Further, he says that a certain degree of rationalism had always marked the town men's existence.

Smelser (1988) has established a relationship between the economy and four aspects of its socio-cultural environment: (i) cultural, (ii) political, (iii) integrative, and (iv) social stratification aspect.

Yinger (1970) in his topic on 'Religion and Economic Development' has analysed whether religious differences help to account for variation in economic development? He says that the doctrine of predestination may be different for different people.

Indian Context

Hinduism and Economic Development

Weber's second thesis has largely been analysed in Indian context and has attracted both oppositions and supports. Major studies in Indian context have been conducted by Kapp (1963) and Misra (1962). Kapp examines the values and belief system of Hinduism (rebirth, *karma*) in affecting economic development. He believes that belief in cosmic causation leads to passivism. Bases of Hinduism, i.e., magic and astrology work as static force in social and economic development. He concludes that the rigid deterministic character of Hinduism is against the principle of economic development, that man makes his own history. Misra finds that the other worldliness of Hinduism stressed the release from the cycle of rebirth and this negatively affected economic growth. Myrdal's (1986) view about Asian religions like Hinduism and Buddhism also support this view.

Andreski (1984) enquires into how Indian religion may have prevented capitalistic developments as one factor among many. He finds major barrier to economic development is caste system and the doctrine of karma associated with it. According to him, the first condition for the development of capitalism were geographical. In India and China costs of transportation formed serious obstacle to capitalistic development. The factor that produced capitalism is the rational permanent enterprise with its rational accounting, technology and law but not these alone. Other complementary factors were the rational spirit, the rationalization of the conduct of life in general and a rational economic ethic. He stresses on, that religious roots of the modern economic outlook is dead and the concept of calling is a relic in the world today.

Saran (1963, 1969b) asserts that Hindu tradition is not conducive to the orthogenetic evolution of a rational modern world.

Some view that religious movements in pre-modern India (Ramakrishna Mission and Vivekananda's practical Vedanta) are transitional, imitative and non-rational (Datta, 1954; Majumdar, 1965; Ray, 1970). Vivekananda's practical vedanta is viewed as an objective need for responding towards rapid erosion of Hinduism due to western impact. Thus, Vivekananda becomes a prototype of the native response to the western challenge leading to depending on one's bias to tradition to modernity or to a tradition-modernity synthesis (Singh, 1973; Srinivas, 1966a; Saran, 1969).

For Hindus change can occur only from the top down. The medium of this change can only be religious; social reform or politics can become relevant to a Hindu only if it comes through his religion (*The Complete Works of Swami Vivekanand,* VIII: 77).

Schoffeleers and Meizers (1978) raise the issue: Is the development of modern capitalism must necessarily be linked to inwardly asceticism? It is observed that the Portuguese Jews in Holland in the post-reformation era were not ascetic but the signs of a modern capitalistic development can be observed in them. The book examines a number of oriental religions like Judaism, Hinduism, Budhism, Jainism and Confucianism in this context. The authors propose that there are other conditions also which are required to arrive at a modern capitalism. It is suggested that the forms and contents of the ethical or religious system is of importance. More than one ethical system within one religious group make it impossible for man to act rationally. Hence, for a meaningful rational life only one ethical system (provided by the religion) is needed. The other way is the total secularization of society so that another ethic (secular) can be introduced.

Some sociologists have argued that Hinduism like Christianity is conducive to change and can easily meet from within the requirements of the modernization process (Srinivas, 1966a; Rudolph and Rudolph, 1967; Singer, 1972). Singer has drawn an analogy between Weber's analysis of Hinduism with his study of the role of the 'Protestant Ethic' in the rise of European industrial capitalism. He finds several parallels between Calvinistic and Hindu eschatology. In both, a vocational ethic enjoins industriousness and dedication to one is calling as a moral duty. Competence and success in one's calling are also linked in both to a trascendent goal of spiritual salvation. He rejects the assertion that Hinduism constitutes a barrier to India's modernization. He writes, "Traditional Indian society has been a changing society, and the Hindus who have been agents of these changes have not been prevented by caste, ritual or religious beliefs from making innovations".

On the same line Rao (1969), Agarwal (1972), Bhowmick (1977), Majumdar and Srinivas (1966), Bose (1975), Vidyarthi and Sinha (1974, 1977b.), Timberg (1978), Narayan (1988b), Nevaskar (1971), Chandra (1964), Singh (1973), Dube (1965a), Karve (1968), Schoffeler and Meizers (1978), Kariyil (1988), and Kusumakar (1982) hold the view that the Hindu religious tradition is fully compatible with modernity. Traditional cultural values of Hinduism did not impede the process of economic development in India. Basic traditional Indian institutions such as caste, joint family, religious affiliation and traditional occupations do not seem to hinder the growth of industrial entrepreneurship. On the contrary, these traditional institutions and their accompanying value systems work out an adaptive relationship towards a viable growth of modern roles and industrial innovations (Singh, 1973).

Dube (1965a) distinguishes cultural factors that affect programmes of economic development into ideological-motivational and institutional-organizational. While the former includes cultural orientations to life, time, wealth, work experiment, innovation, a minimal consensus on such social goals as higher standard of living, education and health, and a system of incentives, rewards, sanctions and control, the latter includes structural units and their articulation, stratification, status system, mobility, pattern of authority and leadership, reference groups and patterns of identification and communication, especially economic, political, religious and educational institutions, and system of resource mobilization and role assignment. Cultural values determine these norms and set the standards of judgement. Culture has elements of both continuity and change. It is unjust to attribute static quality to cultural values.

There is a difference between Hinduism that is practical in daily life and Hinduism of the sacred texts. Inadequate incentives, a restricted system of rewards, and weak sanctions and controls pose problems of the cultural order that block economic development.

The ascriptive order, emphasizes on the sacred, conformity and ritualism, and the segmentary nature of the social structure are the major cultural problems affecting India's economic development. Her basic value system has several elements that could encourage and stimulate economic growth but her structural inadequacies stand in the way of modernization and development. The proximate values of the society do not bar acceptance of several elements of modernity. There is a need to synthesize the old and new value system for speedy development of society.

Rao (1969) evaluates the various aspects of the relation between religion and economic development. He has specially examined the relationship between Hinduism and economic growth through ritual observances and practices. He selects vows and votive offerings as the main ritual observances. Further, he classifies vows into conditional and unconditional. Former being attached to a specific objective. This may include fasting, offering special worship or animal sacrifice. Other forms of worship constitute a category of rituals called *vratas*. The benefit sought are mundane and material. These include attaining wealth, having sons, success in business undertakings and improvement in worldly pursuits.

The this-worldly character of Hinduism is reflected not only in vows and votive offerings but also in a whole range of ritual observances and practices. But this worldliness of Hinduism does not guarantee a positive orientation to economic action. This needs to be empirically investigated.

He stresses that Protestantism as a reformatory movement, inter alia, contributed to a general social climate which encouraged various aspects of economic development in some European countries, and there was no one-to-one relationship between Protestantism and the rise of capitalism. He says regarding the Asian religion, that the unit of comparison should be a reformatory sect of Hinduism and Protestantism instead of Hinduism as such.

Singh (1973) also supports the view that caste and value system of Indian society does not impede the process of modernization. In his analysis, "Relevance of Max Weber for the Understanding of Indian Reality", he raises very important questions: (i) what degree of centrality did the Indian phenomenon occupy in Weber's scheme of analysis? (ii) to what extent do his substantive statements on India merit, or have merit with affirmation? and (iii) what advantages do his theoretical and methodological insights into the social sciences offer to the Indian sociologists in their own analysis of the Indian reality?

Answering his first question, the author says, India occupied a position of auxiliary interest in Weber's historical sociology. The question has been analysed at (i) substantive, and (ii) theoretical levels. At first level Weber's statements and generalization about social institution and ethical systems in India are subjected to various limitations. At second level he finds Weber's contribution as crucial and of everlasting significance.

Gupta (1974b) supports that Hindu tradition is gradually rationalizing itself by incorporating modern values and institutions. While analysing role of Vivekananda's Ramakrishna Mission, he says that it is not important because it has modernized a band of Hindu sanyasins but because it has almost unconsciously laid down a framework for India's only possible processes of social change.

In 1990 a survey was conducted by Sayeed, Somayanjulu, Das, Kumar, and Ramachandran at Christian (St. Mary's Church, Bombay), Hindu (Bhubaneswar Temple, Orissa; Venkateswara Temple, Tirupati; and Jagannath Temple, Puri), and Muslim (Haji Ali Dargah, Bombay) places of worship. The objectives of the survey were:

(i) to study the socio-economic characteristic of visitors,
(ii) to study frequency of their visits, and
(iii) to study the purpose of visit.

Sample was selected randomly. Bishops and managers of Dargah helped but one Roman Catholic refused to disclose about the information as he felt that it was against his religion. In their findings it was observed that local people formed the majority. Young persons came frequently and in large numbers. The visitors are from all educational and occupational categories. The purpose of visit was mostly spiritual. In all the three temples only high caste people were seen in large numbers.

Religion has been studied in its relationship to various aspects. Malefijt (1968) analyses relation of religion with family patterns, political and economic organization, social values and social structure as a whole. Religion, says the author, has a structural interrelationship with all social institutions.

Religion and Society

Relationship between religion and society has been studied by Chatterjee (1981). He maintains that modern development in the economy and technology, educational advance, knowledge explosion etc., have been monopolized by those who are at the top of the religio-social hierarchy. At the same time confrontation between them and the poorer has been intensified.

Religion of all people displays two important features: (i) the dynamic nature of understanding of symbols and meanings, and (ii) the importance of studying beliefs and practices of the people.

The author shows the need of the church in India to understand the dynamic nature of religious and social consciousness of the people and to see religion and society through their eyes.

Religion and Political Life

Relationship between religion and political life has been taken into account by Narang (1956). He establishes a relationship between religion and political life. He believes that all religious movements are political movements. All political progress requires high aspirations, an enterprising spirit, the will to do, the soul to dare and the purity and integrity of private and public life. The common source from which these virtues have originated is religion. The author asserts this relationship between religion and politics as more intensive than anywhere in the world. He has shown how a religious body got transformed into a political-military organization due to persecution to which Sikh community was subjected by the Muslim government.

Religion and Social Change

Relationship between religion and social change is studied with reference to Hinduism in the light of Weberian thesis by Rao (1969), Agarwal (1977) and Bhowmick (1977). Saberwal (1971) has analysed the relationship between religion and secularization.

Religion and Conflict

Relationship between religion and conflict is dealt by Kabir (quoted in Mathur, 1979). He says, throughout Indian history there has been a tendency towards unification on the basis of religion and culture, on the other side fragmentation due to difference in customs and political and economic interests. Other studies have indicated that differences are maintained by the dominant sections for their political and economic vested intersects.

Religion and Modernization

Relationship between religion and modernization is analysed by Bharati (1971). The author deals with "Hinduism and Modernization" in Indian context. It is stated that modernization of Hinduism can be studied from the theological, doctrinal and ideological perspectives as against the social, pragmatic and operational aspects of Hinduism. The author has developed approaches to the study of modernization of Hinduism instead of analysing Hinduism as a force conducive to modernization.

Other studies on religion and modernization conducted are by Dubey, Majumdar, Srinivas, Bose, Vidyarthi, Singh, Atal and Bellah. Singh and others highlight modernity of Sikhism. Sikhism is thoroughly modern and progressive. It rejects orthodoxy, formalism and feudalistic values. Its attitude towards science, technology, industrialization, education and the welfare of state etc., show its modernity..

Singh (1973) rejects that Hinduism is ascetic and other-worldly; that it denies materialism and pursuit of pleasure; or that it inhibits the growth of an enterprising business elite. He says that Hindu ethos is responsive to modernity and that modernization in India can occur through innovations.

Gupta (1971) while analysing the role of religious component in the process of social change attempts to develop a theoretical framework for studying the role of Hinduism in modernization of India. He concludes that the basic pattern of meditation and interchange with other functional subsystems remains fundamentally unchanged at the highest level of generality; that while purely religious interests are social, social life itself is governed by principles which are 'shastric' in form but customary in substance.

Religion and Development

Studies related to religion and development include Sorensen's (1988) work. He has dealt with the obstacles to India's development as:

(i) social inequality,
(ii) failure of ruling classes to instigate real change,
(iii) the failure of democracy,
(iv) the lack of national unity, and
(v) the capacity of the poor to accept poverty.

The author says that religion is not the single most important impediment to socio-economic development in India and it has not been incompatible with profound economic change and the introduction of new methods and procedure, both in industry and agriculture. There is a core element in Indian religion and culture which help prevent development of the poor.

Religion, rationality and social change thesis has been worked out in the context of protest reform as an ideal type of a premodern religious movement (Bellah, 1964; Eisenstadt, 1968). Bellah (1965) discusses the relationship between religious and political institutions, the relations between religious and secular cultural elites and the relations between established religions and heteroxy. In traditional societies religion and politics were not separate. This tended to inhibit progress. Analyzing second area of tension he observes that the secular elites (i.e., intellectuals) were not necessarily religious elites. Third area refers to the degree to which a religious system can respond to new needs and creatively adjust, as well as contribute to social development. Commenting on Hinduism he writes, "Hinduism, which left the mass of Indian people hermetically sealed in caste-bound religious systems only rarely and usually ineffectively challenged through movements based on Hindu religious universalism". Most religions serve the functions of fusion, disfunction and creative tension between religious ideas and the world. Hinduism exhibits all the three tendencies. The author concludes that religion and ideologies are important elements in Asia's development.

Timberg (1978) concludes that religious affiliation and traditional institutions of India do not hinder economic development. Rather, traditional attitudes, caste loyalties, forms of organization and joint-family of the trading groups have facilitated their economic success. Buhler (1963) gives a brief account of the Jain sects, their origin, features of Jain religion and tenets, rituals, traditions, canonical literature, Jain inscription and mythology. According to him, Jain saints (Degambars) wear coloured garments in present days and confine the disuse of clothes at meals but the author has not specified the region where this has been in practice, Degamber saints, known as Munis, are observed as practising nudity as it is a basic condition of asceticism. Jainism has been studied by Mandelbaum (1970), Misra (1972), and Agarwal (1972). Fischer and Jain have given valuable accounts of contemporary Jain religious practices with emphasis on art and ritual, 2,500 years of Jainism, along with image makers, temples, temple rituals, annual festivals, daily life, image installation in a temple and the daily routine of Swetambar monks and nuns.

Kusumakar (1982) highlights the developmental aspect of Jain mythology. Rules of conduct laid down by Mahavira (24th and last Tirthankar of the faith) had a considerable impact upon the downtrodden. Mahavira developed the concept of social equality irrespective of caste or sex. He asserted on the doctrine of karma. All persons he said, could achieve salvation by observing an ethical code of conduct and not by performing rituals. He laid down a path which consisted of right faith, right knowledge and right conduct. His theory of karma is based on the principle of self-reliance. All these doctrines led to the social development of Jain community and the society in general.

Christianity

Oddie (1969) has examined the British and American Protestant missionary policy towards caste within the church during 1850–

1914, to analyse their attitude towards caste outside the church. His paper is based on secondary sources. It is observed that wherever caste was found as barrier to conversion and it led to apostasy, it was condemned. The missionaries played a part in the formation of law affecting and undermining the authority of caste. This has worked as a means of bringing about social change.

Diebe and Peter (1972), Haq (1973), Alice (1982), Chako (1986), and Eisentadt (1968) have touched upon various aspects of Christianity.

Kariyil (1988) has shown in his analysis of the role of religion in material development with special emphasis on the Catholic church shows that the Catholic church in Kerala has positively contributed towards the material development of society.

Sikhism

Sikhism has been studied largely in terms of its history and military character. A few studies concern with the social and ritual practices. Marenco (1976) has analysed that changes in the Sikh community are caused mainly by educational, technological and ideological changes. It is observed that those who migrated to town or cities and became owners and managers of factories also became part of the emerging business managerial class on the basis of common occupation, sources of money, wealth, interests and daily patterns of association. All these changes affected almost all the important caste of the Sikhs.

Writing about the development of Sikh community Farquhar (1967) writes, after the second Sikh war (1848–49), state of Sikh was very poor which served as a hindrance in their way to progress and prosperity.

Banerjee (1942) has shown in his analysis that the distribution of offerings referred to the division of the Sikh society. The booty and the offering were divided into three shares — the first share was given to the descendents of Nanak who were called Sahibdah, the descendents of the successor of Manak were known as the Bhallah and the second share was given to them. The third share was fixed in the name of the Shahidi Singhs.

Narang (1956) has shown how a religious body of Sikh got transformed into a political-military organization due to persecution to which Sikh community was subjected by the Muslim government.

Ghani (1987) writes about the part played by Sikh sect in transforming Punjab. According to him, Sikhs have contributed tremendously in national development by contributing wheat and rice to 50% of the total production of food grains. They also provided essential services as passenger and goods transportation on roads. The Sikhs fed India's starving millions and formed the backbone of the country's defence forces.

Saberbal (1976) has studied social mobility among three castes, viz., Ramgarhias, Ad Dharmis and Balmikis. Differences were observed respective to each caste in the social mobility pattern.

Ramgarhias have entered into industrial entrepreneurship due to their traditional skills in wood and metal. Ad Dharmis have made modest but wide ranging gains in politics, education and bureaucracy and in industry. Balmikis were found less mobile.

Author observed that "mobility is not influenced by caste factor but by its hereditary occupation and the new avenues open to it". The study concentrates on various sociological issues: the modes of mobility, the course of intercaste relations and political culture.

Marenco (1976) shows how lower caste Sikhs move into higher class group on a group-based mobility. He enquires into the social stratification of Sikhs with reference to the coexistence of caste and class. There are two types of mobility among Sikhs: (a) corporate caste mobility with its implications for the reshuffling of the caste hierarchy among the Sikhs, and (b) the emergence of a new type of social class mobility open to individuals rather than groups. There are considerable changes in traditional occupation both on corporate as well as individual level.

Jat Sikhs became the most literate groups in the Punjab. The Chuhra Sikhs changed their name to Mazhabi Sikh, they moved up corporately in the Sikh caste hierarchy. The author observed that the Tarkhan Sikhs who were the owners and managers of factories or engineers enjoyed a greater prestige than did their caste brothers who stuck to their traditional occupation. Most significant change was found among menials and untouchables. Change of occupation corporately changed their status. They became soldiers and left sweeping and scavenging. The study shows the very ethics of Sikhism have modernizing effect on Indian society.

Dhillon (1989) covers the salient features of Sikh religion and its history. He discusses the significance of Darbar Sahib as the nucleus of Sikhism, the nature of Singh Sabha Movement, role of Akali Dal during the emergency and the causes of Punjab crisis. According to him all Sikh agitations (social, religious or political) were launched from the platform of the gurudwaras.

Singh (1968) highlights the integrative aspect of Sikhism. He believes that Sikhism has reduced the communal tensions between Hindus and Muslims. It has reformed many social evils (caste, untouchability etc.) by condemning social disparity.

Singh (1981) discusses the plebeian character of the Sikh revolution. Major focus is on the revolutionary character of the Sikh movement. He concludes that the major block for social development is the caste system. He maintains that Sikh movement was engaged in propagating freedom and equality than in building a new society and in creating through the *panth* a political revolution.

Kapoor (1987) indicates that military action in the bastion of Sikhism provoked a wave of deep anger among Sikhs. The release of Akali politicians began a renewal and increased competition for leadership among them. He discusses various Sikh sects in brief and their political dimensions in detail especially the agitations since 1984.

Singh (1990) argues that rituals .are more avidly performed in culturally backward societies where rules and way of nature are not properly understood. A change is observed in the ritual practices among the Sikh sect. Ritualism plays a dominant role. There are conflicts on ritualism among the Takhat Jathedars. Sikhs have been found observing non-Sikh rituals also.

Bingley (1984) has traced religio-political history and origin of Sikhism, their sacraments, rituals, festivals geographical distribution of Sikh according to their descent. He also found that Sikh women prefer Hindu customs and beliefs.

Gill (1973) discusses social institutions of Sikhism. He says, Sikhism infused a spirit of high type of equality and bravery. This was the result of social democracy without which political democracy, economic democracy and socialism could not work.

Singh has drawn a comparison of the ethics of Hinduism, Islam, Christianity and Buddhism with its major focus on Sikhism but does not analyse their role in society.

Singh (1986) highlights the corruption that has become more intensive in the Sikh organizations. Leaders of the organization are concentrating on accumulating wealth, property and luxury. He says that more than 90% gurudwaras are run by such people. He has observed some important causes of conflict in the Sikh sect. Religious devotion and gradation is measured by the amount of offering one can pay in cash. Parties conflict with each other for the control of important shrines and gurudwaras. Motive behind is money. Offerings are used for political, social and selfish ends of the few in control and power. The object of worship is not spiritual but material gain.

Several incidences of inter-sect conflict among Sikhs have occupied cover page of the newspapers, e.g., extremists Akalis were arrested at Patiala on charges of rioting causing hurt and violation of restrictions for attempting to disturb a 'Satsang' at Nirankari Bhawan. In Amritsar, Bhindranwale threatened Nirankaris for holding Satsang in Punjab.

General Observations

On the basis of above studies, it can be concluded that:

1. Religion plays a significant role in shaping society.
2. Role of religion in economic development is controversial. Weber's thesis about religion too is controversial but majority of votes are against it. Most studies have proved that Indian religions (especially Hinduism) and their associated institutions and value system do not inhibit economic and social development.
3. Concept of 'calling' is also applicable to the pursuits of a priest, soldier, physician and bureaucrat.
4. Some scholars believe that major barriers to economic development are caste system and the doctrine of karma.
5. Forms and contents of the religious system is important. More than one ethical system leads to non-rational behaviour. Secular ethics is the solution for rational development.
6. Religiosity is higher among younger generation. Education does not affect religiosity.
7. Power in religious organization is held by those who are at top of socio-economic strata.
8. Within one sect, gap between rich and poor is more intense.
9. Religion is closely associated with politics. It leads to both unity and conflict within the community.

10. Religious values are in conformity with the modern outlook.
11. Barrier to India's development are social inequality, failure of the ruling class to initiate change, failure of democracy, lack of national unity and the capacity of the poor to accept poverty and government policies.
12. Hinduism, Jainism, Christianity and Sikhism are all conducive to social development.
13. A change in ritual performance is taking place. There is a tendency of observing rituals of the other religions especially among Sikhism. Motive behind is personal.
14. Religious power forms the bases of conflict among Sikh sect. Religious organizations are suffering from corruption.

References

Agarwal, B.C. (1972), "Diksha Ceremony in Jainism: An Analysis of Its Socio-political Ramifications", *Eastern Anthropologist*, 25 (1), pp. 13–20.

——— (1974), "Changing Patterns of Jati among the Jains of M.P.", in *Tribe, Caste and Peasantry*, B.C. Agarwal and K.S. Mathur (eds.) Lucknow, Ethnographic and Folk Culture Society.

——— (1977), *Cultural Contours of Religion and Economics in Hindu Universe*, National Publishing House, New Delhi.

Alice, P.J. (1982), *The Roman Catholic Mission in Agra from* 1781–1947, St. Joseph's Printing School, Agra.

Andreski, S. (ed.) (1983), *Max Weber on Capitalism, Bureaucracy and Religion*, George Allen & Unwin, London.

——— (1984), *Max Weber's Insights and Errors*, Routledge & Kegan Paul, London.

Aron, R. (1967), *Industrial Society: Three Essays on Ideology and Development*, Praeger, New York.

Banerjee, I. (1972), *Evolution of the Khalsa*, Calcutta.

——— (1942), "A Short History of the Origin and Rise of the Sikhs", *Indian Historical Quarterly*, Vol., 18, Brown W. Norman.

Bellah, R.N. (1963), "Reflections on the Protestant Ethic Analogy" in *Asia, Journal of Social Issues*, 19(52–60).

——— (1964), "Religious Evolution", *American Sociological Review*, 29: 63(358–374).

——— (ed.) (1965) "Epilogue", *Religion and Progress in Modern Asia*, Free Press, New York.

Bharati, A. (1971), "Hinduism and Modernization", in R.F. Spencer (ed.), *Religion and Change in Contemporary Asia*, University of Minnesota Press, Minneapolis.

Bhattacharya, M., Dutta, L. Bela (1973), "A Study of Rituals with Reference to Sex, Age, Segments", *Journal of Social Research*, 16 (1) (72–81).

Bhowmick, P.K. (1977), "Cultural Continuity in Social Economic Change: A Study in Religious Complexes in the Rural Setting", *Journal of Social and Economic Studies*, 5(2) (185–99).

Binigley, A.H. (1984), *Sikhs: Religion Political History and Origin of Sikhism, Sacraments and Rituals, Festivals and Customs*, Sumit Publication, New Delhi.

Bose, N.K. (1975), *Structure of Hindu Society*, Trans. from Bengali by Andre Beteille, Orient Longman, New Delhi.

Brentano, quoted by R.H. Tawney in, *Religion and the Rise of Capitalism*, The New American Library, New York, 1926, p. 261.

Buhler, G. (1963), *On the Origin of the Indian Brahmana Alphabet*, (ed. 3) Chowkhamba Sanskrit Series Office, Varanasi.

Chako, Arun, (1986), "Change in Church Perspectives" *News Time*, 27, January

Chandra, B. (1964), "The Problems of Poverty and Indian National Leadership", *Enquiry*, 2(54–106).

Chatterjee, S.K. (1981), "A Note on the Study of Religion and Society", in *Religion and Society*, Vol. 28(3), Sept.

Collins, R. (1980), "Weber's Last Theory of Capitalism: A Systematization", *American Sociological Review*, 45 Dec. (925–42).

——— (1985), *Three Sociological Traditions*, Oxford University Press, New York.

——— (1986a), *Max Weber*, Vol. 3, Sage Publications, Beverly Hills, London.

Datta, B.N. (1954), *Swami Vivekanand: Patriot Prophet* Navbharat Publishers, Calcutta.

Deibe, P.D. and Peter, S.J. (1972); "The Catholic Church and Caste in Rural Tamil Nadu", *Eastern Anthropologist*, 25 (1).

Dhillon, G.S. (1989), *Researches in Sikh Religion and History*, Sumeet Prakashan, Chandigarh.

Dube, S.C. (1965a), "Cultural Problems in Economic Development of India" in *The Economic, Religion and Progress in Modern Asia*, R.N. Bellah (ed.), Free Press, New York.

——— (1977), "Oral Traditions and Cultural Development", *East Asian Cultural Studies*, 16(14).

Eisentadt, S.N. (ed.) (1968), *Protestant Ethic and Modernization: A Comparative View*, Basic Books, New York.

Farquhar, J.N. (1967), *Modern Religious Movements of India*, Munshiram Manoharlal, Delhi.

Fischer, E. and Jain, J. (1977), *Art and Rituals: 2500 years of Jainism*, Sterling, Delhi.

Ghani, J. (1987) *The Sikh Volcano*, Vanguard, Pakistan .

Gill, P.S. (1973), *Trinity of Sikhism: Philosophy, Religion, State*, New Academic Publishing Co., Jullundur.

Graft, F.W. (1987), "Friendship Between Experts Notes on Weber and Troeltsch" in *Max Weber and his Contemporaries*, The German Historical Institute, London.

Gupta, K.P. (1971), "Theoretical Approach to Hinduism and Modernization in India", *Indian Journal of Sociology*, 2(1) (59–91).

——— (1974a), "Sociology of Indian Tradition and Tradition of Indian Sociology", *Sociological Bulletin*, 23(1) (14–43).

——— (1974b), "Religious Evolution and Social Change in India: A Study of Ramakrishna Mission Movement", *Contributions to Indian Sociology (NS)*, 8(25–49).

——— (1978), "Religion and Development: A non-Sociological perspective", *Spectra of Anthropological Progress*, Vol. 1.

Hagen, E.E. (1962), *On the Theory of Social Change: How Economic Growth Begins*, The Dorsey Press Inc. Homewood, Illinois.

Howe, R.H. (1978), "Max Weber's Elective Affinities", *American Journal of Sociology*, 84(366–85).

Jain, J. (1977), "Jain Ritual and Space" in *Urban Space and Ritual*, N. Gutschow and T. Sieverts (eds) Darmstadt: Technische Hoch Schub Darmstadt.

——— (1979), "Rathyatra: The Chariot Festival of the Jains", Arts & Archaeology Research Papers, 16(15–18).

Kapoor, R.A. (1987), *Sikh Separatism*, Vikas Publishing House Pvt. Ltd., New Delhi.

Kapp W.K. (1963), *Hindu Culture. Economic Development and Economic Planning in India*, Asia Publishing House, Bombay.

Kariyil, A. (1988), "Religion and Material Development", *Journal of Dharma*, Vol. XIII, October–November (312–327).

Karve, D.G. (1968), *Hindu Society and Interpretation* Deshmukh, Poona.

Kusumakar, H. (1982), "Colourful Re-enactment of Jain Mythology", *Times of India*, 3 February.

Loomis, C.P. and Loomis, Z.K. (1969), "Socio-Economic Change and the Religious Factor in India", *An Indian Symposium of Views on Max Weber*, Affiliated East West Press, New Delhi.

Majumdar R.C. (1965), *Swami Vivekanand: A Historical Review*, General Printers and Publishers, Calcutta.

Malefitz, A.D.W. (1968), *Religion and Culture: An Introduction to Anthropology of Religion*, Macmillan, New York.

Mandelbaum, D.G. (1970a), "Curing and Religion in South Asia", *Journal of the Indian Anthropological Society*, 5(1–2), (171–186).

——— (1970b), *Society in India: Change and Continuity*, 2 Vols., University of California Press, Berkeley.

Marenco, E.K. (1976), *The Transformation of Sikh Society*, Heritage Publishers, New Delhi.

Marshall, G. (1982), *In Search of the Spirit of Capitalism*, Hutchinson, London (123).

Mathur, S.S. (1979), *A Sociological Approach to Indian Education*, Vinod Pustak Mandir, Agra.

Misra, R.L. (1972), "The Jains in an Urban Setting: The Ascetics and the Laity and the Jains of Mysore City", *Bulletin of the Anthropological Survey of India*, 21(1–2) (1–68).

Misra, V. (1962), *Hinduism and Economic Growth*, Oxford University Press, Bombay, (206).

Mommsen, W.J., and Jurgen.O. (eds) (1949), *The Theory of Economic Development*, Mass, Cambridge.

Munch, R. (1988), *Understanding Modernity*, Routledge, London.

Myrdal, G. (1986), *Asian Drama* (3 vols.)., Pantheon Books, New York.

Nag, A.K, (1973) Christianity and the Role of Church in Mizoram', *The North Eastern Affairs*, 2, (1).

Narang, G.C. (1956), *Transformation of Sikhism*, New Book Society of India, New Delhi (250–55).

Narayan, Swami (1974a), "Pilgrimage to Kashi", *Journal of Social Research*, 17(1) (20–22).

——— (1988b), quoted by Antony Kariyil in *Religion and Material Development, Journal of Dharma*, Volume XIII, October–November (313–22).

Nevaskar, B. (1971), *Capitalists without Capitalism: Jains of India and the Ouakers of the West*, West Fort C.T., Greenwood.

Oddie, G.A. (1969), "Protestant Missionary Caste and Social Change in India, 1850–1914", *Indian Economic Social History Review*, Vol., 6, (259–91).

Poggie, G. (1983), *Calvinism and the Capitalistic Spirit: Max Weber's Protestant Ethic*, MacMillan (47).

Ray, N. (1970), *The Sikh Gurus and the Sikh Society*, Patiala.

Rao, M.S.A. (1969), "Religion and Economic Development", *Sociological Bulletin*, 28(1) (1–5).

Rudolph, L.T. and Rudolph, S.H. (1967), *The Modernity of Tradition: Political Developments in India*, Orient Longmans, Bombay.

Runciman, W.G. (ed.) (1978), *Weber: Selections in Transition*, Translated by E. Mathews, Cambridge University Press, Cambridge.

——— (1976b), *Mobile Men: Limits to Social Change in Urban Punjab*, Vikas Publishing House Pvt. Ltd., New Delhi.

Saberbal, S. (1971), "Secularism a Threat to Religion" Bulletin of the Christian Institute for the Study of Religion & Society, 13(3).

——— (1976), *Mobile Men: Limits to Social Change in Urban Punjab*, Vikas Publishing House, Pvt. Ltd, New Delhi.

Samuelson, K. (1961), *Religion and Economic Action: A Critique of Max Weber*, Trans. E. Geoffrey (French), Harper and Row, New York.

Saran, A.K. (1969b), "Religion and Society: The Hindu View" in *International Yearbook of the Sociology of Religion* (41–55).

Sayeed, U., Somayanjulu, U.V., Das, N.C., Kumar, A. and Ramachandran, P. (1990), "Profile of Visitors to Places of Worship", *Social Action*, January–March, Vol. 40(1).

Schlushter, W. (1981), *The Rise of Western Rationalism: Max Weber's Development History*, (Trans.) Guenther Roth, California University Press, Berkeley.

Schoffeleers, M. and Meizers, D. (1978), *Religion. Nationalism and Economic Action*, Van Garum, Assen, The Netherlands.

Schumpeter, J.A. (1987), in *Max Weber and his Contemporaries*, Harper Collins, Publisher London.

Sen, A. (1989), *Perspective on Capitalism. Marx. Keynes. Schumpeter and Weber.* K. Bhardwaj and S. Kaviraj (eds), Sage Publications, New Delhi.

Shils, E. (1987), "Max Weber: The Enduring Contemporary", in *Max Weber and His Contemporaries*, The German Historical Institute, London.

Singer, M. (1968a), *Tradition and Change in India* (Ed.) B.Cohn and M. Singer, New York (423–452).

Sinha, S (ed.) (1977), "Anthropology in India", Vol. 1: *Cultural Anthropology*, Anthropological Survey of India, Calcutta.

——— (1972b), *When a Great Tradition Modernizes: An Anthropological Approach to Indian Civilization*, Praeger, New York.

Singh, Darshan (1968), *Indian Bhakti Tradition and Sikh Gurus*, Lyall Book Depot, Bhopal.

Singh, F., Singh, T., Singh, G.B.S., Singh, J.P.U. and Singh, S. (1969), *Sikhism*, Punjabi University, Patiala.

Singh, J. (1981), *The Sikh Revolution*, Bahri Publications Pvt. Ltd., New Delhi (115).

Singh, T. (1990), "Ritualism Vs. Reality", *The Sikh Review*, Vol. 3, 8(441) (16–17).

Singh, T. (1986), "Need for Renewal and Reform in Present Working of Sikh Religious, Cultural and Political Institutions", *Sikh Review*, September, Vol. No. 393.

——— (1986), "Crumbling of Sikh Values", *Sikh Review*, October, Vol. 34 (394) (21–22).

Singh, Y. (1973), *Modernization of Indian Tradition: A Systematic Study of Social Change*, Thompson Press, Delhi.

——— (1987b), "Development in India: Continuities and Contradictions" in K.S. Shukla (ed.), *The Other Side of Development*, Sage, New Delhi.

——— (1989c), "Relevance of Max Weber for the Understanding of Indian Reality" in *Perspective on Capitalism*, (224–228).

Sinha, S. (ed.) (1977a), *Anthropology in India*, Vol. 1, *Cultural Anthropology*, Anthropological Survey of India, Calcutta.

——— (1974b), "Sociology of Religion: A Trend Report" in *A Survey of Research in Sociology and Social Anthropology*, Vol. II, Popular Prakashan, Bombay.

Smelser, N.J. (1988), *The Sociology of Economic Life*, Prentice Hall of India, Pvt. Ltd., New Delhi.

Sorenson, G. (1988), "Internal and External Intertwined: Five Obstacles to Development in India", *Guru Nanak Journal of Sociology*, 9(1).

Srinivas, M.N. (1966a), *Social Change in Modern India*, University of California Press, Berkeley.

——— (1976b), *The Remembered Village*, Oxford, Delhi.

Tawney, R.H. (1926), *Religion and the Rise of Capitalism*, The New American Library, New York.

The Hindustan Times, August 28, 1978.

Timberg, T.A. (1978), *The Marwaris: From Traders to Industrialists*, Vikas Publishing House, New Delhi.

Vidyarthi, L.P. (1970), "Socio-Cultural Implications of Industrialization in India: A Case Study of Tribal Bihar", Planning Commission, New Delhi.

Vivekanand, S. (1970), *The Complete Works of Swami Vivekanand*, Mayavati Memorial Edition, Advaita Ashram, Calcutta.

Weber, M. (1930a), *The Protestant Ethic and the Spirit of Capitalism*, Trans. Talcott Parsons, Charles Scribener and Sons, New York.

——— (1968b), *Religions of India: The Sociology of Hinduism and Buddhism*, translation and edited by H.H. Gerth and Don Martindale, Free Press, New York.

——— (1948c), *From Max Weber: Essays in Sociology*, translation and edited by H.H. Gerth and C.H. Mills, Routledge and Kegan Paul, London.

——— (1964d), *Theory of Social and Economic Organization*, translated by A.M. Handerson and T. Parsons, Free Press, New York.

Yinger, M. (1970), *The Scientific Study of Religion*, McMillan Pub. Co. Inc., New York.

3 The Sects

Different religious sects live in the city of Agra. The city has its existence since 1131 AD. Sikandar settled at Agra on the east bank of Yamuna river and built a fort and laid out a city which became the capital of the Empire around 1495–1501. In 1517, Sikandar died at Agra. In 1526 Babur annexed the city. During 1569–1570 Akbar refounded it on the west bank of the Yamuna. In 1666, Agra became the seat of a provincial governor. In 1763, Agra was taken over by the Jats of Bharatpur. In 1803, the district came under British rule as a result of the victories of Lord Lake. From 1843–1857, Agra city was the capital of North-West Provinces (*Gazetteer, 1905*).

The Christians

Christianity bears its origin in Jerusalem with the resurrection of Jesus Christ. It has three major divisions or sects: (i) Roman Catholics, (ii) Protestantism, and (iii) Eastern Orthodoxy, composing of more than 260 sub-divisions.

The Roman Catholic Sect

Roman Catholicism has its head office at Rome in Italy and is dominant in Central and Southern Europe, Ireland and South American countries; whereas Protestantism is prevalent in North Europe, England, Scotland, North America and Australia. Eastern Orthodoxy is mainly confined to USSR, Greece and the Slavic countries.

Catholicism became the official religion of the Roman empire in 380 AD and Christianity achieved legal recognition in 1313 AD. The first great schism occurred in 1054, giving rise to two sects, viz., Roman Catholics and Eastern Orthodoxy (headquartered at

Constantinople) The next significant schism occurred in the 16th century as the reformation movement launched by Luther and put forward by Calvin, Zwingly etc. As a consequence, Protestant churches were established in Germany, England and Scotland. Thus, the western church got bifurcated into Roman Catholicism and Protestantism.

Christianity came to India in the first century AD. It is believed that Jesus, at the age of 13 years came to India (Jain, *V.S.* 2476: 16). In around 48–49 A.D. St. Thomas, an apostle of Jesus, came to North India (Subramanyam, 1970: 8) and in 52 AD he came to South India and set up seven churches in Kerala. Christianity came to India in three ways: as an outcome of missionary work, as a result of Portuguese domination over India and as a result of the British colonial expansion. Fr. John of Monte Carvino was the first missionary who came to India in 1291 AD. He was followed by four Franciscans in 1320 and Vasco de Gama reached India with some traders and priests in 1498.

History of Christianity in Agra began with the arrival of two priests at Fatehpursikri in 1580 and the other missionary arrived here in 1591. During this period some conversions took place. Agra became the first diocese under the Capuchins. The Vicariate of the Mughal had been created by the Jesuits by 1773.

Christians were already established in Agra in the days of the Mughal empire. It is said that Akbar adopted the son of an Armenian merchant, Jacob, and attributed the birth of Jehangir in 1570 and erected a church in the Cathedral compound of Agra in 1600. Efforts were made at Agra to spread the Christian community. The Franciscans and Dominicans were the first orders followed by Jesuits and Augustinians and later by Carmelites, Theatines, Hospitallers and Orantorians. On Akbar's request the Jesuits came to Agra and built two churches one each at Agra and Lahore.

During Akbar's period there were many Christians. In 1601 first Jesuits came to Agra and established their permanent headquarters here. It is from here they moved in every direction. During 1602 there were two major Christian communities one at Lahore and the other at Agra. Since 1580, Agra became the centre of Catholic mission.

Jehangir allowed the Jesuits to build a college at Agra with the freedom to preach and convert. He granted twelve bighas of land at Agra for a cemetery and a garden. In 1610, three nephews of Jehangir were baptised. Begum Sumroo of Sardhana was also baptised at the Agra Cathedral. In 1611, Padre Santoos Chapel was formed. During 1611–18 a number of foreign missionaries came to Agra and it became cosmopolitan. There were three cemeteries: (i) Lashkarpur, (ii) Poiyaghat, and (iii) Old Roman Catholic graveyard.

In 1613–14, churches of Agra and Lahore were closed down but were restored in 1615. A fire damaged the church in 1616 and during mid-17th century, church was in ruins. In 1621 Dutch established their trade at Agra and built a factory. A Jesuit college was also established.

Jehangir was succeeded by Shahjahan whose attitude towards the missionaries was not favourable. He besieged the Portuguese settlement at Hoogli in 1631 and 4,400 Christians were sent to Agra to be sold as slaves. The Christian congregation in Agra numbered about 400 which included Armenians and Europeans. Till 1635, the Jesuits were harassed their houses were raided and priests were jailed but later that were released on condition of putting down their churches. Between May 1648 and August 1649, only 49 pagans were baptised. The Catholic strength depended upon the presence or absence of Imperial Court.

Agra church was raided in 1758 by Afghans under Ahmad Shah. This church was later repaired by Fr. Francis Xavier, and in 1794 saw only two converts. During this time Agra had no resident priest except Fr. Juvenal.

During 1773, Agra had about 300 families and 1,000 Catholics, majority of whom were either Armenians or Anglo-Indians residing mainly in Padre Santoos Chapel which is now known as Padre-Tola. During the same year Jesuits were suppressed. There was no priest in Agra and the mission property was resumed by the government and was subsequently given to Fr. Francis Xavier in 1775. During 1781–1807 Agra was world renowned for its oriental court. In 1784, Agra, under the name of vicariate of Tibet-Hindustan, was separated and Capuchins were given the charge. During 1806, Cantonment cemetery was built.

In 1812, Armenians were in majority at Agra and had their own priest. In 1820, the Bishop of Agra assumed the title of Vicar Apostolic of Tibet-Hindustan. Agra gained significance during this period. According to Pezzoni's report dated 20 October 1825, the number of Catholics during 1824 in Agra were 300 out of a total of 3,550 (8.5%) in various parts of India.

According to the statistics submitted to the congregation of propaganda in 1825, number of European Catholics was 2,000 while in Pezzoni's report of 1830, it was 4,000 and of the native Christians was 5,000. A large number of Europeans (due to scarcity of priests) drifted away into Protestantism. Pezzoni started a seminary with three Europeans and three natives but in vain.

In 1835, the Old Cathedral was enlarged. Mughal Catholics lived together as a community adjacent to the church (*Franciscan Annals* 1918: 128) The Catholic population rose to 13,922 and beṣides, there were 3,499 Catechumens, three creches, six orphanages, two old-age homes, seven hospitals and eight dispensaries (Vannini 1981). In 1838, Pezzoni founded an institution for girls at Agra. In 1840, Agra Cathedral had 800 and Agra Cantonment (with Mathura as its outstation) 750 Catholics (*Madras Catholic Directory*, 1863).

In 1841, the 'Association for the Propagation of the Faith' was established by Dr. Borghi, at the same time a convent of Jesus and Mary was opened in 1842 (now known as St. Patrick's College). There were two Catholic chapels (*Gazetteer*, 1841: 123). In Civil Lines their number increased. Total number of Catholics were 18,000, other denominations being 10,000 (Borghi). In 1942 their number rose to 30,000 (Fr. Joachim of St. Anatolia).

In 1945, first Catholic press in North India was started and Catholic Book Society was set up. In 1846 foundation stone for the new Cathedral was laid, and St. Peter's College was established. In same period, St. Patrick's Church was built in Agra Cantonment. This church was opened to public in 1948. Borghi also established St. Aloysius Boarding School for girls, St. Joseph's School for Indian Christians (1862), and St. Anthony's Day School (1901), St. Francis School (1912), St. Claire's School in 1958, St. Daminso Convent (1960) and MagSaysay Shishu Bhawan and Premdan in 1961 at Agra. Number of pupil (Christians) was too low, 12 out of which 3 were Protestants. The strength rose subsequently in 1843 as mentioned in the letter written by Messanger Bishop Borghi to M. Rossat on 28 June 1843.

"Our Boarding School was opened only five months ago and already we have 32 boarders and 7 or 8 applications for vacancies" (Smith, 1980). Since Borghi's time Indianization of the church began. In 1863 there were five educational institutions in Agra (*Catholic Directory* 1864). Number of Christians during 1865 was 2,392 in Agra city (Census, 1861). Michael Angelo started the 'Catholic

Table 3.1: Number of Christians in Agra District/City from 1862 to 1981

Year	District	City
1862	2,392	–
1872	536	–
1881	4,997	1,587
1891	4,758	1,486
1901	5,522	2,343
1911	7,229	2,622
1921	6,818	–
1931	4,758	4,469
1941	–	–
1951	5,182	3,725
1961	5,291	–
1971	6,903	5,473
1981	6,903	5,829

Source: Data is from Censuses, Gazetteers and Catholic Directories of the corresponding years.

Temperance Society' (1868) to prevent excessive drinking by the soldiers and founded a monastery at Agra which became an asylum for the missionaries.

During 1872, in Agra division (Agra, Mathura, Farrukhabad, Etah, Etawah, and Mainpuri) out of a total population of 5,038,136 total number of Christians was 2,536 (*Gazetteer*, 1876); It rose to 3,756 in Agra in 1877–78 and in Agra city during 1881 was 1,587 (11.97%) but in Agra district it was 4,997. In 1887, Agra vicariate had 1,500 Catholics, 24 churches and one Cathedral (at Agra).

According to 1891 census (Table 3.1), there were 4,758 Christians in Agra district but in the city their number was 1,486 (6.34%) less than 50% of the preceding census whereas their total number in 1881 in India blessing was 13,264 and in 1891 it was 23,406 (Census, 1891). In Agra Municipality Christians numbered 1,723 and in Cantonment their number was 2,292 (Census, 1891). In 1394 first Provincial Council was held at Agra. During 1901, there were 5,522 Christians in Agra, Roman Catholics numbered 346, Europeans 2,539 and Eurasians being 640 and 3,343 in Agra city (*Catholic Directory*, 1909). Their number increased in 1907. There were 4,558 European and Eurasian Catholics; native Catholics numbered 4,308 and 366 baptisms took place in the Archdiocese. In 1908, St.Francis

Printing Press was opened at Agra. In 1909 the number of Catholics was 9,422 in the Archdiocese of Agra. On the January 1, 1910 the first issue of *Franciscan Annals of India* was published. St. Francis Convent and Founding Homes (1912) were opened. More than 7,000 babies were baptised and more than 1,000 abandoned girls were brought up in the faith (Catholic). The rate of increase in the Catholic population was 40.5% during 1901–1911 but between 1911–12 it decreased to 29.3% due to First World War.

Messers John and Co. owned six factories out of 19 under the Factories Act during 1914. During 1917 Agra Mission had 8,010 Catholics, 463 conversions, 21 residences, 34 churches and chapels, nine cemeteries, 38 schools, four colleges, seven orphanages, 868 baptisms, 84 confirmations, 53 marriages, 151,115 communions and 167 burials (*Annals*, 1918: 38). On April 7 the Archbishop administered confirmation to 75 children on Saturday and on Sunday to 17 children and one adult (*Franciscan Annals*, 1918: 167).

Table 3.2 : Percentage of Increase in the Catholic Population during 1901–1921

Ecclesiastical Province	*Roman Catholics*		
	1901	*1911*	*1921*
Agra, Simla	32,107	45,107	58,537
Total population in 1901		Increase 1901–11	Increase 1911–21
121, 298, 119		40.5%	29.3%

Source: *Catholic Directory*, 1922, pp. 171–172.

The above Table 3.2 indicates that percentage increase in the Catholic population during 1901–11 was higher (40.5%) than in the period 1911–21 (29.3%).

The total Catholic population in North India showed a phenomenal increase rate of 80.8% between 1898–1922. During this period there were 33 schools in the Archdiocese of Agra. In 1923, St. Mary's Church was erected by John family (*Gazetteer*, 1921). There were 11,187 Catholics, 31 priests, 14 religious brothers, 56 sisters and 15 novices. Around 405 children of Catholic parents, 191 dying children of non-Catholic and 271 Hindus and Protestants were baptised.

During 1927, total number of Roman Catholics in Agra was 2,040 of which 787 were in Cathedral, 805 in St. Mary's Church and 448 in St. Patrick's Church. Besides, there was a chapel at Kheria. The Archdiocese of Agra in 1929, managed by 26 Capuchin Fathers, 5 secular Priests, 14 brothers and 56 sisters, 271 Hindus and Protestants were received into the Church. There has been 76 marriages, 341 confirmations, 282 burials, and 198,643 Holy communions.

During 1931–35, eight more schools were opened. Catholic population in the Archdiocese of Agra was 13,922; Catichumens 3,499; creches 3; orphanages; old-age homes 2; hospitals 7 and dispensaries 8. The Archdiocese had 12,359 Catholics in 1937 (*Catholic Directory*, 1935: 122). According to report submitted to the Propaganda by Borghi on 15 December 1941, the number of Catholic population was 18,000 other Christians were 10,000. In 1944, Catholic Bishop's Conference was founded. The Catholic population increased to 16,000 and number of priests to 48; there were 62 nuns and 22 brothers in Agra Archdiocese (*The Examiner*, 1946). Number of Catholics in 1946 in Agra Cathedral was 2,000. The annual amount collected during this year was Rs 984, Mission Sunday Rs 1180.15. Total amount was Rs 2164.15, out of this Rs 991 was contributed by the schools of Agra Diocese. It indicated a significant contribution of the schools to the mission.

Catholic Association of India was organized for safeguarding the rights of the Catholics. Its organizing committee consisted of a president, a secretary and eight members. In April 1947, its membership rose to 87 persons (*Francisean Annals*, 1947). On Sunday, 27 July 1946 inaugural meeting of the Catholic Association of Agra was held. At the beginning it had over 150 members. There also existed an Indian Christian Association. In 1951, Agra City had 3,725 Christians out of a total of 375,665 (0.99% of the total population) (Census, 1955: 138–39). There were 3,853 Catholics (1956) in Agra. St. Claire's School was founded. There were 5,291 Christians (529 in rural and 4,762 in urban) in Agra district in 1961 (*Gazetteers*, 1965). Number of Catholics in Agra was 4,000 in 1964 (Subramanyam, 1970: 113). A slight increase (4,965) is observed during 1969. In 1972, there was a decline (4,553) in their number but the population increased (5,123) in 1980 *(Catholic Directory*, 1956–1980).

According to history of Indian Capuchin Province 1922–1972, there were 2,000 Catholics in Agra and it has one monastery. One more seminary, viz., St. Lawrence has been established in St. Mary's Church compound in 1991 and a hospital was to be started in the coming year.

Table 3.3 gives the number of baptisms and funerals between 1980–1990 in the Cathedral of Agra. Strength of Catholics in the Cathedral in 1990 was 1,776. Table 3.3 shows that in the Cathedral number of baptisms has been declining.

Table 3.3: Number of Baptisms and Funerals from 1980 to 1990 in the Agra Cathedral

Year	*Baptisms*	*Funerals*
1980	56	14
1981	37	07
1982	24	11
1983	26	07
1984	27	09
1985	36	08
1986	12	08
1987	27	09
1988	22	06
1989	24	12
1990	10	–

Source: Baptismal and Funeral Registers, 1980–1990 (unpublished), The Cathedral, Agra.

During 1989, there were 12 million Catholics in India, 3 million belonged to Oriental rite (St. Thomas Christians or 'Syrians' and 9 million to Latin rite (NCOC, 1989). Roman Catholics constitute 1.68% of the total Indian population. Agra has 7,880 Roman Catholics. Roman Catholics mission is running following educational institutions in India during 1990 (*Catholic Directory*, 1990).

Agra has two seminaries, two junior colleges, two intermediate colleges, four high schools, two junior high schools, four technical and industrial schools, fifteen middle and primary schools; number of Catholic children in the school is 213 with one hostel for girls, two dispensaries, one mobile clinic and one printing press.

Various associations involved in social welfare activities are:

1. Apostolate of Our Lady of Fatima
2. Catholic Anjuman & Burial Society
3. Catholic Association of Agra

Table 3.4: Number of Institutions Run by Roman Catholic Mission in Agra Archdiocese during 1990

Institutions	*Number*	*Strength of Pupils*
K.G. and Nursery	3,785	4,55,079
Primary	7,319	23,26,555
Secondary Schools	3,765	17,89,104
Colleges	240	2,13,392
Social Welfare Activities		
Technical and Training Schools		1,514
Hostels and Boarding Houses		1,765
Orphanages		1,085
Creches		228
Hospitals		704
Dispensaries and Health Centres		1,792
Leprosaria		111
Rehabilitation Centres		102
Homes of Aged, Destitutes and Handicapped		455

Source: Report, National Conference of Catholics, 2–5 June, 1989.

4. Catholic Enquiry Centre (not functioning).
5. All India Catholic Universities Federation at Aligarh.
6. Society of the Holy Childhood.
7. Society of St.Vincent de Paul.
8. Agra Social Service Society. It undertakes the following tasks:

   (a) M.C.H. sponsored by Catholic Relief
   (b) I.C.H. Society
   (c) Health Services
      (i) Hospitals
      (ii) Dispensaries
      (iii) Health visiting
      (iv) Mobile clinic
   (d) Education includes adult education
   (e) Home construction (rehabilitation scheme)
   (f) Road construction
   (g) Agricultural work

Roman Catholicism through its philosophy of social action has influenced social change. In 1950, the UN organized the Economic and Social Councils to work for higher standards of living and full employment in underdeveloped countries. World Bank, FAO, UNESCO, WHO, UNICEF, The Aid India Consortium, International Union of Welfare of Children, The Ford Foundation, The Rockfeller Foundation, are aiding in the development of India.

The Catholic Church in India has a modernizing role. Bishops have been training the Christians to control population growth by natural means of family planning (ICRB, 1964). Catholic Reforms Movement have influenced Indian Social Reform Movements e.g., restriction on child marriage, widow remarriage; introduction of nunneries and convents has promoted education of girls. This has raised the status of women.

The Protestant Sect

Unlike Roman Catholicism, Protestantism started lately. The first Protestant missionary arrived in India in 1706, but the endeavour was ecumenical. Before 1800 Protestant Missionary was solely confined to Europe (Jones, 1963: 17). Protestantism began in the real sense in India with the landing of Schwartz in 1750. He was followed by William Carey (a cobbler) who was sent out by the Baptist Society in 1792 (Wand, 1952). He translated the new Testament in Bengali, thus Indianization of Christianity began In 1792 Baptist Missionary Society was formed (Hole, 1896: 19). Henry Martyn landed in 1806 at Calcutta and translated the New Testament into Hindustani. He made one convert. According to the Charter of the East India Company in 1813, a Bishop was appointed. He founded the Bishop's College at Calcutta. In 1830, the first missionary, Alexander Duff was sent out by the established church, started many schools for the education of higher castes. Missionaries supplied teachers for elementary schools as well as for higher education. With a joint effort about 40 colleges were founded in addition to 11 Roman Catholic colleges and 23 seminaries.

There were various Protestant churches in India. Important among these are Anglican, Methodist, Congregationalist, Presbyterian. These have united into Church of South India, i.e., C.S.I. and C.N.I. which includes the Council of the Baptist, Churches in North India, the Church of the Brethren in India, the Disciples of Christ, the Church of India, the Methodist Church (British and Australian Conference) and the United Church of North India.

The beginning of the Protestantism in Agra dates back from the early 19th century. In 1811 Baptist Church was established and its associated school was started in 1812. The Church has been reconstructed.

Table 3.5 indicates very poor proportion of Christian population attached with the Baptist Church. It was observed during the field-work that members of the Church have been shifting to other churches of the Protestant Sect.

Table 3.5: Record of the Baptisms and Marriages Conducted in the Baptist Church, 1943–1990

Year	*Baptisms*	*Marriages*
1943	DNA	1
1944	-do-	1
1946	-do-	2
1947	-do-	3
1948	-do-	2
1949	-do-	nil
1950	-do-	1
1954	-do-	1
1966	-do-	1
1967	-do-	1
1969	2	2
1970	nil	nil
1971	4	-do-
1972	2	-do-
1973	2	-do-
1974	6	1
1975–83	nil	nil
1984	-do-	2
1985	5	2
1986	8	nil
1987	2	-do-
1988	nil	-do-
1989	3	-do-
1990	4	-do-

Source: Baptismal and Marriage Register of the Baptist Church, 1943-1990 (unpublished), Baptist Church of Agra.

In 1813, the British Parliament obliged the East India Company to allow British citizens (including missionaries) access to the territories controlled by the Company. Before that churches were planted by the Company's Chaplains.

The most important work was done by Henry Martyn and Daniel Carrie. Among the Indians, Sheikh Salah (Abdul Masih) worked for many years (1812–1825), with his work Anglican Church in North India began in a true sense. There was then a Presidency of Agra.

Church Missionary Society (CMS) work was started in April 18, 1813. Its first service was held on June 20, 1813. On October 30, Divine Service was performed in a building known at that time as Bishop Corrie's Chapel. On Easter Sunday 1826, Holy Communion was administered on various Christian communities (e.g., Europeans, Indian Christians, Romanists, Armenians etc.). A procession was carried out for the first time of male members only. At the thanks giving function there were over 400 people present.

Construction of St. George's Church began in 1828 and was consecrated by Bishop Wilson on his first visit to Agra on 14 December 1836. He confirmed 20 candidates on his second visit to Agra in 1840. Rev. W.H. Tribe, confirmed 130 candidates including 97 soldiers.

In 1883, a school was built which was demolished by the Municipality in 1917. The same year the Anglican set up a Chapel on Hospital Road. In the commencing year Havelock Church was established in Agra Cantonment. Church at Sikandra was erected in 1842. In 1845 'North India Bible Society' was founded. During 1847, there were around 300 people in Katra congregation. In 1849, a printing press was set up. At the same time Presbyterian Church and a cemetery at Delhi Gate were created but were sold to Dr. Sarkar in 1935. Now there is a market and Sarkar's Nursing Home at that place.

In 1850, St. John's College was started as a school on Hospital Road which was later on shifted to M.G. Road in 1913. First Confirmation (Protestant) was held in 1911. In 1854, St. Paul's Church was established. Foundation of St. John's Church was laid by John Calvin in March 1855. Rev. David Corrie established the Church mission in 1812, at Agra. In 1813, Corrie's Chapel was built in Bootat ka Katra. The Church was opened for public in 1857 (HBODOL, 1900). It has two congregations: (i) Indian and European, and (ii) Anglo-Indians. In 1856, Methodist Church was built with the arrival of Dr and Mrs Butler to Agra (CMT, 1960). According to the centenary celebrations brochure of the Christian Missionary Society, Agra, first Methodist missionary came to Agra after 1857. During this period the church was demolished and was restored in 1860 out of the funds raised by Protestant community and a steeple was added to the church in 1861. In 1863, Agra Scottish Presbyterian Mission was closed and sold in 1935.

The English Church was rebuilt in 1888. The old property was sold and the money was used in building the new church. The medical home for girls was established in 1888.. Some houses were bought adjacent to the church. The English Church had faced many upheavals. The number of Church members decreased due to their transfer to other stations or their shifting to new quarters. The number further decreased when Agra had no pastor. In that condition the pulpit was supplied by the ladies of the faith (foreign missionaries).

On the Christmas of 1901, 68 Baptisms took place from adjoining villages. Between 1893 and 1902 the entire Trans Yamuna came into the fold (Smith, 1980: 5). Attendance was 250 in the morning and 75 in evening. In 1905, Rev Fisher reopened the Church with an evening Sunday service and the attendance rose to 100 from 30. In 1914 the Church became linked with St. John's School and the girl's school Queen Victoria succeeded the parish school for the girls. Like-wise, St. John's Girls School is the successor of the three early city schools. In 1910, St. John's High School was opened. During 1923–1940, two most significant activities of the Church began, (i) Khristiya Sewak Samaj, and (ii) Zenana Mission (Holman, 1950: 118). There was no other duty during 1940–1945 apart from Sunday worship in the Church. There existed a local inter-denominational body for United Evangelistic action and promotion of the Christians in Agra, (mentioned above as 'Khristiya Sewak Samaj'). In 1923 Holman Institute was founded which was raised to High School in 1985. In 1971, an English medium unit was started which also is a high school at present. There were about 225 students and 34 Christian staff members in the school. During and after 1959, the Women's Christian Temperance Society (WCTU), the Women's Society of Christian Service (WSCS) and the Methodist Youth Fellowship (MYF) all grew during this period. A Sunday school for the youth and adults was being run regularly. In 1953, Agra was made a separate district. There were 1,450 members in the Church but 250 were regular subscribers. The yearly budget of the Church was Rs 80,000 for its maintenance. It contributes Rs 7,000 per year to Home Mission. The Church provided scholarship to needy and bright students.

In 1875, Diocesan Primary School was started by the CMS. In 1886 St. George's High School was opened. On 9, April 1976 Diocese of Agra was set up. Other important educational institutions were St. John's Primary School and St. Paul School (1978), Q.V. Nursery School (1960) and the Holman Primary School.

During 1980 there were 283 adults and 76 children members of C.N.I. Protestant sect is contributing significantly in the field of educational development of Agra, thus influencing social -economic uplift of the masses in general and of the Christians in particular.

Table 3.6 reveals that the strength of the Methodist Church has been increasing as compared to the Baptist Church. This is due to better management of the Methodist Church.

Table 3.6: Number of Baptisms and Marriages held in the Central Methodist Church of Agra during 1914–89

Year	*Baptisms*	*Marriages*
1914–1924	4	–
1925–1935	30	–
1936–1946	137	–
1947–1957	393	18
1958–1968	401	60
1969–1979	371	115
1980–1990	280	13

Source: Baptismal and Marriage Registers of the Methodist Church of Agra 1914-1990 (unpublished).

The Jains

Data regarding the history of Jainism is not available before the year 1891, neither is there any record available with the institutions of Jains. Jain Samaj rarely had the tradition of writing history (Singh, 1935). On the basis of records available it can be said that Jainism is one of the oldest religion of India. It originated in the 9th century BC. (Jain, 1926). Faruquhar mentions 6th century BC (Farquhar, 1967)

Jainism is the oldest religion of not only India but of the whole world. Besides India, it was popular in other countries also. Number of Jain Munis travelled throughout Iraq, Siam, Phillistine during 8th century BC. Up to 17th century (Vikram era) Jain temples, nurseries, followers of Jainism, Shrisangha Muni were present. Whole population and King were Jains. In Afghanistan (in ancient times it was included in Gandhar) Jain Tirthankar idol was found. In 1582 Jain Swetambar Tapagacchacharya Shri Heervijay Suri reached Fatehpursikri on an invitation by Akbar. Along with 67 Munis he spent his 'Chaturmas' at Agra. Degambar Muni came to Agra in 1619 and established a new panth 'Terapanthai' in 1623.

There are twenty-four Tirthankars among Jainism. The 22nd Tirthankar's (Neminath) period is supposed to be 84,000 years before Parsvanath (23rd Tirthankar), born about 3,038 years before the present era (Jain , 1926). Mahavira, the last Tirthankar was born in 599 BC; Kund-Kund Acharya was born in 108 BC. It indicates that Jainism is more ancient than Christianity and Sikhism.

Jainism was one but got bifurcated due to twelve years famine probably after 3rd or 4th century of Mahavira's Nirvana. Some differences occurred among Jains. A meeting was held at Mathura and the society got bifurcated into two sects on the debate of wearing clothes by the Saints, these were Degambars whose Saints observe nudity, and Swetambars whose Saints wore white clothes, former being older whose existence is traced to 4th century BC and the latter to about 80 AD (Suda, 1978).

During 1891 (see Table 3.7) the Jain community in the United Provinces belonged to entirely Degambars (Census, 1891: 183). Number of Jains in Agra district during this period was 13,462, i.e., 0.9% of the total Indian population and in the city it was 3,211, i.e., 2.83 times of the district figures for Christians. There is no separate enumeration of Degambars and Swetambars available. Total number of Jains in India were 1,500,000.

These sects further got divided into various sub-divisions. Swetambars developed Chaityvasa (Veer Samvat 882), Brahmadupik (V.S. 1755), Ratuk (V.S. 2032), Veeja (V.S. 2040), Parsvachandra-Surigaccha (V.S. 2042), Luca (V.S. 1978), and Luka Sangha (V.S. 2003). Later developments are Sthanakvasi (1473 AD) held their conference in 1905, Terapanthi, Bhikapanthi, Teen Thoi Wale etc. (Singh, 1935).

Among Degambars there developed Dravida Sangha, Vyapania Sangha, Kastha Sangha, Mathura Sangha, Bhillak Sangha, Tera pantha, Bees pantha, Taran pantha, Bhattarak pantha etc.

Figures (1891) indicate that Jains have stayed in Agra since the inception of the city itself around 1495 (*Gazetteer*, 1921). In the same period statue of Munisuvratnatha dated V.S. 1065 was found in Agra. Pandit Roopchandji Pandey arrived at Agra in the 17th century. Swetarnbaracharya Mahamahopadhyaya Megh Vijay wrote 'Yuktipraboth' during his stay at Agra in 1757 Vikram era (1700). In 1863 Swetamabrachrya Atmaramji observed his Chaturmas at

Table 3.7: Population of Jains vis-a-vis the Total Population in Agra District and City

	District Population		*City Population*	
Year	*Total*	*Jains*	*Total*	*Jains*
1872	1,076,005	–	149,008	–
1881	974,656	11,476	160,203	–
1891	1,003,796	13,462	168,622	3,211
1901	1,060,528	12,953	188,022	–
1911	1,021,847	11,210	185,449	2,754
1921	924,155	10,242	185,532	–
1931	1,048,316	13,162	229,764	3,828
1941	DNA	DNA	284,149	DNA
1951	1,501,391	16,376	375,665	7,724
1961	1,862,142	17,710	508,680	8,240
1971	2,308,638	21,255	634,622	9,361
1981	2,852,942	23,179	747,318	7,094
1991	2,704,545	–	891,800	–

Source: Census and gazetteers of the corresponding years. Please see references.

Agra and received education from Ratanchandji Maharaj (Jain, 1989). In 1893, Degambars held their first annual conference, as a result 'Jain Young Men's Association' was formed. In 1894 'All India Degambar Jain Mahasabha' was established. Thereafter, *Jain Gazetteer* (1895) was started. It is a main weekly paper of Degambar Jains. It published nearly 8,000 copies per week which are circulated allover the world. This Mahasabha has also organized 'Indian Degambar Tirtha Kshetra Committee'. Degambars also support other newspapers as 'The Degambar Jain', 'Jain Mitra', and a women' s paper 'Jain Nari Hitkari'.

A slight decline is observed during 1901 (Jain population in Agra district was 12,953 which was 0.97% of total of India which was 1,334,000). In Agra tehsil their number was 4,095. In the corresponding years 1911 (in India T = 1,248,000) and 1921 their number went down to 11,210 and 10,242 respectively, in the district. In 1931 their number rose to the figures equal to the year 1891 (i.e., 13,462) Jain Sabha was established in 1939. It is a registered body. A further decline in the number of Jains in Agra district (11,301) is observed during 1951 but in the city it was 7,724 (2.05%) of the total population (Census, 1951: 256). During this period, there were three

Jain schools in Agra city. Number of Jains rose to 13,526 in 1961. They mostly belong to the Vaish caste. On the whole, they were traders, businessmen, moneylenders, and bankers. They belonged to Degambar, Swetambar and Sthanakvasi sects. The majority being Degambars.

During succeeding years their number increased considerably. In 1964 it was 17,710 in Agra district, rural Jain population being 4,184 and urban being 13,526 (*Gazetteers*, 1965: 82). A further increase (21,255) is observed in 1971 in the district, whereas in the city it was 9,361 (*Census*, 1971: 202–203). It increased further to 23,179 in 1981 (*Census*, 1981: 6, 16–17). With the rise in number of Jains, various organizations developed within the society. 'All India Jain Youth Federation' was established on 1, January, 1976 (Bharilla, 1981). It has about 213 branches and 3,200 members (ibid.). During 1968–69 'Bharatvar Shiya Veetrag Vigyan Pathshala Samiti' was established for the evangelism of the masses. A Swetambar Jain temple has been established on December 5, 1988. A group of Swetambar saints reached here on December 8, 1988. Agra has one women's association which is working against dowry among Jains. It has influenced local Jains. Another body is 'Jain Youth Association' whose main objective is to prevent alcoholism (liquor consumption) among the Jain youths.

There are number of Jain dharamshalas, one charitable association for feeding the birds, one school for the teaching of Jainism–attendance here is very low; only about 5–6 students come here. There are around 50 temples in the city, some of them are of ancient origin, about 600–700 years old. According to one elderly person aged 89 years, there was a temple of Jains around 500 years back at the present Kamla Nagar-Sultanganj crossing which was destroyed by Aurangzeb. The idol of Lord Parsvanath was brought by the Jains and a temple was established at Tajganj which is supposed to be the oldest Jain temple in Agra. The other historical temples are at Sikandra (400 years old) Roshanmohalla (500 years old), Nunihai (500 years old), and Motikatra (400 years old).

Agra forms one of the oldest centres of Jains. Old established families indicate that, it is the oldest among the other religions under present study. Jainism is contributing significantly to the educational development of the city inhabitants. There is one degree college for girls, one intermediate college each for boys and girls, and around five primary schools. There is one Oswal Jain boarding house.

The Jain contribution to medieval Indian logic is well known. Jainism constitute one of the most significant systems of Indian thought. It is a religion of multifarious activities. It has produced great geniuses in every branch of literature. It has produced great mathematicians like Mahaviracharya who worked on oriental mathematics. There have been great historians and biographers.

Thus, it can be concluded that it is a dynamic force in the development of the city inhabitants in general and Jains in particular. Their money is spent more on religious activities. Apart from this, Jain Samaj has created a Mahavidyalaya at Banaras in which Jain priests receive modern training, an orphanage in Delhi, hostels and a widow's home in Bombay. The All India Jain Association is governed by its officers and a managing committee. Chief Officer is the General Secretary assisted by three Joint Secretaries one from each Degambar, Swetambar and Sthanakvasi sects. Its objectives are:

(i) union and progress of Jain community
(ii) the propagation of Jainism, and
(iii) to encourage female education

Jainism is very active in Agra. A huge procession is carried out every year on Mahavir Jayanti. During Paryushan Parva various sacraments are performed with great pomp and show. Persons (mainly businessmen) belonging to upper strata are donating large amounts for religious purposes. Also, they are donating regularly (annually) to the lepers asylum at Agra. Prizes are given to the meritorious Jain students. Recently, they have started participating in politics also. It shows that Jains are not only religious but also are active socially and politically as economic power is already in their hands. Like Christians, Jains also have a system of stratification. Religious hierarchy of Jains is as follows:

1. Acharya and Upadhyaya are the chief officers of the Jain church. The authority to initiate, confirm and the like vests with the Acharya.
2. Organization of nuns has four officers, viz., Pravartini, Ganavacchedini, Abhiseka and Pratihari.

In addition to Acharya and Upadhyaya there are Pravartaka, Sthavira, Ganin, Ganavacchedaka and Ratnadhika. All the officers of Jain church are expected to be highly qualified and experienced persons.

The Sikhs

Sikhism originated in the Punjab with the birth of Guru Nanak (1469–1539). The name 'Sikh' signifies a 'disciple'. Formation of sect took place when the disciples were persecuted by the administration. Torture, harassment and persecution of Sikhs had been started by the then Muslim rulers which made their group come together and take up arms against Muslims. Their tenth Guru, Guru Govind Singh (1660–1708) gave this sect a military character and the name 'Singh' meaning the lion was given. Like Jainism and Christianity, Agra also formed an important and one of the oldest settler of Sikhism. Guru Das (1540–1560) spent some years preaching in Agra (Singh, 1971). Guru Nanak visited Agra (Lohamandi) on the 4th day of Bhadon of the year 1566 Vikram Samvat. In 1665 Guru Tegh Bahadur came to Agra and was arrested here with his devotees. In this sense Agra forms an important historical centre of Sikhism.

In the 18th century, the Sikh religion was a conglomeration of sects (Archer, 1946). Major sect was Nanakpanthi. In 1909, Keshdhari and Sahajdhari sects were formed (Macauliffe, 1909). The Nanakpanthi, he said, was the major sect of the Sahajdharis. This division was mainly based upon caste. Followers of Guru Govind Singh were mainly Jats, while Sahajdharis were mainly drawn from Hindu high castes like the Kshatriyas and Aroras. Certain Sikh sects began movements for religious reforms, e.g., Namdharis and Nirankaris. Singh (1966) said, "the Nirankaris are fast loosing their separate identity and may, within a few decades merge back into the Hindu or Sikh parent body". Later researches have proved him wrong. Although of recent origin, Sikhism is expanding considerably (see Table 3.8) in India as well as in Agra. History of Sikhism in Agra is purely religious (Cunningham, 1915). According to 1881 census, Sikhs numbered 1,853,426 in India and in 1901 their number was 2,195,339 (*Encyclopaedia*, Vol. xiii, p. 789). Data regarding number of Sikhs in Agra is available after 1891, onwards (Table 3.8). In 1891 there were 540 Sikhs in Agra district and 485 in Agra City (*Census*, 1891). Followers of Guru Hargovind (1606–1645) lived in Agra and Gwalior (Court, 1985). Guru Tegh Bahadur (1621–1675)

Table 3.8: Sikh Population in Agra District and City during 1872–1991

Year	District	City
1872	–	–
1881	409	–
1891	540	485
1901	120	61
1911	138	105
1921	211	–
1931	–	–
1941	DNA	DNA
1951	1543.5	9094
1961	10699	–
1971	9075	7880
1981	10565	1336
1991	–	

Source: The table has been compiled from census and gazetteers of the corresponding years. Please see the references.

came to Agra. He sat in a garden and sent his valuable seal ring and a shawl through a disciple to the market saying, "take them to some confectioner and bring me some food".

The confectioner thinking that it was perhaps a stolen property took him to the Kotwal. The Kotwal took that ring and came to Tegh Bahadur in the garden and began to ask, "who are you and from where have you come from". Tegh Bahadur replied, "from Anandpur to wander about". He made several converts at Agra.

Another popular story is about an old woman aged about 80 years who weaved a 'than' for Guru Tegh Bahadur. When he visited her house, she presented it to the Guru and also gave her house for the purpose of Sikh worship. Since then the gurudwara is known as 'Maithan' gurudwara which is the oldest one (about 276 years old) and the area surrounding it is called Maithan. Guru Govind Singh (1666–1708) reached Agra in August 1707, to meet Bahadur Shah. He stayed here for four months. He addressed the Sikh congregation every morning and evening.

During 1901, the number of Sikhs in the district was 120 and in the Tehsil it was 89 and in the city it was 61 only (*Gazetteer*, 1921: 68) At this time Sikhs were mainly in government service, in the army and police and were not natives of the district. In the Indian

National Army 60% of the officers and soldiers were Sikhs. All Sikh agitations were launched from the platform of the gurudwara. There were nine gurudwaras in the Agra city. On 30, October 1902, Agra Singh Sabha was associated to the Chief Khalsa Diwan (Singh, 1983) In 1920 Shiromani Akali Dal was established along with Shiromani Gurudwara Prabandhak Committee (SGPC). During 1909, Anand Marriage Act was sponsored.

In Agra district the number of Sikhs rose from 138 to 211 during 1911–1921. Data is not available for the period 1921–1941. A sharp increase in their number is observed during 1951. In the district it was 15,435 whereas in the city 9,094 (2.42% of the total) A slight decrease (10,435 in urban and 264 in rural area, total = 10,699) is observed in 1961. Their number declined to 7,880 in 1971 and increased to 10,565 in 1981. According to the head office of the Sikh's Gurudwara (Guru-ka-Tal) the number of Sikhs in Agra district during 1991 was 60,000. Due to 1984's riots Sikhs have migrated from Punjab to Agra.

Although of recent origin, Sikhism has played a significant role in the socio-religious regeneration of the Sikh community. The Sikh Sabha Movement (1873) had three social goals to build society, to use society as a base to wage an armed struggle and to capture political power by the Khalsa (Singh, 1981).

Sikhism discards caste system as well as the concept of pollution and purity (untouchability) attached to it . It has also uplifted the status of women. Guru Amar Das abolished the custom of purdah and sati (Singh, 1962) Its plebian base aimed at uplifting the downtrodden. Sikhism has also started schools whose main aim is to promote proselytisation. It also had an objective of producing a class of teachers and evangelist.

The gurudwaras not only helped to spread the teachings of the religious leaders, but also formed a platform for discussion of general problems concerning the welfare of the Sikh Panth and as training grounds of social service, public deliberations and other kinds of practical religion as well. History of Sikhism mainly revolves around these gurudwaras.

Agra has around 24 gurudwaras of which three constitute the historical gurudwaras, viz., Maithan, Lohamandi and Guru-ka-Tal. The last one constitutes a major centre of worship. Attached to this is a dispensary which provides free medical aid to all, irrespective of caste and religion.

There is a big farm which supports Langar (the meals supplied in the name of God) and is one of the source of income. Gurudwara Maithan is running a school. Other gurudwaras are small and are regarded by the community as local.

References

Alice, P.J. (1982), *The Roman Catholic Mission in Agra from 1781–1947*, St. Joseph's Printing School, Agra.

Alzog, Rev. J.D.D. (1882), *Manual of Universal Church History*, Vol.IV, Third Period A.D. 1648–1878, Trans. by The Rev. F.J. Fabisch and The Rev. Thomas, S. Byrne, M.H. Gill and Son, Dublin.

Annual Guide and Gazetteer (1841), The Bengal and Agra, Vol. 1, Willian Rustom & Co., Calcutta, p. 123.

Archer, J.C. (1946), *The Sikhs*, Princeton, New Jersey.

Baarth, A. (1969), *The Religions of India*, Trans. Rev. J. Wood, S. Chand and Co., Delhi.

Badely Bishop B.T. (1931), *Visions and Victories in Hindustan: Story of the Mission Stations of the Methodist Episcopal Church in Southern Asia*, Diamond Jubilee Edition, Methodist Publishing House, Madras (Chennai).

Bharilla, H.C. (1981), *Yugpurush Shri Kanj Swami, Kund Kund Kohan*, Degambar Jain, Tirtha Suraksha Trust, Jaipur, p. 36.

Catholic Directory of India (1935) p. 122.

Catholic Directory of India for the Year 1956–1980 and 1990, St. Paul Publications, New Delhi,

Catholic Encyclopaedia, Vol. XIII, The Encylopaedia Press, Inc. New York, p. 789.

Catholic Reference Book, (1964–65).

Census of India, 1861.

Census of India, (1891) Vol. XVI, Part-I, 1894, (p. 147).

Census of India (1951), *Agra Distt. Census Handbook*, (pp. 138–39 and 256).

Census of India (1971), Agra City Urban Agglomerate, (p. 202–203).

Census of India (1981), (p. 6, 16–17).

Cook, H.T. (1975), *The Sikh Wars: The British Army in the Puniab 1845–1849*, Thomson Press India Ltd., Publication Division, New Delhi.

Cort, J. (1986), "Recent Descriptive Accounts of the Contemporary Jains: A Review Essay", *Man in India*, 66(2), June, (p. 180–86).

Court, M.H. (1985), *History of the Sikhs*, (trans.) ; Amar Prakashan, Delhi (p. 26).

Cunningham, J.D. (1915), *History of the Sikhs*, Indian Edition, S. Chand, New Delhi.

D'Souza, D. (1982), *The Growth and the Activities of the Catholic Church in North India: 1757–1858*, St. Ann's Friary, Mangalore.

Duggad, H. (1979), *Madhya Asia Aur Punjab Mein Jain Dharma*, Jain Prachin Sahitya Prakashan Mandir, 'Shahdara, Delhi, (p. 18).

Encylopaedia Catholic, Vol. XIII, The Encyclopaedia Press Inc.

Farquhar, J.N. (1967), *Modern Religious Movements in India*, Munshiram Manoharlal, Delhi.

Franciscan Annals (1918), April, (p. 128).

——— (1918), VoL IX, May, Nos. 5, (p. 167).

——— (1918), No V., (p. 38).

——— (1947), Vol. LXXXXIII, No. 1, Agra, Feb., (p. 4).

Gazetteers of the North West Province, (1876), Vol. IV, Agra Division, Part.1.

Gazetteer, Agra (1921), Vol. VIII, (p. 68 and 142).

Gazetteer, U.P. District (1965), Agra, (p. 82).

Gazetteer Imperial (1905), United Province, Agra Division, (p. 24).

Gibbs, M.E. (1972), *The Anglican Church In India 1600–1970*, ISPCK, Delhi.

Gopalan, (1973), *Outlines of Jainism*, Wiley Eastern Pvt. Ltd., New Delhi.

Gupta, H.R. (1952), *History of the Sikhs*, Vol. 1, Simla.

——— (1973), *History of the Sikh Gurus*, U.C. Kapur & Sons, New Delhi.

——— (1978), *History of the Sikhs*, Vol. II, Munshiram Manoharlal Publishers, New Delhi.

——— (1989), *The Sikh Gurus*, Vol. 1, Delhi.

Handbook of Diocese of Lucknow (1900), G.A. Ford.

Hole, Rev. C. (1896), "The Early History of the Church Missionary Society for Africa and the East to the End of A.D. 1814," Church Missionary Society, London.

Holman, S.C. (1950), *What God Hath Wrought*, The Book Room, Boston.

Hughes, A .W. (1871), *Outlines of Indian History*, Bell and Daily, London.

Indian Catholic Reference Book, (1964), The Catholic Association of Bombay.

Jain, J.B. (*V.S.* 2476), *Itihas Mein Mahavir Ka Sthan*, Shri Mahavir Prakashan, Etah, (p. 16).

Jain, P.R. (1989), *Shri Vijyanand Suri, Mahatara Sadvi*, Sh. Mrigavatiji Foundation, Delhi.

Jain, K.P. (ed.) (1926), *Samkshipta Jain Itihas*, Moolchand Kishanchand, Jain Vijay Printing Press, Surat.

Jones, T.K., Jr. (1963), *Our Mission Today*, World Outlook Press, New York.

Khurana, G. (1985), *British Historiography on The Sikh Power in the Punjab*, Mansell Publishing Co. Ltd., London and New York.

Macaulifee, M.A. (1909), *The Sikh Religion*, Oxford University Press, Delhi.

Madras Catholic Directory, (1863).

——— (1864).
——— (1909).
Mcleod, W.H. (1968), *Guru Nanak and the Sikh Religion*, The Clarendon Press, Oxford.
National Convention of Catholics (1989) 2–5 June.
Polhacamury, T. Archbishop (1961) *The Religion of the Jains*, Trans. from German by Amulya Chandras and T.C. Burke, Sanskrit College, Calcutta.
Singh, A. (1935), *Jail Mein Mera Jainabhayas*, Achal Grantha Mala, Agra (p. 21 and 23)
Singh, G. (ed.) (1962), *Early European Accounts of the Sikhs*, R.K. Maitra, Calcutta, (p. 21 and 23).
Singh, H. (1966), *Guru Gobind Singh*, The Guru Gobind Singh Foundation, Chandigarh, (p. 25).
Singh, H. (1983), *Religions of India*, Clarion Books, New Delhi, (p. 147).
Singh, J. (1981), *The Sikh Revolution*, Bahri Publications Pvt. Ltd., New Delhi, (p. 115).
Singh, K. (1971), *History of the Sikhs*, Vol. I & II, 1469–1839, Oxford University Press, Delhi.
Singh, Trilochan (1967), Guru Tegh Bahadur, Gurudwara Prabandhak Committee, Sis Ganj, Chandni Chowk, Delhi.
Smith, Thomas (1980), "Christianity and Christian Institutions in Agra", St. John's Church, Agra, Post Centenary Silver Jubilee, Souvenir.
Subramanyam, K.N. (1970), The Catholic Community in India, MacMillan, New Delhi.
The Christian Missionary Today (ed.), (1960), The Joint Section of Education and Cultivation of the Board of Missions of the Methodist Church, p. 93.
The Examiner, (1946). Vannini F.F. (1981), Hindustan Tibet Mission, OFM. Cap., New Delhi.
Vannini, F.F. (1976), *The Bell of Lhasa*, OFM Cap., New Delhi
——— (1976), *The Religious Sects of the Hindus*.
Wilson, H.H., (1977) *A Sketch of the Religious Sects of the Hindus*, Cosmo Publications, New Delhi, (p. 276–347).

Reports

Gazetteer, Agra, Vol. VIII, 1905, p. 65, 68 & 72.
Census of India, 1921, Vol. XVI, pt. 11, Govt. Press, 1923, 30–31.
Census of India, 1881. p. 11.
Census of India, 1891, Vol. L; Printers to the Queen's Most Excellent Majesty, 1892, 62–63.

Census of India, 1911, Vol. 15, pt. 1, Printed by F. Luper, (p. 30), Supdt. Government. Printing Press, 1912, 32–33 and 152–158.
Census of India, 1921, Vol. XVI, 30–31.
Census 1931, Vol. XXIII. pt 1.
Census of, India, 1951 Vol. 2, pt. II, Supdt. Printing and Stationary, 1953, (251–56 & 560–61)
Census of India, Agra Distt. Census Handbook, 1965, (p. 5).
Census of India, 1971, Distt. Census Handbook, (202–203).
Census of India, 1981, (pp. 16–21)
Census of India, 1991.
The Christian Missionary Today (ed.) 1960, The Joint Section of Education and Cultivation of the Board of Missions of the Methodist Church, p. 93.
Note: There is a difference between figures according to provisional populations table and primary census abstract.

Unpublished Sources:

Baptismal and Marriage Register of the Baptist Church 1943–1990, Baptist Church of Agra.
Baptismal and Funeral Registers of the Cathedral (1980–1990). The Cathedral, Agra.
Baptismal and Marriage Registers of the Methodist Church of Agra (1914–1990), Central Methodist Church, Agra.
Report by Borqhi, 15.12.1841, Archives, The Cathedral, Agra. Report by Fr.. Joachim of St Anatolia, Archives, The Cathedral, Agra.
References regarding Population of Christians, Jain and Sikh Population from 1862 to 1991 in Agra Distt/City.

4 Social and Religious Practices of the Sects

In every society, particularly in Indian society, religion plays a vital role in an individual's life and generally, most of his day-to-day decisions are guided by his affiliation to a particular religion. Religion as a dominating factor governs most of an individual's activities or we can say that social behaviour of an individual is coloured with religious values. Religion shapes domestic, economic and political institutions. It manifests in certain movements as rise of capitalism (Troeltsch, 1931; Weber, 1966; Tawney, 1926; Fanfani, 1939). It has profound effect upon culture. It is the key element in the life of civilization whose very existence is endangered when religion fails (Dawson, 1949; Tonybee, 1947; Demant, 1952).

Religion performs dual functions, viz., on the one hand, it sustains the social system whereas on the other it serves as a vehicle of social change (Gupta, 1974b). It has a structural relationship with all social institutions (Malefitz, 1968). Religion is closely linked with politics (Narang, 1956). Rituals as an integral part of religion play significant role in the organized life of a sect and their performance sometimes closely link an individual to its sect. Rituals have been defined as "the religious means by which the purity of an individual and the social life becomes guaranteed" (Desai, 1978:58). Particular sets of rituals are dictated to a particular caste or sub-caste group so that distinct differences in the respective rituals which those social groups and sub-groups follow enable to distinguish them from one another (ibid.). It has been observed that differences in ritual performance lead to division of a sect or a religious group. Rituals are so significant in one's life that even minor variation leads to formation of a sub-sect within a sect.

The aim of the present chapter is (i) to analyse as to what extent age, sect, education, occupation and income help to account for variation in religiosity and ritualism of an individual, and (ii) what changes have been taking place in the religious behaviour of people and what are the causes of change? In the present analysis, the term 'religiosity' refers to religious behaviour which is defined as "a whole configuration of behaviour pattern, including feelings, attitudes, emotions etc., all of which are presumably somehow summated and responded to an entity" (Glenn, 1962). For the study of religiosity among various sects following questions have been raised:

1. How strong do you feel about your religion?
2. How frequently do you visit your place of worship?
3. How much time do you spend per week in you religious organization?
4. How much money do you contribute per year to your religious organization?
5. How frequently do your participate in your religion's organizational activities?
6. Have you ever worked for raising funds for your religious organization?
7. Do you feel that religious differences lead to segmentation with your own group?
8. How strongly do you favour that with the changing society religious practices should also change?

Ritualism has been studied in the light of the following questions:

1. Have you ever worked in organizing rituals in your religious organization?
2. How strictly do you believe in life cycle rituals?
3. Do you observe seasonal rituals? They include among Christians 15th August, Novina; among Jains Daslakshan, and Paryushan; and among Sikhs Baisakhi and Sankrant?
4. Do you observe various sacraments?

Along with this a separate list of various rituals of the respective sects was prepared and each individual was asked to respond upon these. Causes of change in ritual observance have been analysed with the help of open-ended questions aided by interview. For the above purpose two four-point scale has been constructed on religiosity and ritualism.

Religiosity

A careful examination of our data (Table 4.1) reveals that feeling about one's own religion is greatest (88%) among the age group of 56 years and above followed by the age group of 46–55 years (86%) and

Table 4.1: How strongly do you feel about your religion?

Variable	*Categories*	*Very Strong*		*Strong*		*Less Strong*		*Not at all Strong*		*Total*	
		'f'	*%*	*'f'*	*%*	*'f'*	*%*	*'f'*	*%*	*'f'*	*%*
Age	⩽–35 years	35	71	6	12	4	8	4	8	49	100
	36–45	66	81	11	13	2	2	3	4	82	100
	46–55	67	86	7	9	4	5	0	0	78	100
	56 ⩾	80	89	4	4	5	5	2	3	91	100
	Total	**248**	**83**	**28**	**9**	**15**	**5**	**9**	**3**	**300**	**100**
Sect	Roman Cath.	40	80	8	16	2	4	0	0	50	100
	Protestant	35	70	7	14	4	8	4	8	50	100
	Degambar	40	80	3	6	4	8	3	6	50	100
	Swetambar	47	94	3	6	0	0	0	0	50	100
	Sikh	86	86	7	7	5	5	2	2	100	100
	Total	**248**	**83**	**28**	**9**	**15**	**5**	**9**	**3**	**300**	**100**
Edu-cation	Basic or Less	33	89	3	8	1	3	0	0	37	100
	Matriculate	58	87	6	9	3	4	0	0	67	100
	Intermediate	45	83	7	13	2	4	0	0	54	100
	Graduate	63	80	7	9	5	6	4	5	79	100
	P.G. & Higher	49	78	5	8	4	6	5	8	63	100
	Total	**248**	**83**	**28**	**9**	**15**	**5**	**9**	**3**	**300**	**100**
Occu-pation	Business	117	89	8	8	6	4	1	1	132	100
	Teaching	29	78	5	14	2	5	1	3	37	100
	Govt. Service	56	78	10	15	1	9	5	3	72	100
	Engineering	7	64	2	18	1	1	1	9	11	100
	Preaching	11	100	0	0	0	0	0	0	11	100
	Admn. (pvt.)	8	73	1	9	1	9	1	9	11	100
	Others	20	77	2	8	4	15	0	0	26	100
	Total	**248**	**93**	**28**	**9**	**15**	**5**	**9**	**3**	**300**	**100**
Income	⩽ Rs 2000	62	78	8	10	6	5	3	4	79	100
	2000–5000	87	84	9	9	5	4	3	3	104	100
	5000–10000	69	87	5	6	4	5	1	1	79	100
	10000–more	30	79	6	16	0	0	2	5	38	100
	Total	**248**	**83**	**28**	**9**	**15**	**5**	**9**	**3**	**300**	**100**

36–45 years (81%). Frequency (72%) of those who feel very strong about their religion is minimum among the 35 years or less age group.

Among Christians these include Baptism, Holy Communion, marriage and burial. In Jains these are: (a) Chathi, (b) Dasthon, (c) marriage, and (d) death and among Sikhs major life cycle rituals are Janam, Amrat, Anand and Uthala corresponding to a,b,c and d.

Frequency of those who do not at all feel strong (8%) about their religion (Table 4.1) is maximum in the age group of 35 years or below, then 4% in the age group of 36–45 years and 3% in the age group of 56 years and more. Our observations indicate that religiosity is observed more among the higher age groups.

Sectwise distribution (Table 4.1) indicates that the frequency of those who feel very strong (94%) is highest among the Swetambar sect of Jains, next highest frequency (86%) is among the Sikh sect. It is still lower (80%) both in Roman Catholic and Degambar and lowest (70%) among the Protestants.

On the basis of education it is observed (Table 4.1) that highest (89%) ratio of those who feel very strong or strong is in the lowest education group and lowest (78%) among the postgraduate and higher group of education. Those who do not feel strong about their religion is 5% among the graduates and 8% in the postgraduate and higher education group.

It is also indicated (Table 4.1) that feeling of religiosity is highest (100%) among the preaching class followed by business class (89%) and in government service and teaching class (78%) each. This is due to the fact that this class consists mainly of the Sikhs and feeling of religiosity is observed comparatively higher among them (Table 4.1). Private administrative group and those who have been categorized as 'others' have shown lower (73% and 77%) proportions. Engineering occupation forms minimum frequency (64%) of those who feel very strong. Those who feel not at all strong (9%) are both among the engineering and private administrative occupation, 3% each in teaching and government services. It is still low (1%) among business and nil in preaching and in others. It indicates that occupation is one of the factors which determines religiosity. It is apparent from Table 4.1 that the income group of Rs 2,000–5,000 p.m. has maximum (87%) proportion of those who feel very strong about their religion, and minimum (78% and 79%) ratio of such persons is highest among the lowest income groups (≤ Rs 2000) and Rs 10,000 and above. Thus, we can say that income does not constitute significant factor in determining religiosity. But those who do not at all feel strong are maximum (5%) in higher income group and next (4%) in the income group of Rs 2,000 and below and (3%) in the income group of Rs 2,000–5,000 p.m. Their frequency (1%) is minimum in the income group of Rs 5,000–10,000 p.m.

Therefore, it can be concluded that age, sect, education and occupation but not income are important factors in determining religiosity of an individual. Since higher income groups have shown higher religiosity we can say that religion does not hamper economic development. This is also indicated by previous studies (Singh, 1973; Rao, 1969; Dube, 1965).

Table 4.2 indicates that highest frequency (64%) of those who visit their places of worship daily or weekly (after clubbing frequencies of daily and weekly) is among the age group of 56 years and above and lowest (43%) among the youngest age group of 35 years and below. It also shows that proportion of those who never visit their places of worship is nearly equal among all age groups. It has different reactions. Those who belonged to the oldest age group cannot go very frequently to their place of worship due to their old age, although they have a desire to go.

Sectwise distribution shows that the Sikhs have the highest (66%) ratio of the persons visiting their places of worship regularly (the term regularly has been used because the Sikhs and the Christians have Sunday worship as most significant whereas the Jains have daily worship. The frequency (40%) is lowest among the Protestants. Table 4.1 also indicates lowest degree of religiosity among the Protestants and highest among the Sikhs. Among the Jains, the Degambars visit more (54%) frequently as compared to the Swetambars (50%). Among all the three religious groups, the Sikhs form the highest frequency of the religious sect followed by the Jains and the Christians, who are regular visitors to their place of worship.

Educationwise distribution indicates that those in the matric group form (67%) (maximum) who go more frequently (i.e., daily or weekly) to their places of worship as compared to the uneducated (62%) and postgraduate and higher education (63%) groups. Those in the graduate group form minimum (i e., 37% only) in this regard. Observations on the basis of Table 4.1 are found in contrast to Table 4.2. It implies that feeling of religiosity does not indicate attendance in the church (refers to all places of worship).

Table 4.2: How frequently do you visit your religious centre?

Variable	*Categories*	*Daily*		*Weekly*		*Frequently*		*Occasionally*		*Never*		*Total*	
		'f'	*%*	*'f'*	*%*	*'f'*	*%*	*'f'*	*%*	*'f'*	*%*	*'f'*	*%*
Age	⩽–35 years	9	18	12	25	8	16	18	37	2	4	49	100
	36–45	23	28	16	19	13	16	26	32	4	5	82	100
	46–55	23	29	20	26	13	17	18	23	4	5	78	100
	56 ⩾	31	34	27	30	11	12	17	19	5	5	91	100
	Total	**86**	28	**75**	25	**45**	15	**79**	26	**15**	05	**300**	**100**
Sect	Roman Cath.	16	32	10	20	5	10	19	38	0	0	50	100
	Protestant	8	16	12	24	8	16	17	34	5	10	50	100
	Degambar	20	40	7	14	9	18	12	24	2	4	50	100
	Swetambar	9	18	16	32	9	18	11	22	5	10	50	100
	Sikh	33	33	30	30	14	14	20	20	3	3	100	100
	Total	**86**		**75**		**45**		**79**		**15**		**300**	**100**
Education	Basic or less	19	51	4	11	7	19	3	8	4	11	37	100
	Matriculate	31	46	14	21	4	6	14	21	4	6	67	100
	Intermediate	9	17	15	28	11	20	19	35	0	0	54	100
	Graduate	15	19	14	18	14	18	38	35	6	7	79	100
	P.G. & Higher	12	19	28	44	9	14	13	21	1	2	63	100
	Total	**86**		**75**		**45**		**79**		**15**		**300**	**100**
Occupation	Business	54	41	14	11	20	15	41	31	3	2	132	100
	Teaching	3	8	19	51	5	14	8	22	2	5	37	100
	Govt. Service	12	17	25	35	15	21	16	22	4	5	72	100
	Engineering	0	0	0	0	3	27	2	18	6	5	11	100
	Preaching	6	55	3	27	1	9	1	9	0	0	11	100
	Admn. (Pvt.)	2	18	6	55	0	0	3	27	0	0	11	100
	Others	9	34	8	31	1	4	8	31	0	0	26	100
	Total	**86**		**75**		**45**		**79**		**15**		**300**	**100**
Income	⩽ Rs 2000	13	29	28	35	10	13	28	23	0	0	79	100
	2000–5000	16	15	33	31	23	21	19	28	13	5	104	100
	5000–10000	37	47	10	13	6	8	24	30	2	2	79	100
	10000–more	20	53	4	10	6	16	8	21	0	0	38	100
	Total	**86**		**75**		**45**		**79**		**15**		**300**	**100**

Our observations (Table 4.2) indicate that attendance in religious centres is highest (82%) (after combining percentages of daily and weekly goers) among the preaching class followed by those in 'others' (65%) and business (52%) and lowest (0%) among the engineering class. Proportion of people who never visit their places of worship is highest (55%) among the engineering class then 5% both in teaching and in government service.

Among various income groups, it is observed that church attendance is highest (64%) among the income group of Rs 2,000 p.m. then higher income group (63%) followed by 57% among Rs 5,000–Rs 10,000 p.m. income group, then 46% (i.e., minimum) in the income group of Rs 2,000–5,000 p.m. Thus, we may say that, income does not affect an individual's church attendance.

A careful examination of Table 4.3 reveals that persons in the age group of 56 years and above who spend three hours or more per week are 26.4% while the persons of the middle age group (45–55 years) spend one hour (41%), persons belonging to 36–45 years age group never visit the place of worship (42%) whereas in the age group of < 35 years they form 33% and in the age group of 46–55 years their frequency is still lower. It is minimum (20%) in the age group of 56 years and more.

Similar observations were made by Sayeed et al. (1990), but their study showed that frequency of persons visiting religious places decreased with the increasing age. On the contrary, present observations indicate that frequency is higher among the youngest and eldest age group. This implies that as the responsibilities of life increase, an individual tends to remain confined to his/her domestic affairs and as soon as one gets free from it he/she gets involved in religious activities.

During the interview it was observed that younger people go to visit religious places generally for fun but the older people go for religious pursuit and for passing their time. Our data (Table 4.3) shows that those who spend maximum time of one hour is maximum among Sikhs (49%) followed by Protestants (46%) , Roman Catholics (40%), Swetambar (38%) and minimum Degambars (32%). Frequency (10%) of persons spending two hours is maximum among Degambars and of those who spend more than or equal to three hours form highest frequency among the Sikhs (27%), then among Swetambers (20%), Degambar (16%), Roman Catholic (12%) and Protestants (6%) constitute minimum frequency. Those who spend no time in religious centre are maximum among Protestant (44%), followed by Roman Catholics (40%), Swetambar (36%), Degambar (24%) and among the Sikh (19%) sect. Thus the Sikhs form the highly religious group followed by the Jains and the Christians. We may infer that variation in sects have different effects upon religiosity.

Table 4.3 also reveals that persons in higher education groups, i.e., postgraduate and higher (36%) and graduates (35%) do not spend

Table 4.3: How much time per week do you spend in your religious organization?

Varia-ble	*Categories*	*≤ 1 hour*		*2 hour*		*≥ 3 hour*		*No time*		*Total*	
		'f'	%	'f'	%	'f'	%	'f'	%	'f'	%
Age	≤ 35 years	24	49	4	8	5	10	16	33	49	100
	36–45	27	31	5	6	16	19	34	42	82	100
	46–55	32	41	3	4	19	24	24	31	78	100
	56 ≥	44	47	6	7	24	26	17	20	91	100
	Total	**127**		**18**		**64**		**91**		**300**	**100**
Sect	Roman Cath.	20	40	4	8	6	12	20	40	50	100
	Protestant	23	46	2	4	3	6	22	44	50	100
	Degambar	16	32	5	10	8	16	12	24	50	100
	Swetambar	19	38	3	6	10	20	18	36	50	100
	Sikh	49	49	4	4	27	27	19	19	100	100
	Total	**127**		**18**		**64**		**91**		**300**	**100**
Educa-tion	Basic or less	13	35	2	5	15	41	7	19	37	100
	Matriculate	26	39	2	3	22	33	17	25	67	100
	Intermediate	29	54	3	5	6	11	16	30	54	100
	Graduate	30	38	6	8	15	19	28	35	79	100
	P.G. & Higher	29	46	5	8	6	10	23	36	63	100
	Total	**127**		**18**		**64**		**91**		**300**	**100**
Occupation											
	Business	40	30	3	2	38	29	20	39	132	100
	Teaching	20	54	5	14	6	16	6	16	37	100
	Govt. Service	47	65	3	4	4	6	18	25	72	100
	Engineering	2	18	1	9	0	0	8	73	11	100
	Preaching	0	0	1	9	9	82	1	9	11	100
	Admn. (Pvt.)	5	45	2	16	2	18	2	18	11	100
	Others	13	50	3	12	5	19	5	19	26	100
	Total	**127**		**18**		**64**		**91**		**300**	**100**
Income	≤ Rs–2000	41	52	5	6	17	22	16	20	79	100
	2000–5000	52	50	8	8	11	10	33	32	104	100
	5000–10000	22	28	3	4	24	30	30	38	79	100
	10000–more	12	32	2	5	12	31	12	32	38	100
	Total	**127**		**18**		**64**		**91**		**300**	**100**

any time, whereas in the basic or below group, 41% spend more than three hours time, Persons in the educational group of intermediate (54%) and higher (46%) spend less time (i.e., one hour). Above observations indicate that higher the level of education less is the time spent in religious place. Hence, education also affects religiosity. On the basis of occupation it is observed that persons involved in engineering form highest (73%) proportion of those who do not spend any time in their religious places followed by business class (39%). Lower percentage of business class is due to the fact that mostly they have made places of worship in their homes due to lack of time. Altars (equivalent of temple) were found in most of the houses of the Christians also. Even among other sects especially the Sikhs it was observed during interview that people avoid going to places of worship due to fear or due to lack of time. Frequency (38%) of those who do not spend any time in their place of worship is highest in the income group of Rs 5,000–Rs 10,000 p.m. and those who spend maximum time (>3 hours) highest (31%) among the upper income group (Rs 10,000 p.m.). We may say that besides income, there are other factors that are responsible for people's participation in religious activities. Reason for upper income group spending more time in religious pursuits is due to the fact that they are controlling the religious organizations; and also because it is related to profit in business, thus are ought to spend more time. Whereas, persons belonging to middle income groups belong to service class who have no time for religious activities.

A cursory look at Table 4.4 indicates that highest (23%) frequency is in the age group of 36–45 years who contribute more than or equal to Rs 10,000 per annum followed by 56 years and above age group (20%). Persons in the age group of 35 years and below constitute higher proportion (18%) of those who do not contribute at all to the religious organizations. This ratio (4%) is minimum among the age group of 56 years and above.

About 34% Degambars, 28% Swetambars and 21% Sikhs contribute more than or equal to Rs 10,000 and highest proportion (26%) of those who do not contribute at all is among the Protestants followed by Roman Catholics (18%). Monetary contribution made by various religious groups is maximum among the Jains and minimum among the Christians. This indicates their respective economic conditions along with religiosity. Graduates (Table 4.4) form 13% proportion of those do not contribute at all and those in the education

Table 4.4: How much money per year do you contribute to your religious organization?

Variable	*Categories*	*≤ Rs 100*		*≤ Rs 1000*		*≥ Rs 10000*		*Nothing*		*Total*	
		'f'	%	'f'	%	'f'	%	'f'	%	'f'	%
Age	≤–35 years	19	39	18	37	3	6	9	18	49	100
	36–45	24	29	32	39	19	23	7	9	82	100
	46–55	29	37	28	36	15	19	6	8	78	100
	56 ≥	38	42	31	34	18	20	4	4	91	100
	Total	**110**	**37**	**109**	**36**	**55**	**18**	**26**	**9**	**300**	**100**
Sect	Roman Cath.	19	38	20	40	2	4	9	18	50	100
	Protestant	17	34	19	38	1	2	13	26	50	100
	Degambar	14	28	18	36	17	34	1	2	50	100
	Swetambar	20	40	16	32	14	28	0	0	50	100
	Sikh	40	40	36	36	21	21	3	3	100	100
	Total	**110**	**37**	**109**	**36**	**55**	**18**	**26**	**9**	**300**	**100**
Education	Basic or less	13	35	12	32	12	13	0	0	37	100
	Matriculate	23	34	26	39	12	18	6	9	67	100
	Intermediate	25	46	19	35	10	19	0	9	54	100
	Graduate	22	28	32	40	15	198	10	13	79	100
	P.G. & Higher	27	43	20	32	6	10	10	16	63	100
	Total	**110**	**37**	**109**	**36**	**55**	**18**	**26**	**9**	**300**	**100**
Occupation	Business	18	14	58	44	49	37	7	5	132	100
	Teaching	20	54	13	35	1	3	3	8	37	100
	Govt. Service	45	63	18	25	4	5	5	7	72	100
	Engineering	5	46	4	36	0	0	2	18	11	100
	Preaching	5	45	1	9	0	0	5	45	11	100
	Admn. (Pvt.)	3	27	5	46	1	9	2	18	11	100
	Others	14	62	10	38	0	0	2	0	26	100
	Total	**110**	**37**	**109**	**36**	**55**	**18**	**26**	**9**	**300**	**100**
Income	≤ Rs 2000	55	70	2	2	0	0	22	28	79	100
	2000–5000	48	46	54	52	0	0	2	2	104	100
	5000–10000	6	8	51	64	21	27	1	1	79	100
	10000–more	1	3	2	5	34	89	1	3	38	100
	Total	**110**	**37**	**109**	**36**	**55**	**18**	**26**	**9**	**300**	**100**

groups postgraduate and higher form 16%. Persons who are least qualified form 13% of those who contribute more than or equal to Rs 10,000 p.a. and minimum (10%) ratio is among the postgraduate and higher qualified group. It shows that feeling of charity decreases with the increasing qualification but education alone does not determine an individual religious behaviour.

Occupationwise distribution shows that ratio of persons contributing highest amount (i.e., ⩾ Rs 10,000) is highest (37%) among the business class and negligible (0%) among engineering, preaching and administrative (private) classes. Highest (63%) proportion of those who contribute Rs 100 per year is among the government servants followed by others class (62%), teaching (54%) and preaching class (45%) (Table 4.4).

Thus, it can be concluded that charity is related with ones economic condition and business class being the wealthiest, contributes liberally to the religious organization. This is also because by contributing to religious bodies they save their income tax and also earn reputation in society.

Table 4.4 reveals that lowest contribution, Rs 100 per year or less, is highest (70%) among the lowest income group (Rs 2,000 p.m. or less) and maximum amount (Rs 10,000 or more) is contributed by the upper income group (89%). Percentage of those who do not contribute at all is highest (28%) among the lowest income group. It indicates that limited resources do not permit an individual to donate more amount. It was also observed during the field observations that there are very few persons who contribute one- tenth of their income for religious purposes. Business class donate for material gains.

Our data (Table 4.5) shows that highest (69%) frequency of those who always participate in religious activities is among the age group of 56 years and above and lowest (37%) among the age group 35 years or below. People in the age groups of 35 years and below and 36–45 of years form the highest (10%) proportion of those who have never participated in such activities.

Thus, it can be said that a change is taking place in people's religious behaviour. This proportion (people participating in religious activities) is highest (68%) among the Sikhs followed by the Jains (57%) and the Christians (46%). Among the Christians, Roman Catholics (56%) are more active than the Protestants (36%), whereas among the Jains, the Swetambars (62%) take more active participation than the Degambars (52%).

Their proportion (70%) is highest in the lower educated groups (below basic) and matriculates (69%), it is lowest (49%) in the post-graduate and higher education group. This group also forms highest (14%) proportion of those who never participate in religious activities.

Table 4.5: How frequently do you participate in your religious organizational activities?

Variable	Categories	Always		Frequently		Sometimes		Never		Total	
		'f'	%	'f'	%	'f'	%	'f'	%	'f'	%
Age	≤ 35 years	45	37	14	29	12	24	5	10	49	100
	36– 45	46	56	14	17	14	17	9	10	82	100
	46–55	44	56	14	18	14	18	6	8	78	100
	56 ≥	63	69	10	11	14	15	4	5	91	100
	Total	**171**	**57**	**52**	**17**	**54**	**18**	**23**	**8**	**300**	**100**
Sect	Roman Cath.	28	56	10	20	9	18	3	6	50	100
	Protestant	18	36	15	30	12	24	5	10	50	100
	Degambar	26	52	9	18	9	18	6	12	50	100
	Swetambar	31	62	7	14	11	22	1	2	50	100
	Sikh	68	68	11	11	13	13	8	8	100	100
	Total	**171**	**57**	**52**	**17**	**54**	**18**	**23**	**8**	**300**	**100**
Education	Basic or less	26	70	14	11	5	24	2	5	37	100
	Matriculate	46	69	17	25	4	6	0	0	67	100
	Intermediate	28	52	7	13	16	29	3	6	54	100
	Graduate	40	54	13	16	17	22	9	11	79	100
	P.G. & Higher	32	49	11	17	12	19	9	14	63	100
	Total	**171**	**57**	**52**	**17**	**54**	**18**	**23**	**8**	**300**	**100**
Occupation	Business	78	59	26	20	24	18	4	3	132	100
	Teaching	21	57	6	19	7	16	3	8	37	100
	Govt. Service	39	54	11	15	14	20	8	11	72	100
	Engineering	1	9	2	18	2	18	6	55	11	100
	Preaching	11	100	0	0	0	0	0	0	11	100
	Admn. (pvt.)	7	64	2	18	1	9	1	9	11	100
	Others	14	54	5	19	6	19	1	8	26	100
	Total	**171**	**57**	**52**	**17**	**54**	**18**	**23**	**8**	**300**	**100**
Income	≤ Rs 2000	45	57	14	18	10	13	10	12	79	100
	2000–5000	51	49	19	18	26	25	8	8	104	100
	5000–10000	47	59	14	18	13	16	5	6	79	100
	10000–more	28	74	5	13	5	13	0	0	38	100
	Total	**171**	**57**	**52**	**17**	**54**	**18**	**23**	**8**	**300**	**100**

Besides preaching (100%) this ratio (64% and 59%) is higher among administrative (private) and business classes respectively. On the other hand, engineering class constitutes 55% of those who have never participated in these activities. Thus, it may be concluded that nature and type of occupation are also a significant factors in determining religiosity. Almost 74% (Table 4.5) in the income group of Rs 10,000 p.m. or more, 59% in the income group of Rs 5,000–10,000, 57% in the income group of Rs 2,000 or below per month, and 49% in the income group of Rs 2,000–Rs 5,000 p.m. participate always in religious activities. Those who never participate form maximum frequencies (i.e., 12% and 8%) in the income groups of Rs 2,000 and Rs 2,000–5,000 p.m. respectively. Thus, it can be concluded that age, sect, education, occupation and income constitute significant factors in determining religiosity.

Religiosity measured in terms of people attitude towards change in traditional religious practices show (Table 4.6) that 41% (i.e. maximum younger people (i.e., those in the age group of ⩽35 years) favoured change in religious practices whereas in the eldest age group form minimum proportion (9%). Table also shows that is religiosity is observed more among the elderly people than the younger people.

A total of 58% Roman Catholics, as compared to 36% Protestants, 58% Swetambars and 66% Degambars and 67% Sikhs, do not favour change in religious practices. Thus, we observe that Roman Catholics are more orthodox than the Protestants and the Degambars on certain issues are more religiously orthodox than Swetambars and vice versa whereas Sikhs are less orthodox than the Jains and more than the Christians. In other words we may say that, the Sikhism is a reformed religion which does not have traditional practices on the other hand Roman Catholicism prohibits marriage of the priest and the Degambars recommend nudity of the saints. Most people objected against these practices.

Religious orthodoxy increases as the level of education decreases. Among different occupations maximum (i.e., 64%) proportions of those who do not favour change in religious practice are formed by government service and preaching then 61% by others. In administrative (private) service minimum frequency (i.e., 36%) is of those who do not favour change in religious practices.

Further, it is maximum (i.e., 61%) in the income group of < Rs 2,000 p.m. and minimum (52%) in Rs 10,000 or more p.m. income group. That is religious orthodoxy is observed more among the lower economic stratum than the upper. On the basis of above data we may infer that religious orthodoxy is affected by age, sect, education, occupation and income of the individual.

Most of the persons among the Christians and the Sikhs have made a place of worship in their homes as they have been unable to visit

Table 4.6: How strongly do you favour that, with the changing society religious practices should also change?

Variable	*Categories*	*Very Strongly*		*Strongly*		*Do Not Favour*		*No Comments*		*Total*	
		'f'	*%*	*'f'*	*%*	*'f'*	*%*	*'f'*	*%*	*'f'*	*%*
Age	≤–35 years	20	41	10	20	19	39	0	0	49	100
	36–45	20	24	12	15	48	59	2	2	82	100
	46–55	12	15	17	22	49	63	0	0	78	100
	56 ≥	8	19	21	23	60	66	2	2	91	100
	Total	**60**	**20**	**60**	**20**	**176**	**59**	**4**	**1**	**300**	**100**
Sect	Roman Cath.	10	20	10	20	29	58	1	2	50	100
	Protestant	18	36	12	24	18	36	2	4	50	100
	Degambar	7	14	10	20	33	66	0	0	50	100
	Swetambar	13	26	8	16	29	58	0	0	50	100
	Sikh	12	24	20	40	67	67	1	1	100	100
	Total	**60**	**20**	**60**	**20**	**176**	**59**	**4**	**1**	**300**	**100**
Education	Basic or Less	6	16	5	14	26	70	0	0	37	100
	Matriculate	10	15	9	13	46	69	2	3	67	100
	Intermediate	11	20	9	17	34	63	0	0	54	100
	Graduate	19	24	21	27	38	48	1	1	79	100
	P.G. & Higher	14	22	16	25	32	51	1	2	63	100
	Total	**60**	**20**	**60**	**20**	**176**	**59**	**4**	**1**	**300**	**100**
Occupation	Business	30	23	25	19	77	58	0	0	132	100
	Teaching	11	30	6	16	20	54	0	0	37	100
	Govt. Service	9	13	16	22	46	64	1	1	72	100
	Engineering	5	45	1	0	6	55	0	0	11	100
	Preaching	1	9	3	27	7	64	0	0	11	100
	Admn. (pvt.)	2	18	4	37	4	36	1	9	11	100
	Others	2	8	6	23	16	61	2	8	26	100
	Total	**60**	**20**	**60**	**20**	**176**	**59**	**4**	**1**	**300**	**100**
Income	≤ Rs 2000	18	23	10	12	48	61	3	4	79	100
	2000–5000	15	14	27	26	61	59	1	1	104	100
	5000–10000	18	23	14	18	47	59	0	0	79	100
	10000–more	9	24	9	24	20	52	0	0	38	100
	Total	**60**	**20**	**60**	**20**	**176**	**59**	**4**	**1**	**300**	**100**

their places of worship as they are busy with their jobs and with business or due to distance of their place of residence from places of worship or due to old age.

Ritualism

Ritualism has been conceived as an act of performing rituals. Ritual is defined in the dictionary of social sciences as a concentrated, focused marshalling of symbols redolent with arrays of meaning. Like myth, ritual through metaphor and metonymy makes statements about and allows the exploration of major relational systems in the socio-cultural context of experience. Transfer of power or of goods, assertions, establishment of new alliance of legitimacy or the breaking of old ones, the progression through personal or social developmental phases are bonds marked by rituals, According to Hindu Dharmshastra, the individual comments has to pass through many Samskaras-sarira. These are intended to sanctify the body. They are supposed to purify the person of a human being in this life and for the life after death. Each of these Samskaras is preceded by a symbolic sacrifice.

Table 4.7 indicates that maximum frequency (35%) of those who have ever worked in organizing rituals in their religious organization is in the age group of 56 years then 27% each among the age groups of 36-45 and of 46–55 years and lowest (12%) in the age group of 35 years.

About 60% Protestants and 40% Roman Catholics have ever worked for organizing rituals in their religious organization. Degambars are more (88%) ritualistic than Swetambars (70%). Sikhs are more (59%) ritualistic than Christians (50%) and less than Jains (79%). Those who have never worked in organizing rituals are maximum (60%) in Roman Catholic sect followed by 41% among Sikh sect and 40% in Protestant. It is minimum (i.e., 2%) in the Degambar sect of Jains. Thus, we may say that Degambers are more ritualistic than the Swetambars and Catholics. Jains are more ritualistic than Sikhs and Protestants are more ritualistic than Roman Catholics whereas Christian's are least ritualistic.

Minimum (13%,14% and 15%) ratios in the education groups of basic or less, P.G. & Higher, and Intermediate have ever worked in organizing rituals. About 29% each among the matriculates and Graduates have ever worked in organizing rituals. Education does not show any significant variation with education.

Besides preaching (0%), others (31%) and business (32%) occupations forming minimum frequencies of those who have never worked in organizing rituals in their religious organizations. Engineering form highest (82%) ratio after government service (44%) and teaching (46%) who have been never worked in organizing rituals in their

Table 4.7: Have you ever worked in organizing rituals in your religious organization?

Variable	*Categories*	*Yes*		*No*		*Total*	
		'f'	%	'f'	%	'f'	%
Age	⩽-35 years	23	12	26	53	49	100
36–45	50	27	32	39	82	100	
46–55	50	27	28	36	78	100	
56 ⩾	65	35	24	29	91	100	
Total	**188**	**100**	**112**		**300**	**100**	
Sect	Roman Catholics	20	40	30	60	50	100
	Protestant	30	60	20	40	50	100
	Degambar	44	88	6	12	50	100
	Swetambar	35	70	15	30	50	100
	Sikh	59	59	41	41	100	100
	Total	**188**	**100**	**112**		**300**	**100**
Education	Basic or Less	25	13	12	32	37	100
	Matriculate	54	29	13	20	67	100
	Intermediate	29	15	25	46	54	100
	Graduate	54	29	25	32	79	100
	P.G. & Higher	26	14	37	59	63	100
	Total	**188**	**100**	**112**		**300**	**100**
Occupation	Business	90	68	42	32	132	100
	Teaching	20	9	17	46	37	100
	Govt. Service	40	56	32	44	72	100
	Engineering	2	18	9	82	11	100
	Preaching	11	100	0	0	11	100
	Admn. (Pvt.)	7	64	4	36	11	100
	Others	18	69	8	31	26	100
	Total	**188**	**100**	**112**		**300**	**100**
Income	⩽Rs–2000	31	39	48	61	79	100
	2000–5000	73	70	31	30	104	100
	5000–10000	54	68	25	32	79	100
	10000–more	30	79	8	21	38	100
	Total	**188**	**100**	**112**		**300**	**100**

religious organization. Incomewise distribution indicates that 39% in the income group of Rs 2000 p.m., 70% in Rs 2000–5000 p.m. and 79% in Rs 10,000 and more have ever worked in organizing rituals in their religious organizations and dominated by economic elites of society. Age, sect, occupation, and income effect religiosity of an individual.

Life Cycle Rituals

Baptism/Chathi/Janam Samskar (a)

A careful examination of our data (Table 4.8) reveals that in the age group of less than or equal to thirty-five years 20% believe very strictly, 24% strictly, 27% less strictly and 29% do not believe in birth ritual. In the age group of 36–45 years, 27% believe very strictly, 29% believe strictly, 30% less strictly and 13% not at all believe in birth ritual. In the age group of 46–55 years, 29% believe very strictly, 27% believe strictly, 32% believe less strictly and 1% do not at all believe in birth ritual. In group 56 years and more 36% believe very strictly, 27% believe strictly, 29% less strictly and 8% do not at all believe in birth rituals.

Among different sects it is observed (Table 4.8) that 44% among Roman Catholics and 38% Protestants believe very strictly, 40% Roman Catholics and 28% Protestants believe strictly, 12% Roman Catholics and 24% Protestants believe less strictly and 4% Roman Catholics and 10% Protestants do not believe in birth ritual. Likewise, 44% Degambars and 32% Swetambars believe very strictly, 44% Degambars and 36% Swetambars believe strictly, 8% Degambars and 24% Swetambars believe less strictly and 4% Degambar and 8% Swetambars do not at all believe in birth ritual. 9% Sikhs believe very strictly, 8% believe strictly, 55% believe less strictly and 28% do not believe in birth rituals. On the basis of above observations (Table 4.8) we may conclude that the Jains are more ritualistic than the Christians and the Christians are more ritualistic than the Sikhs.

In the education group of basic or below, 54% believe very strictly, 22% strictly, 19% less strictly and 5% not at all believe in birth ritual. In the education group of matriculate, 33% believe very

Table 4.8: How strictly do you believe in life cycle rituals?

Age group		*Very Strictly*				*Strictly*				*Less Strictly*				*(Not at All)*			
	t.f.	*a*	*b*	*d*	*c*	*a*	*b*	*d*	*c*	*a*	*b*	*d*	*c*	*a*	*b*	*d*	*c*
≤ 35	49	10	6	8	7	12	14	14	12	13	12	13	15	14	15	14	5
		(20)	(16)	(16)	(14)	(24)	(29)	(29)	(24)	(27)	(24)	(27)	(31)	(29)	(31)	(29)	31)
36–45	82	16	21	18	18	24	25	27	26	25	25	27	26	11	11	10	12
		(27)	(26)	(22)	(22)	(29)	(30)	(33)	(32)	(30)	(30)	(33)	(32)	(13)	(13)	(12)	(15)
46–55	78	23	23	22	21	21	21	22	23	25	26	24	23	9	8	11	11
		(29)	(29)	(28)	(27)	(27)	(27)	(28)	(29)	(32)	(34)	(31)	(29)	(12)	(1)	(14)	(14)
≥ 56	91	33	34	31	30	25	25	27	26	26	25	26	24	7	7	6	11
		(36)	(37)	(34)	(33)	(27)	(27)	(35)	(29)	(29)	(28)	(29)	(26)	(8)	8	7	12
Total	**300**	**88**	**86**	**79**	**76**	**82**	**85**	**90**	**89**	**88**	**90**	**88**	**88**	**41**	**41**	**41**	**49**
Roman Cath.		50	22	25	23	22	20	17	15	14	6	6	5	7	5	5	7
			(44)	(50)	(46)	(44)	(40)	(34)	(30)	(28)	(12)	(12)	(10)	(14)	(4)	(4)	(14)
Protestant		50	19	16	14	18	14	14	12	11	12	15	18	17	5	5	6
			(38)	(32)	(28)	(36)	(28)	(28)	(24)	(22)	(24)	(30)	(36)	(34)	(10)	(10)	(12)
Degambar		50	22	21	22	21	22	21	17	24	4	6	9	3	2	2	2
			(44)	(42)	(44)	(42)	(44)	(42)	(34)	(28)	(8)	(12)	(18)	(6)	(4)	(4)	(4)
Swetambar		50	16	15	11	9	18	15	17	20	12	14	14	14	4	6	8
			(32)	(30)	(22)	(18)	(36)	(30)	(34)	(40)	(24)	(28)	(28)	(28)	(8)	(12)	(16)
Sikh		100	9	9	9	6	8	18	29	18	55	47	44	47	28	26	18
Total		**300**	**88**	**86**	**79**	**76**	**82**	**85**	**90**	**89**	**88**	**90**	**88**	**88**	**41**	**41**	**41**

(Table 4.8 Contd...)

(Table 4.8 Contd...)		a	b	d	c	a	b	d	c	a	b	d	c	a	b	d	c
Basic or Less	37	20	18	18	19	8	10	10	9	7	6	6	7	2	3	3	2
		(54)	(49)	(49)	(51)	(22)	(27)	(27)	(24)	(19)	(16)	(16)	(19)	(5)	(8)	(8)	(5)
Matriculate	67	22	21	21	20	18	22	18	18	22	19	24	22	5	5	5	7
		(33)	(31)	(31)	(30)	(27)	(33)	(27)	(27)	(33)	(28)	(36)	(33)	(7)	(7)	(7)	(10)
Intermediate	54	19	19	16	17	20	19	20	21	22	13	13	12	3	3	5	4
		(35)	(35)	(30)	(32)	(37)	(35)	(37)	(39)	(22)	(24)	(24)	(22)	(6)	(6)	(9)	(7)
Graduate	79	18	19	16	13	22	21	25	25	23	26	23	23	16	13	15	18
		(23)	(24)	(20)	(16)	(28)	(27)	(32)	(32)	(29)	(33)	(29)	(29)	(20)	(16)	(19)	(23)
P.G. & Higher	63	9	9	8	7	14	13	17	14	25	24	24	24	15	17	13	18
		(14)	(14)	(13)	(11)	(22)	(21)	(21)	(22)	(40)	(38)	(38)	(38)	(24)	(27)	(21)	(29)
Total	**300**	**88**	**86**	**79**	**76**	**82**	**85**	**90**	**89**	**88**	**90**	**88**	**88**	**41**	**41**	**41**	**49**
Business	132	54	50	46	41	31	33	36	41	41	42	43	41	5	7	8	9
		(41)	(38)	(24)	(31)	(24)	(25)	(27)	(31)	(31)	(32)	(33)	(31)	(4)	(5)	(6)	(7)
Teaching	37	9	9	8	9	12	11	12	13	9	10	9	9	7	7	8	6
		(24)	(24)	(22)	(24)	(32)	(30)	(32)	(35)	(24)	(27)	(24)	(24)	(19)	(19)	(22)	(16)
Govt. Service	72	15	17	16	14	18	23	20	14	22	21	22	21	17	11	14	23
		(21)	(24)	(22)	(19)	(25)	(32)	(28)	(19)	(31)	(29)	(31)	(29)	(24)	(15)	(19)	(32)
Preaching	11	4	3	3	4	5	5	5	5	2	2	2	2	1	1	0	0
		(36)	(27)	(27)	(36)	(46)	(46)	(46)	(46)	(18)	(18)	(18)	(18)	(9)	(9)	0	0
Engineering	11	0	1	1	2	4	3	3	3	2	2	2	2	5	5	5	4
		(0)	(9)	(9)	(18)	(36)	(27)	(27)	(27)	(18)	(18)	(18)	(46)	(46)	(46)	(0)	36

Admn. (Pvt.)	11	1	1	2	2	3	3	3	3	2	2	2	2	5	5	4	4
		(9)	(9)	(18)	(18)	(27)	(27)	(27)	(27)	(18)	(18)	(18)	(18)	(46)	(46)	(36)	(36)
Others	26	5	5	3	4	9	7	11	8	11	9	10	11	1	5	2	3
		(19)	(19)	(12)	(15)	(35)	(27)	(42)	(31)	(42)	(35)	(39)	(42)	(4)	(19)	(8)	(36)
Total	**300**	**88**	**86**	**79**	**76**	**82**	**85**	**90**	**89**	**88**	**90**	**88**	**88**	**41**	**41**	**41**	
≤ Rs 2000	79	28	27	27	28	22	21	20	18	16	19	20	20	13	12	12	
		(35)	(34)	(34)	(35)	(28)	(27)	(26)	(23)	(20)	(24)	(26)	(26)	(16)	(15)	(15)	
2000–5000	104	23	22	23.	24	42	40	41	40	32	33	33	35	7	9	7	
		(22)	(21)	(22)	(23)	(40)	(39)	(39)	(39)	(31)	(32)	(32)	(34)	(7)	(9)	(7)	
5000–10000	79	24	25	21	25	12	13	21	16	25	24	19	23	18	17	18	
		(30)	(32)	(27)	(32)	(15)	(16)	(27)	(20)	(32)	(30)	(24)	(29)	(23)	(22)	(23)	
10000–more	38	13	12	8	5	6	11	8	13	16	12	18	10	3	3	4	
		(34)	(32)	(21)	(13)	(16)	(29)	(21)	(34)	(42)	(32)	(47)	(26)	(8)	(8)	(11)	
Total	**300**	**88**	**86**	**79**	**76**	**82**	**85**	**90**	**89**	**88**	**90**	**88**	**88**	**41**	**41**	**41**	

a-Birth ritual–Baptism/Chathi/Janam Sanskar
b-Holy communion/ Dasthon/Amit Sanskar.
c-Matrimony
d-Burial/Death/Uthala

strictly, 27% believe strictly, 33% believe less strictly and 7% do not believe in birth ritual. Among the intermediates, 35% believe very strictly, 37% believe strictly, 22% believe less strictly and 6% do not believe in birth ritual. In the education group graduates, 23% believe very strictly, 28% believe strictly, 29% believe less strictly and 20% do not believe in birth ritual. In the postgraduate and above education group, 14% believe very strictly, 22% believe strictly, 40% believe less strictly and 24% do not believe in birth ritual.

It is also indicated (Table 4.8) that 41% in the business occupation group believe very strictly, 24% believe strictly, 31% believe less strictly and 4% do not believe in birth ritual. In the teaching group, 24% believe very strictly, 32% strictly, 24% less strictly and 19% do not believe in birth ritual. Among government servants, 21% believe very strictly, 25% believe strictly, 31% less strictly believe and 24% do not believe in birth ritual.

In preaching group, 27% believe very strictly, 46% believe strictly, 18% believe less strictly and 9% do not believe in rituals. Among Engineering 36% believe very strictly, 18% less strictly and 46% do not believe in birth ritual. 9% in the administrative group believe very strictly 35% believe strictly, 42% believe less strictly and 4% do not believe in birth ritual.

In the income group of < Rs 2,000 p.m., 35% believe very strictly, 28% believe strictly, 20% believe less strictly and 16% do not believe in birth ritual. 22% in the income group of Rs 2,000–5,000 p.m. believe very strictly, 40% believe strictly, 31% believe less strictly and 7% do not believe in birth rituals, whereas in the income group of Rs 5,000–10,000 p.m. 30% believe very strictly, 15% believe strictly, 32% believe less strictly and 23% do not believe in birth ritual.

Holy Communion/Dasthon/Amrat Sanskar (b)

Age and Birth Ritual

Our data reveals (Table 4.8) that 16% in the age group of 35 years believe very strictly, 24% believe less strictly and 31% do not believe in birth ritual. In the age group of 36–45 years 26% believe very strictly, 30% believe strictly, 13% do not believe in birth ritual. In 46–55 years group 29% believe strictly, 34% believe less strictly 27% believe strictly 10% do not believe in birth ritual. Among the persons belonging to the age group of 56 years or more 37% believe very strictly, 27% believe strictly, 28% believe less strictly and 8% do not believe in birth ritual.

Sect and Life Cycle Ritual

Sectwise distribution (Table 4.8) shows that 50% among Roman Catholics and 32% among Protestants believe very strictly, 34% Roman Catholics and 28% Protestants believe strictly, 12% Roman Catholics and 24% Protestants believe less strictly and 4% Roman Catholics and 10% Protestants do not believe in receiving holy communion. Among Jains, 42% Degambars and 30% Swetambars believe very strictly, 42% Degambars and 30% Swetambars believe strictly, 12% Degambars and 28% Swetambars believe less strictly and 4% Degambars and 12% Swetambars do not believe in performing Dasthon ritually. Among Sikhs, only 9% believe very strictly, 18% believe strictly, 47% believe less strictly and 26% do not believe in Amrat Sanskar.

Occupation and Life Cycle Ritual

Persons in various occupation groups who do not believe in life cycle ritual, (Table 4.8) are maximum (46%) in engineering and private administration groups followed by 24% among government service, then 19% in teaching and 4% in 'others' and minimum (7%) among the business group. It is nil in preaching groups.

Income and Life Cycle Ritual

In different income groups we observe maximum frequency (i.e., 27%) in the income group of Rs 5,000–6,000 p.m. than 26% in income group of Rs 10,000 and more p.m. It is minimum (i.e., 5%) in the income group of Rs 2000–5000 p.m.

Matrimony (c)

Age and Matrimony

Maximum frequency (31%) of those who do not believe in matrimonial rituals is in the age group of 35 years followed by 15% in the age group of 36–45 years and 14% in the age group of 46–55 It is minimum (i.e., 12%) in the age group of 56 years and more.

Sect and Matrimony

Among various sects Sikhs form the highest frequency (29%) who do not believe in matrimony rituals followed by 14% Roman Catholics and Swetambars both. Degambars form minimum frequency (4%) after Protestants (8%) who do not believe in matrimony rituals.

Education and Matrimony

Further, maximum frequency (29%) of those who do not believe in matrimony ritual is in the education group of postgraduate and higher. Then 23% in graduates, 10% in matriculates, 7% in intermediates and minimum (i.e., 5%) in the basic or below group (Table 4.8).

Occupation and Matrimony

Engineering (36%) and administrative (36%) form the least ritualistic occupational groups. No one among preaching and 7% (second minimum after preaching) among business category do not believe in matrimony ritual performance (Table 4.8).

Income and Matrimony

In the income group Rs 10,000 and above, 27% (maximum) in the income group of Rs 5,000–10,000 p.m., 16% in the income group of Rs 2,000 or less p.m. and 5% (lowest) in the income group of Rs 2,000–5,000 p.m. do not believe in matrimony rituals.

Burial/Death/Uthala (d)

Age and Death Ritual

Maximum frequency (29%) of persons who do not believe in various death rituals is in the age group of <35 years. Persons in the age group of 46–55 years form 14%, in the age group of 36–45 years there 12% persons and in the age group of > 56 years frequency (7%) is minimum.

Sect and Death Ritual

Roman Catholics (46%) and Degambars (44%) constitute maximum frequencies followed by Protestants (28%) and Swetambars (22%).

Sikhs form minimum frequency (9%) of those who very strictly believe in Uthala Sanskar. Further those who strictly believe are more (30%) in the Roman Catholics than in Protestants (24%). Among Jains both Degambar and Swetambar form equal (34%) proportions whereas, Sikhs form 29% of those who strictly believe in Uthala rituals.

About 18% Sikhs, 14% Roman Catholics, 12% Protestants do not believe in death rituals. Among Jains, Swetambars form higher ratio as compared to Degambars who form minimum (4%) among all the sects in the present study.

Education and Death Ritual

In the different groups of education those in the postgraduate and higher form maximum frequency (21%) followed by graduates (19%). Those in the intermediate (9%) , below basic (8%) and matriculate group (7%) (show marginal differences) do not at all believe in performing death rituals.

Occupation and Death Ritual

Variations are observed on the basis of occupations. Highest frequency (46%) of those who do not believe in death ritual is in the engineering group then 36% in administrative and 22% in teaching. Persons in government services constitute 19%, Preaching 0%, in 'others' 8%. It is second minimum (i.e., 6%) in business group.

Income and Death Ritual

Highest frequencies of persons who do not believe in death ritual are in the income group of Rs 5,000–10,000 p.m. (23%) and < Rs 2, 000 p.m. (15%). Persons in the income group of Rs 10,000 or more constitute 11% and in the income group of Rs 2,000–5,000 p.m. form minimum frequency (7%).

On the basis of above observations we may say that a change has been taking place in people's attitudes toward ritual performance. Birth rituals are observed more strictly than matrimony. In all the cases i.e., Christian, Jain and Sikh sects marriage has been made simple. Ritual performance has been replaced by social performance. That is, birth of a child is celebrated with great pomp and show. It is a time when people develop more and more contacts with others

During such celebrations, exchange of gifts take place. Unlike, traditional time, ways of observing birth and other rituals have changed. People host parties (usually dinner), circulate the invitation cards. We see western impact upon ritual performance in India.

Seasonal Rituals

Further our data shows (Table 4.9) that observance of seasonal rituals is more (Novina 38%) among Roman Catholics than Protestants (30%). Unlike life cycle rituals, observance of Daslakshan (fasts) is 38% among Degambars whereas it is only 28% among Swetambars, 43% Sikhs observe Baisakhi and 30% of them observe Sankrant. Observance of seasonal rituals is comparatively higher among Sikhs than sects of Jainism and Christianity.

Sacraments

Table 4.9 also shows that performance of prayer (80%) and fasts (28%)are highest among Protestants than Roman Catholics (58%) and (20%) but percentage of other sacraments (Rosary 40%, Lord's supper 16%) is higher among Roman Catholics than the Protestants (Rosary 34%, and Lord's Supper 12 %). In Jains, 60% Degambars and 26% Swetambars count Rosary, 34% Degambars and 10% Swetambars perform Prakashal (bathing of Lord's idols), 36% both Degambars and Swetambars perform Pooja regularly, 20% Degambar's and 18% Swetambars perform Aarti, and 10% Degambars and 2% Swetambars had ever gone on pilgrimage. Among Sikhs 60% do 'path' at their homes and 35% perform other sacraments. It can be concluded that performance of sacraments is higher among Degambars and Sikhs than other sects.

We may infer that observance of life cycle rituals is maximum among all the sects under present study though minor variations occur from sect to sect. Observance of matrimonial rituals is comparatively less in most of the cases, Marriage has been made simpler in present days but birth and death rituals are performed with full vigour. In the observance of seasonal rituals, Roman Catholics are found more ritualistic but in the observance of various sacraments, Rosary is counted more by Roman Catholics than the Protestants, whereas Protestants are more prayer and fast bound than the Roman

Catholics. Among Jains, Degambars are less ritualistic than Swetambar sect. Although Sikhism does not preach ritual performance even then they are fairly ritualistic due to local impact of Hinduism. Sikh ritualism plays a dominant role (Singh, 1990).

Shils (1987) also observed in western societies that regular attendance at service of worship has decreased. Ritual and ceremonial have been forced into more and more confined occasions, their elaborateness has been simplified. This indicates a secular, rationalizing outlook.

Table 4.9 Seasonal Rituals and Sacraments Observed by Various Sectors

Sector		*15th August*		*Novina*		*Not at all*					
		'f'	*%*	*'f'*	*%*	*'f'*	*%*				
Christians											
Seasonal Rituals	1. Roman Catholic	10	20	19	38	21	42				
	2. Protestant	0	0	15	30	35	70				
Jains		*Daslakshan*		*Paryushan*		*Not at all*					
Seasonal Rituals	1. Degambars	19	38	0	0	31	62				
	2. Swetambars	0	0	14	28	36	72				
Sikhs		*Baishakhi*		*Sankrant*		*Not at all*					
Seasonal Rituals	Sikh	43	43	30	30	27	27				
Christians		*Rosary*		*Prayer*		*Fast*		*Lord's Supper*			
Sacraments	1. Roman Catholics	20	40	29	58	10	20	8	16		
	2. Protestants	17	34	40	80	14	28	6	12		
Jains		*Rosary*		*Prakshal*		*Pooja*		*Aarti*		*Vandana*	
Sacraments	1. Degambar	30	60	17	34	18	36	10	20	5	10
	2. Swetambar	23	46	5	10	18	36	9	18	1	2
Sikh		*Path*		*Others*							
Sacraments	Sikh	60	60	35	35						

Change in Ritual and Ceremonial Performance

Causes of change in the performance of rituals among various sects (Table 4.10) have been studied. 10% Christians, 24% Jains, and 14% Sikhs said that lack of religious training among younger generation is one of the major cause for the decline of ritual observance. 31% Christians, 36% Jains and 88% Sikhs said that lack of time and money is the more important cause. 8% Christians, 10% Jains and 10% Sikhs said that modern education is responsible for the decline of rituals performance. Other major causes are impact of globalization, modernism. Media and terrorism 18% Sikhs only commented on it, 15% out of a total of 300 said that there is no change in ritual performance, and 10.5% gave no comments.

It is obvious from the above observations (Table 4.10) that lack of time and money is one of the most important causes for the decline in the observance of rituals and sacraments among all the sects, but among Sikhs terrorism is also important. People of this sect (Sikhs) avoid to show in public any such performance out of fear of insecurity due to 1984 incident. Those Sikhs who have big shops have also kept idols and calendars of Hindu gods and goddesses to show positive attitude towards Hinduism outwardly. Inter-religious practices among the Sikhs have been observed. Sikh women show their preference for Hindu customs and beliefs (Bingley, 1984) Inter-religion worship is also observed in famous places of worship, e.g., Hindus also visit Gurudwaras, Jains light scent sticks at Muslims graveyard. During interview, they said that these are evil spirits so we bow before them for our safety as some of the colonies have been built upon graveyards. Christians are fairly rigid in bowing before other than their own religious God. Similarly, elderly people of Jain and Sikh do not believe in other religion's supremacy.

Finally, we may conclude that a change is observed on the basis of age from religious orthodoxy to secularism and liberalism. On the basis of sect, Sikhs are found highly religious whereas Protestants as least religious.

Educationwise data shows that graduates have shown a change in religious matters. Data based on occupation shows that business class besides preaching is the most religious along with 'others' in contrast to engineering. Income has also indicated its significance in determining religiosity. Upper income group is generally holding

Table 4:10 Cause of Change in Ritual Practices

Categories	*Roman Catholic*		*Protestant*		*Degamber*		*Swetambar*		*Sikh*	
	F	%	F	%	F	%	F	%	F	%
Lack of religious training	5	10	5	10	12	24	12	24	7	7
Lack of time and money	18	36	13	26	20	40	16	32	44	44
Materialism	4	8	4	8	3	6	1	2	4	4
Modern education	2	4	6	12	6	12	4	8	5	5
Impact of other cultures	3	6	2	4	3	6	6	12	12	12
Scientific outlook	0	0	4	8	2	4	8	16	5	5
Impact of television	2	4	2	4	3	6	1	2	5	5
Terrorism	0	0	0	0	0	0	0	0	9	9
Others	2	4	3	6	1	2	0	0	0	0
No change	7	14	3	6	0	0	0	0	5	5
No comments	7	14	8	16	0	0	2	4	4	4

Table 4.11 Scores on Religiosity According to Age

Scores	*Age Group*				*Grand Total*
	⩽ 35 years	*36–45*	*46–55*	*56 years*	
		& above			
L	38	45	39	41	163
H	11	37	39	50	137
Total	49	82	78	91	300

Tabulated = 7.82, calculated =14. 403, d.f. = 3. Level of significance =5%

power over religious organizations. It is found more religious on important issues. This class is the deciding body of the society (religious) at large. Table 4.11 shows proportion of those who have secured high scores (medium of religiosity is 18) on religiosity are 22% in the ⩽ 35 years age group 45% in the 36–45 years age group, 50% in the 45–55 years age group and 55% in ⩾ 56 years age group. It reflects that higher age group people have shown more religiosity as compared to those in the younger age groups.

Association between age and religiosity is significant. Proportions of those who have secured high score on religiosity indicate (Table 4.12) that, Roman Catholic sect show higher frequency (56%) than the Protestant sect, (26%) and Swetamber sect (64%) than Degamber sect (42%) reflect higher frequency. Here, Jains form the highly religious group, Christians form second highly religious group and Sikh forms the least religious group. Hence, we may say that, Sikhs are highly socially, developed religious group and Christians are less developed than Sikhs but are more developed than Jains.

It also indicates (Table 4.12) that ritualism is affected significantly by variation in sect affiliations.

Nearly 57% in the category basic or less, 54% in matriculates, 37% in intermediates, 38% in case of graduates and 46% of post-

Table 4.12 Scores on Religiosity According to Sect

Scores	*Sects*					*Grand Total*
	Roman	*Protestant*	*Degambars*	*Swetambars*	*Sikh*	
L	22	32	29	18	62	163
H	28	18	21	32	38	137

Tabulated = 9.49 Calculated = 13.448, d.f. = 4. Level of significance = 5%

graduate and higher education group have secured high scores on religiosity. No significant variation regarding religiosity in case of different educational categories with the increasing or decreasing level of education is seen (Table 4.13).

Table 4.13 Scores on Religiosity According to Education

Scores	*Education*					*Grand Total*
	Basic or less	*Matricu-lates*	*Interme-diates*	*Graduates*	*P.G. & Higher*	
L	16	31	33	49	34	163
H	21	36	21	30	29	137

Tabulated = 9.49, Calculated = 6.479, d.f. = 4. Level of significance = 5%

Almost 50% in business, 91% in preaching and 55% in administrative (private) occupational categories as compared to teaching (38%), engineering (45%) and in government service (39%) form higher frequencies of those who have secured high scores on religiosity. We may say that persons in engineering, teaching and government service are more developed than those in preaching, business and administrative (private) occupations. We may conclude that nature of occupation significantly affects religiosity (Table 4.14).

Table 4.14 Scores on Religiosity According to Occupation

Occupation	*Scores*		*Grand Total*
	L	*H*	
Business	66	66	132
Government	44	28	72
Teaching	23	14	37
Engineering	6	5	11
Preaching	1	10	11
Administrative (pvt.)	5	6	11
Others	18	8	26
Total	163	137	300

Tabulated = 2.59, Calculated = 14.997, d.f. = 6. Level of significance = 5%

Frequencies of persons securing high scores on religiosity are 41% in Rs < 2,000 per month, 39% in Rs 2,000–5,000 per month, 52% in Rs 5,000–10,000 and 61% in Rs 10,000 or above per month. Associations between income and religiosity is not significant (Table 4.15).

Table 4.15 Scores on Religiosity According to Income

Scores	*Income (Rs per month)*				*Grand Total*
	2000 or Less	*2000–5000*	*5000 10000*	*10000 or more*	
L	74	63	38	15	163
H	32	41	41	23	137
Total	79	104	79	38	300

Tabulated = 7.82, Calculated = 7.C98, d.f. = 3. Level of significance = 5%

Persons securing high scores on ritualism (median value or ritualism is) are 24% in 35 years age group, 33% in 36–45 years age group 29% in 46–55 years age group and 56% in 56 years age group. Thus higher age group people may be regarded as more ritualistic hence less developed socially, than the younger age groups. Associations between age and ritualism has been found statistically significant. Therefore, we may infer there is a significance association between age and ritualism (Table 4.16).

Table 4.16 Scores According to Age on Ritualism

Scores	*Age Group*				*Grand Total*
	⩽ 35	*36–45*	*46–55*	*56 & above*	
L	37	55	55	41	188
H	12	27	23	50	112
Total	49	82	78	91	300

Tabulated = 7.82, Calculated = 18.253, d .f = 3. Level of significance = 5%

Both Roman Catholic and Protestant sects have secured equally high scores (54%) on ritualism. Thus, both may be regarded as equally, socially developed. Swetambar sect reflects higher frequency (72%) than Degambar (22%). Here, Christians form the higher frequency (54%) of persons securing high scores on ritualism. Jains form second highest frequency (47%) and Sikhs from minimum frequency (11%) of those who have secured high ritualism. Hence Christians may be regarded as least developed. Second developed groups Sikhs constitute the most developed religious groups (Table 4.17).

Table 4.17 Scores According to Sect on Ritualism

Scores	*Sects*					*Grand Total*
	Roman Catholics	*Protes-tant*	*Degam-bars*	*Swetam-bars*	*Sikhs*	
L	23	23	39	41	89	188
H	27	27	11	36	11	112
Total	50	50	50	50	100	300

Tabulated = 9.49, Calculated = 50.002, d.f. = 4. Level of significance = 5%

On the basis of high scores secured by various categories of education, we observe that, 43% in the basic or less, 40% in matriculates, 35% in intermediate, 37% in case of graduates and 33% in postgraduate and higher education category form the larger concentrations. But association between education and ritualism has not been found significant (Table 4.18).

Table 4.18 Scores According to Education on Ritualism

Scores	*Education*					*Grand Total*
	Basic or less	*Matricu-lates*	*Interme-diates*	*Graduates*	*Higher*	
L	21	40	35	50	42	188
H	16	27	19	29	21	112
Total	37	67	54	79	63	300

Tabulated = 9.49, Calculated = 1.35, d.f. = 4. Level of significance =5%

In the different categories of occupation, an overwhelming majority is in the preaching occupation (91%), other category (77%) and in the administrative (private) (55%) occupations have secured high scores on ritualism and a comparatively lower ratio is the occupational categories such as business (38%) government service (35%) teaching (32%) and engineering (27%) (Table 4.19).

Persons securing high score on ritualism form larger part (42%) in the Rs <2,000 per month income group whereas second largest frequency (39%) is formed by Rs 5,000–10,000 per month income group. And comparatively lower frequencies are formed by Rs 2,000–5,000 per month and Rs 10,000 and above per month income groups. It reflects that ritualism is not affected significantly by variations in income (Table 4.20).

Table 4.19 Scores According to Occupation on Ritualism

Occupation	*Scores*		*Grand Total*
	L	*H*	
Business	82	50	132
Government services	47	25	72
Teaching	25	12	37
Engineering	8	3	11
Preaching	1	10	11
Administrative (private)	5	6	11
Others	6	20	26
Total	188	112	300

Tabulated = 12.59, Calculated = 29.385, d.f. = 4. Level of significance = 5%

Table 4.20 Scores According to Income on Ritualism

Scores	*Income (Rs per month)*				*Grand Total*
	2000 or less	*2000–5000*	*5000–10000*	*10000 or more*	
L	46	69	48	25	188
H	33	35	31	13	112
Total	79	104	79	38	300

Tabulated = 7.82, Calculated = 1.549, d. f. = 3. Level of significance = 5%

Sikhs have secured higher score on religiosity as well as on ritualism. Therefore, they constitute the highly developed religious group. Association between religiosity and ritualism is significant. Therefore, it can be said that income and ritualism are not significantly associated.

On the basis of various values of X^2 calculated, we may infer that Age and Religiosity Table 4.11 ($X^2 = 14.403$ @ 3 d. f.), Sect and

Table 4.21 Scores on Religiosity and Ritualism

	Ritualism		*Grand Total*
	L	*H*	
H	81	56	137
L	31	132	163
Total	112	188	300

Tabulated = 3.84, Calculated = 51.71, d.f. = 1. Level of significance =5%

Religiosity Table 4. 12 (X^2 = 13.4 4 8) and Occupation and Religiosity Table 4.14 (X^2 = 14997) are significantly associated but Education and Religiosity Table 4.13 (X^2 = 6.479) and Income and Religiosity, Table 4.14 are significantly related with each other infer (on the basis calculated) that age, sect and occupation affect religiosity. Age and Ritualism Table 4.16 (X^2 = 18.253), Sect and Ritualism Table 4.17 (X^2 = 50.002) and Occupation and Ritualism Table 4.19 (X^2 = 29.385) are significantly associated but Education and Ritualism Table 4.18 (X^2 = 1.35) and Income and Ritualism Table 4.20 (X^2 = 1.549) have no significant association with each other. Association between Religiosity and Ritualism Table 4.21 (X^2 = 51.171) has also been found as significant. Hence, religiosity and ritualism affect each other.

References

Benedix, R. (1960), *Max Weber: An Intellectual Portrait*, Heinman, London, p. 196.

Bingley, H. (1984), *Sikhs: Religio-Political History and Origin of Sikhism, Sacraments and Rituals, Festivals and Customs*, Sumeet Publications, New Delhi.

Brentano, quoted by P.C. Gilbert, *Fundamentals of Sociology*, Orient Longmans, New Delhi, p. 206.

Dawson, C. (1949), *Religion and Culture, Gifford Lectures*, Sheed & Ward, London.

Desai, A.R. (1978), *Rural Sociology in India*, Popular Prakashan, Bombay (Mumbai).

Demant, V.A., (1952), *Religion and the Doctrine of Capitalism*, Faber & Faber, London.

Dube, S.C., (1985), "Cultural Problems in the Economic Development of India," in *Religion and Progress in Modern Asia*, R.N. Bellah (Ed.), The Free Press, New York.

Fanfani (1939), *Catholicism, Protestantism and Capitalism*, Sheed & Ward, London.

Glenn, M.V. (1962), *Sociology of Religion*, McGraw Hill, London.

Glenn, N.D. and Hyland, R. (1967), "Religious Preference and Worldly Success: Some Evidence from National Survey", *American Sociological Review*, 32, No. 1, 1967, pp. 73–85.

Gupta, K.P. (1974b), "Religious Evolution and Social Change in India: A Study of Rama Krishna Mission Movement". *Contributions to Indian Sociology* (N.S) 8: 25–49.

Malefitz, A.D.W. (1968), *Religion and Culture: An Introduction to Anthropology of Religion.* Mac Millan, New York., p. 290.

Narang, G.C. (1956), *Transformation of Sikhism*, New Book Society of India. New Delhi.

Parvathamna, C. (1978), "Religion and Social Change" in *Dimensions of Social Change* (ed.), by M.N. Srinivas, Allied Publishers, Bombay.

Rachfahl, K., quoted by R.I. Johnstone (1975), *Religion and Society in Interaction*, p. 166.

Rao, M.S.A. (1969), "Religion and Economic Development", *Sociological Bulletin,* 18(1) (1–15).

Sayeed et al. (1990) "Profile of Visitors to Places of Worship", *Social Action,* Jan.-March. Vol. 40(1).

Shils, E. (1961), *The Intellectual Between Tradition and Modernity: The Indian Situation*, Mouton & Co., New York.

Singh, T. (1990) "Ritualism vs. Reality", *The Sikh Review,* 38(441)., pp. 16–17.

Singh, Y. (1973), *Modernization of Indian Tradition: A Systematic Study of Social Change*, Thomson Press, Delhi.

Sombart, quoted by P. Gisbert, op. cit., p. 206.

Tonybee, A. (1947b), *Study of History, 1934–61*, 12 Vols, abridged to 2 vols. by D.C. Somervelle, Oxford University Press, London, p. 487.

Troeltsch, E. (1931), *The Social Teaching of the Christian Churches*, (Trans.) by Olive Wyon, George Allen and Unwin Ltd., London.

—— (1958), *Protestantism and Progress*, Beacon Press.

Weber, M., (1966). *The Theory of Social and Economic Organisation*, (Trans.) A.M. Handerson & Talcott Parsons, The Free Press, New York. pp. 154–157.

5 Sect and Society

Sociology of religion centres around the interplay between religion and society. Religion interacts with society in many ways. Religion shapes society and vice versa. It has a dominant effect upon one's feelings and helps shape attitudes (Bingley, 1984). For instance, Sikhism preaches equality, Christianity teaches universal love and Jainism insists upon non-violence and equality among all.

Social reality is significantly influenced by religion (Troeltsch, 1931). Religion is bound up with the totality of the social process and the concreteness of individual existence (especially in Asia), where religion still shapes the traditional forms of culture, and being so deeply involved in social and personal life has profound implications for the course of historical development, encouraging or inhibiting economic, political and social modernization (Bellah, 1965). Social change is brought about by the interplay of many forces and religion is one such force (Parvathamma, 1977).

Sect is a voluntary association of only those who, according to the principle, are religiously and morally qualified. If one finds voluntary reception of his membership, by virtue of religious probation, he joins the sect voluntarily (Weber, 1966).

As a crystallized form of religion, sect may set limits of an individual's social interaction. Some people remain confined to their sect boundaries, whereas others may come across it. Factors leading to such variations may be exogenous or endogenous. Among the endogenous factors are the rituals of a specific sect. Exogenous may include several social and economic determinants that may be common to all sects, e.g., age, education, occupation, income and common habit. On the basis of external factors, sects may exhibit similar tendencies but variations are found from one religious sect to another and even within different sects of one religious group. These variations may account for different degrees of social development of various sects.

The objective of the present chapter is to analyse the interplay between religious sect and society. That is, how does a sect shape society and vice versa on one hand and the impact of age, sect, education, occupation and income of an individual upon sectarianism on the other, with a view that higher the feeling of sect, more be the tendency segregation from other sects or the larger society. This, in turn, may function as a block in social development. For this purpose, following questions have been raised:

1. How strongly do you feel about your sect?
2. Do you maintain relations with your sect members only?
3. How frequently do you visit your sect members?
4. How much time do you spend per week for the sect?
5. Do you feel that sect helps/constraints an individual's progress?
6. Did you ever get support from your family, relatives or sect?
7. Do you feel that your children should be married within your own sect?
8. How frequently do you visit to other people than your sect members?
9. How strictly do you invite other sects' members?

Sectarianism here means the feelings and actions of an individual towards his sect and sect members.

Intra-Sect Relations

Sectarianism

Table 5.1 indicates that maximum frequency (71%) of those who feel very strong about their sect is among the eldest age group, i.e., 56 years and more and minimum (57%) among the youngest age group (35 years or less). Those who do at all feel strong about their sect form highest ratio (10%) among the youngest age group (35 years or less) and more older equal 1% and 2% among the higher age groups respectively. Thus, we may say that sectarian feeling is observed more among the higher age groups than the younger people.

Table 5.1 also indicates that sectarianism is maximum (78%) among Swetambar sect of Jains, followed by 73% Sikhs and 62%

Table 5.1: How strongly do you feel about your sect?

Variable	*Categories*	*Very Strong*		*Strong*		*Less Strong*		*Not at all Strong*		*Total*	
		'f'	*%*	*'f'*	*%*	*'f'*	*%*	*'f'*	*%*	*'f'*	*%*
Age	⩽ 35 years	28	57	12	25	4	8	5	10	49	100
	36–45	56	68	12	15	12	15	2	2	82	100
	46–55	51	65	19	25	7	9	1	1	78	100
	56 ⩾	65	71	16	18	8	9	2	2	91	100
	Total	**200**	**67**	**59**	**19**	**31**	**10**	**10**	**4**	**300**	**100**
Sect	Roman Cath.	31	62	9	18	7	14	3	6	50	100
	Protestants	28	56	12	24	5	10	5	10	50	100
	Degambar	29	58	16	32	4	8	1	2	50	100
	Swetambar	39	78	5	10	5	12	0	0	50	100
	Sikh	73	73	17	17	9	9	1	1	50	100
	Total	**200**	**67**	**59**	**19**	**31**	**10**	**10**	**4**	**100**	**100**
Education	Basic or less	31	84	1	3	3	8	2	5	37	100
	Matriculate	46	69	13	19	4	6	4	6	67	100
	Intermediate	27	50	17	31	10	19	0	0	54	100
	Graduate	53	67	17	21	6	8	3	4	79	100
	P.G. & Higher	43	68	11	17	8	13	1	2	63	100
	Total	**200**	**67**	**59**	**19**	**31**	**10**	**10**	**4**	**300**	
Occupation	Business	91	69	28	21	11	8	2	2	132	100
	Teaching	22	59	4	11	7	19	4	11	37	100
	Govt. Service	49	68	19	27	3	4	1	1	72	100
	Engineering	6	55	2	19	3	27	0	0	11	100
	Preaching	11	100	0	0	0	0	0	0	11	100
	Admn. (pvt.)	5	45	2	18	2	18	2	18	11	99
	Others	16	62	4	15	5	19	1	4	26	100
	Total	**200**	**67**	**59**	**19**	**31**	**10**	**10**	**4**	**300**	
Income	⩽ Rs 2000	50	63	18	23	11	14	0	0	79	100
	2000–5000	66	64	18	17	14	13	6	6	104	100
	5000–10000	58	73	13	17	4	5	4	5	79	100
	10000–more	26	69	10	26	2	5	0	0	38	100
	Total	**200**	**67**	**59**	**19**	**31**	**10**	**10**	**4**	**300**	

Roman Catholics. It is observed least 56% among Protestants and 58% among Degambars. If we draw a comparison, we find that Sikhs are highly (73%) sectarian followed by Jains (68%) and Christians (59%). Within a particular religion it is observed that 10% Protestants as compared to 6% Roman Catholics, and 2% Degambars as against 0% Swetambars and 1% Sikhs do not at all feel strong about their sect.

Among various education groups feeling about sect is maximum (84%) in the least qualified people, then 69% among matriculates, 68% in the higher educated group, 67% among graduates and lowest 50% in the intermediates. Frequencies of those who feel strong about their sect is maximum (31%) among intermediate and lowest (3%) in the basic or below group. Persons feeling less strong is maximum 19% in the intermediate and lowest 6% among the matriculates, persons feeling not all strong is 5% in the basic or below, 4% in the graduates, 2% among the higher education group and no one in the intermediate group (Table 5.1).

Here, we do not find any significant increase or decline in the feeling of sect according to education. There may be certain other associated factors that may affect sectarianism.

Sectarianism on the basis of income does not indicate significant results. Lowest income groups Rs 2,000 p.m. and below and Rs 2,000–5,000 p.m. constitute 63% and 64% and Rs 5,000–10,000 p.m. form 73% whereas Rs 10,000 p.m. and above indicates fairly higher proportion (69%) but less than the preceding income group.

Table 5.2 shows that percentage of persons spending one hour time per week for their sect is maximum 21% among the age group of 36–45, years, 20% among Roman Catholics and Sikhs, 46% among intermediates, 36% among administrative and 19% in the income group of Rs 2,000 p.m. or less.

Those who spend 2 hours per week form lowest (4%) proportion on the whole. Persons spending three hours or more per week are maximum (33%) among the age group of 56 years and above, 36% among Degambars, 62% among the basic or less education group and 91% among preaching followed by 35% among teaching and 47% in the income group of Rs 10,000 p.m. or more.

Those who spend no time for their sect form maximum concentration, i.e., 61% among the age group of 35 years or less, 31% among the Protestants, 84% among the higher qualified group and 91% among engineering and 57% in the income group of Rs 2,000–5,000 p.m. On the basis of above observations it can be concluded that age, sect and income but not education and occupation affect sectarianism.

Sectarianism decreases with the decreasing age and increases with the decreasing education. Three hours time is spent mostly by Sikhs

Table 5.2: How much time do you spend for your sect per week?

Varia-ble	*Categories*	*≤ 1 hour*		*2 hour*		*≥ 3 hour*		*No time*		*Total*	
		'f'	%	'f'	%	'f'	%	'f'	%	'f'	%
Age	≤–35 years	7	14	2	4	10	21	30	61	49	100
	36–45	17	21	4	5	22	39	47	82	82	100
	46–55	14	18	2	2	24	31	38	49	78	100
	56 ≥	15	17	4	4	30	33	42	46	91	100
	Total	**53**	**18**	**12**	**4**	**86**	**29**	**149**	**49**	**300**	**100**
Sect	Roman Cath.	10	20	2	4	16	32	22	44	50	100
	Protestant	9	18	2	4	8	16	31	62	50	100
	Degambar	6	12	1	2	1	36	25	50	50	100
	Swetambar	8	16	3	6	9	18	30	60	50	100
	Sikh	20	20	4	4	35	35	41	41	100	100
	Total	**53**	**18**	**12**	**4**	**86**	**29**	**149**	**49**	**300**	
Educa-tion	Basic or less	2	5	1	3	23	63	11	30	37	100
	Matriculate	20	30	4	6	23	34	20	30	67	100
	Intermediate	25	46	3	6	11	20	15	28	54	100
	Graduate	5	6	3	4	21	27	50	63	79	100
	P.G. & Higher	1	2	1	2	8	12	53	84	63	100
	Total	**53**	**18**	**12**	**4**	**86**	**29**	**149**	**49**	**300**	
Occupa-tion	Business	20	15	3	2	42	32	67	51	132	100
	Teaching	6	16	3	8	13	35	13	41	37	100
	Govt. Service	16	22	3	4	16	22	37	52	72	100
	Engineering	1	9	1	1	1	1	10	91	11	100
	Preaching	0	0	0	0	10	91	1	9	11	100
	Admn. (pvt.)	4	36	1	9	2	18	4	37	11	100
	Others	6	23	2	8	3	11	15	58	26	100
	Total	**531**	**8**	**12**	**4**	**86**	**29**	**149**	**49**	**300**	
Income	≤ Rs 2000	15	19	4	5	25	32	35	44	79	100
	2000–5000	19	18	6	6	20	19	59	57	104	100
	5000–10000	13	16	2	3	23	29	41	52	79	100
	10000–more	6	16	0	0	18	47	14	37	38	100
	Total	**53**	**18**	**12**	**4**	**86**	**29**	**149**	**49**	**300**	**100**

(35%), then by Jains (27%) and minimum 24% by Christians. Variations in the span of time spent for the sect is due to the nature of religious organizations. For instance, Christians usually have one hour's service in the church, Sikhs have services in the gurudwaras for the longest period whereas Jains fall in between the two.

Those who do not spend any time form highest proportions, i.e., 61% in the 35 years or less age group, 31% among the Protestants, 84% among the higher education group, 91% in engineering and 57% among the income group of Rs 2,000–5,000 p.m. Income does not seem to be related with sectarianism.

Sect's Help

Table 5.3 indicates that persons in the youngest age group (35 years or less) form highest ratio (76%) of those who feel that 'sect helps in progress' of an individual followed by 55% in the age group of 36–45 years and 56 years and above. Their percentage is a little low (51%) among the age group of 46–55 years. On the contrary, ratio of those who feel that sect 'constraints' an individual's progress is also highest (12%) among the youngest age group (35 years and less) and nil in the age group of 56 years and above.

A total of 45% in the age group of 56 years, and above, 39% in the age group of 36–45 years, and in the age group of 46–55 years and 12% in the age group of 35 years and less gave no comments. We may infer that this category feels that sect either does not help or does not affect an individual's progress.

About 66% Roman Catholics as against 48% Protestants, and 56% Swetambars as compared to 46% Degambars and 64% Sikhs feel that sects helps in progress. That is Roman Catholics are more sectarian than Protestants and Swetambars are more as compared to Degambars. Sikhs are most sectarian (64%) than Christians (57%) and Jains (51%).

In all, 63% each among the intermediate and higher education group, 91% among preaching and 63% among the lowest (Rs 2,000 p.m.) and the highest income group (Rs 10,000 p.m. or more) form the highest proportion or those who feel that sect helps in progress

Intra-Sect Relations

Table 5.4 reveals that highest ratio (87%) of those who necessarily maintain relations with their own sect members is among the age group of 56 years and more, then 86% among the age group of 46–55 years followed by 77% among the age group of 36–45 years and is minimum (71%) among the 35 years and less age group.

Sectwise distribution indicates that sectarian feeling is highest (90%) among Degambar sect of Jains, then 87% among the Sikhs and

Table 5.3: Do you feel that sect helps/constraints an individual's progress?

Variable	*Categories*	*Helps*		*Constrains*		*No Comments*		*Total*	
		'f'	%	'f'	%	'f'	%	'f'	%
Age	⩽–35 years	37	76	6	12	6	12	49	100
	36–45	45	55	5	6	32	39	82	100
	46–55	40	51	8	10	30	39	78	100
	56⩾	50	55	0	0	41	45	91	100
	Total	**172**	**57.33**	**19**	**6.33**	**109**	**36.33**	**300**	**100**
Sect	Roman Cath.	33	66	15	30	2	4	50	100
	Protestant	24	48	2	4	24	48	50	100
	Degambar	23	46	0	0	27	54	50	100
	Swetambar	28	56	2	4	20	40	50	100
	Sikh	64	64	0	0	36	36	100	100
	Total	**172**	**57.33**	**19**	**6.33**	**109**	**36.33**	**300**	**100**
Educa-tion	Basic or less	19	51	4	11	14	11	37	100
	Matriculate	36	54	8	12	23	34	67	100
	Intermediate	34	63	1	2	19	35	54	100
	Graduate	43	54	6	8	30	38	79	100
	P.G. & Higher	40	63	0	0	23	37	63	100
	Total	**172**	**57.33**	**19**	**6.33**	**109**	**36.33**	**300**	**100**
Occupa-tion	Business	66	50	5	4	61	46	132	100
	Teaching	25	68	2	5	10	27	37	100
	Govt. Service	39	54	4	6	29	40	72	100
	Engineering	6	55	0	0	5	45	11	100
	Preaching	10	91	1	9	0	0	11	100
	Admn. (pvt.)	8	73	1	9	2	18	11	100
	Others	18	69	6	23	2	8	26	100
	Total	**172**	**57.33**	**19**	**6.33**	**109**	**36.33**	**300**	**100**
Income	⩽Rs 2000	50	63	4	6	25	31	79	100
	2000–5000	56	54	15	14	33	32	104	100
	5000–10000	42	53	0	0	37	47	79	100
	10000–more	24	63	0	0	14	37	38	100
	Total	**172**	**57.33**	**19**	**6.33**	**109**	**36.33**	**300**	**100**

84% among Swetambars. Among Christian sects 74% Roman Catholics and 66% Protestants necessarily maintain relations with their own sect fellows. Degambars are observed as highly sectarian because they usually do not dine with other castes. Both Sikh (87%) and Jains (87%) are observed as more sectarian than the Christians.

Education (Table 5.4) shows significant variations. Frequency of persons who maintain relations with their own sect members is highest (89%) among basic or less qualified group followed by 85%

Table 5.4: Do you maintain relations with your sect members only?

Variable	*Categories*	*Necessarily Yes*		*Not Necessarily*		*G. Total*	
		'f'	%	'f'	%	'f'	%
Age	⩽–35 years	35	71	14	29	49	100
	36–45	63	77	19	23	82	100
	46–55	67	86	18	14	78	100
	56 ⩾	79	87	12	13	91	100
	Total	**244**	**81**	**56**	**19**	**300**	**100**
Sect	Roman Cath.	37	74	13	26	50	100
	Protestant	33	66	17	34	50	100
	Degambar	45	90	5	10	50	100
	Swetambar	42	84	8	14	50	100
	Sikh	87	87	13	13	100	100
	Total	**244**	**81**	**56**	**19**	**300**	**100**
Education	Basic or less	33	89	4	11	37	100
	Matriculate	57	85	10	15	67	100
	Intermediate	46	85	8	15	54	100
	Graduate	63	80	16	20	79	100
	P.G. & Higher	45	71	18	29	63	100
	Total	**244**	**81**	**56**	**19**	**300**	**100**
Occupation	Business	116	88	16	12	132	100
	Teaching	29	78	8	22	37	100
	Govt. Service	55	76	17	24	72	100
	Engineering	7	64	4	36	11	100
	Preaching	11	100	0	0	11	100
	Admn. (pvt.)	8	73	3	27	11	100
	Others	18	69	8	31	26	100
	Total	**244**	**81**	**56**	**19**	**300**	**100**
Income	⩽ Rs 2000	61	77	18	23	79	100
	2000–5000	82	79	22	21	104	100
	5000–10000	67	85	12	15	79	100
	10000–more	34	89	4	11	38	100
	Total	**244**	**81**	**56**	**19**	**300**	**100**

among both matriculates and intermediates, 80% among graduates and lowest (71%) among the higher education group. It shows that with the increase in the level of education of an individual his sectarian feelings decrease (Table 5.4).

About 88% among business besides 100% in preaching form the highest ratio of those who maintain relations with their own sect members. 64% (minimum) among engineering, maintain relations with their sect members only. A scan of the Table 5.4 shows that on the whole sectarianism is considerably high (not less than 64% in any occupational group) among all the occupations.

Data based on income indicates that 89% among Rs 10,000 or above, 85% among Rs 5,000–10,000, 79% among Rs 2,000–5000 and 77% in the income group of Rs 2,000 p.m. or less maintain relations with their sect members (Table 5.4). We may infer that in the higher income group sectarianism observed is also high. On the basis of our observations it can be said that highest income group was found mainly among Jains and Sikhs and these sects also indicated higher sectarian feeling on other issues. To sum up, it can be said that sectarianism is related with age, sect, education, occupation and income.

Intra-Sect Marriage

Age of an individual does not show (Table 5.5) any significant variation vis-a-vis his/her choice of marrying children within the same sect.

Membership in a sect sometimes becomes so binding for an individual that he/she is forced to marry their children within their own sect although this binding may be more strict in some sects than in others. There are many factors which force an individual to marry her/his children within his/her own sect. Some of the significant factors are: adjustment which is most important for Protestants (30%) (Table 5.5) and Roman Catholics (24%) than the other sects. Religion is crucial for both the sects of Jain-Swetambars 20%, Degambars 18%, then to Roman Catholics (18%) as compared to Protestants 16%, 14% Roman Catholics, 12% Protestants, 22% Degambars, 10% Swetambars, and 60% Sikhs reported other causes that have significant bearing upon the intra-sect marriage. Cultural importance is 18% in Roman Catholics and more or less equally significant for both the sects of Jain, i.e., Swetambars (22%) and Degambars (20%).

Table 5.5: Do you feel that your children should be married within your own sect?

Variable	*Categories*	*Adjustment*		*Religious*		*Cultural*		*Social Bond*		*Other*		*No Comments*		*Total*
		'f'	*%*	*'f'*	*%*	*'f'*	*%*	*f*	*%*	*f*	*%*	*f*	*%*	*f*
Age	⩽ 35 years	10	20	1	29	8	16	4	8	16	33	10	20	49
	36–45	15	18	3	23	18	22	16	20	12	15	18	22	82
	46–55	16	21	8	14	16	21	13	17	12	15	13	17	78
	56 ⩾	20	22	16	13	9	10	14	15	19	21	13	19	91
	Total	**61**	**20**	**28**	**9**	**51**	**17**	**47**	**16**	**59**	**20**	**54**	**18**	**300**
Sect	Roman Cath.	12	24	3	6	9	18	9	18	7	14	9	18	50
	Protestant	15	30	1	2	12	24	8	16	6	12	8	16	50
	Degambar	8	16	8	16	10	20	9	18	11	22	4	8	50
	Swetambar	8	16	9	18	11	22	10	20	5	10	8	16	50
	Sikh	18	18	7	7	9	9	11	11	30	60	25	25	50
	Total	**61**	**20**	**28**	**9**	**51**	**17**	**47**	**16**	**59**	**20**	**54**	**18**	**100**
Education	Basic or Less	12	32	12	32	2	5	6	16	1	3	4	11	37
	Matriculate	14	21	6	9	13	19	7	10	14	21	13	19	67
	Intermediate	18	33	3	6	0	0	6	11	17	31	10	18	54
	Graduate	13	16	5	6	24	30	12	15	11	14	14	18	79
	P.G. & Higher	4	6	2	3	12	19	16	20	16	25	13	21	63
	Total	**61**	**20**	**28**	**9**	**51**	**17**	**47**	**16**	**59**	**20**	**54**	**18**	**300**

Occupation	Business	18	14	8	6	26	20	34	26	36	1	10	8	132
	Teaching	12	32	4	11	2	5	2	5	7	5	10	27	37
	Govt. Service	14	19	0	0	21	29	3	4	9	3	25	35	72
	Engineering	9	82	0	0	0	0	0	0	2	18	0	0	11
	Preaching	0	0	9	8	0	0	0	0	2	18	0	0	11
	Admn. (pvt.)	5	45	0	0	0	0	0	0	3	27	3		11
	Others	3	11	7	27	2	8	8	30	0	0	6	27	26
	Total	**61**	**20**	**28**	**9**	**51**	**17**	**47**	**16**	**59**	**20**	**54**	**23**	**300**
Income	≤ Rs 2000	14	18	14	18	11	14	5	6	3	0	32	40	79
	2000–5000	18	17	10	9	24	23	14	13	32	4	6	6	104
	5000–10000	17	22	2	3	11	14	24	30	19	11	6	8	79
	10000–more	12	32	2	5	5	13	4	11	5	0	10	26	38
	Total	**61**	**20**	**28**	**9**	**51**	**17**	**47**	**16**	**59**	**20**	**54**	**18**	**300**

Social bond is most crucial for Swetambars (20%) than Degambars (18%), then to Roman Catholics (18%) as compared to Protestants (16%). Due to wider differences in culture, intra-sect marriage is broadly favoured by head of the household, but due to changing time and children's attitude some said that it will depend upon children's own choice. It indicates that authority of the father in present time is declining. Among Jains, people said that if their children will marry out of their sect, then they will not accept them as their children. If parents accept their children then the sect members outcaste them. This has been really true with one of a well-known (both economically and socially) family of a Degambar. Sectarian feeling was observed to be more intense among people residing in a compact group of their own sect laws. Once an individual settles in a heterogeneous setting, his values and opinions about sect becomes diluted.

For the education group, basic or less, adjustment (32%), religious (32%), social bond (16%) which constitute almost highest frequencies are the major factors which force them to marry their children within their own sect. Cultural factor is significant for graduates (30%). Postgraduate and higher form maximum (20%) ratio who feel to marry their children within their sect due to social bond.

For engineering profession, adjustment is the most important (82%) factor, for government servants, cultural is the most significant reason (29%), for business class, social bond is more important (26%), and for 'others' religious and social bond (27% and 30%) are important reasons for marrying their children within their own sect.

Income shows variations with respect to intra-sect marriage. Adjustment is more important (32%) factor for the upper income group whereas religious (18%) for the lower income group (Rs $\leqslant$ 2,000 p.m.), cultural is important for the income group of Rs 2,000–5,000 p.m.(23%), and social bond (30%) for the income group of Rs 5,000–10,000 p.m.

A general overview of Table 5.5 indicates that out of a total of 300, most important factor is adjustment (20%), then cultural (17%), social bond (16%) and some other factors (15%). No comments were given by 18% people. But at the time of interview the researcher felt what most of them preferred intra-sect marriage due to social and ritualistic (religious) differences. Thus sect set the boundaries of an individual's social milieu and significantly shapes the society.

Inter-Sect Relations

Observations on individuals inviting other sect members are significantly different than the previous Table 5.5.

Table 5.6: How strictly do you invite other sects' members?

Variable	*Categories*	*Very Strictly*		*Strictly Strictly*		*Less Strictly*		*Not at all*		*Total*	
		'f'	%	'f'	%	'f'	%	'f'	%	'f'	%
Age	⩽ 35 years	12	24	13	27	19	39	5	10	49	100
	36–45	26	32	26	32	16	19	14	17	82	100
	46–55	29	37	29	37	8	10	12	16	78	100
	56 ⩾	36	40	32	35	12	13	11	12	91	100
	Total	**103**	**34**	**100**	**33**	**55**	**18**	**42**	**14**	**300**	**100**
Sect	Roman Cath.	12	24	11	22	18	36	9	18	50	100
	Protestant	15	30	17	34	9	18	9	18	50	100
	Degambar	19	38	18	36	4	8	9	18	50	100
	Swetambar	18	36	18	36	8	16	6	12	50	100
	Sikh	39	39	36	33	16	16	9	9	100	100
	Total	**103**	**34**	**33**	**43**	**55**	**18**	**42**	**14**	**300**	**100**
Educa-	Basic or less	11	30	16	43	2	5	8	22	37	100
ion	Matriculate	19	28	20	30	8	12	20	30	67	100
	Intermediate	24	44	12	22	15	28	3	6	54	100
	Graduate	25	32	29	37	18	23	7	8	79	100
	P.G. & Higher	24	38	23	37	12	19	4	6	63	100
	Total	**103**	**34**	**100**	**33**	**55**	**18**	**42**	**14**	**300**	**100**
Occupa-	Business	56	42	45	34	14	11	17	13	132	100
tion	Teaching	16	43	11	30	9	24	1	3	37	100
	Govt. Service	14	19	27	38	17	24	14	19	72	100
	Engineering	1	9	5	45	5	45	0	0	11	100
	Preaching	1	9	0	0	3	27	7	64	11	100
	Admn. (pvt.)	5	45	5	5	1	9	0	0	11	100
	Others	10	38	7	7	6	23	3	12	26	100
	Total	**103**	**34**	**100**	**100**	**55**	**18**	**42**	**14**	**300**	**100**
Income	⩽ Rs–2000	20	25	33	42	20	25	6	8	79	100
	2000–5000	32	31	35	34	22	21	15	14	104	100
	5000–10000	37	47	22	28	9	11	11	14	79	100
	10000–more	14	37	10	26	4	11	10	26	38	100
	Total	**103**	**34**	**100**	**33**	**55**	**18**	**42**	**14**	**300**	**100**

A maximum of 40% in the age group of 56 years and above, 39% among Sikhs, 44% among intermediates, 45% in administrative (private), and 47% in the income group of Rs 5,000–10,000 p.m. invite very strictly, (Table 5.6).

A total of 36% each among Degambars, Swetambars and Sikhs, 43% in basic or less education group, 45% in engineering, and 42% in the income group of Rs 2,000 p.m. or less invite strictly. Further 39% in the age group of 35 years or less, 36% in Roman Catholics, 28% in intermediates, 45% in engineering, and 25% in Rs 2,000 p.m. or less income group invite less strictly and 17% in the age group of 36–45 years, 18% each among Roman Catholics, Protestants and Degambars, 30% among matriculates, 64% among preaching class and 26% in the income group of Rs 10,000 p.m. and above do not at all invite other than their sect members at their homes (Table 5.6).

A careful examination of Table 5.6 reveals that 40% in age group of 56 years and above, 37% in the age group of 46–55 years, 32% in the 36–45 years age group, and minimum (24%) frequency is in the age group of ⩽ 35 years who invite other sects' members very strictly. Maximum frequency (37%) of those who strictly invite other sects members is in age group of 46–55 years. Those who invite other sect's members less strictly form highest ratio (39%) in the age group of <35 years. Those who do not at all invite other sects members is highest (17%) in the age group of 36–45 years.

Among various sects Roman Catholic form minimum frequency (24%) of those who very strictly invite other sects' members. Roman Catholic also form minimum frequency (i.e., 22%) of those who invite strictly and maximum (36%) of those who less strictly invite and also (18%) of those who 'not at all' invite the other sects' members.

Persons securing high scores on sectarianism (median value of sectarianism is 18) form comparatively larger proportions (i.e., more

Table 5.7: Scores of Age Groups on Sectarianism

Age Group (years)

Scores	*35 & above*	*36–45*	*46–55*	*56 & above*	*Total*
L	35	46	38	34	153
H	14	36	40	57	147
Total	49	82	78	91	300

Tabulated = 7.82, Calculated = 15.97, d.f. = 3

than half) in the age groups of 46–55 years and 56 years and more (51% and 63%) than in the ⩽ 35 years and 36–45 years age groups (29%, 44%). We observe that lower age groups reflect low on sectarianism than those in the higher age groups. Association between age and sectarianism is significant.

Table 5.8: Scores of Various Sects on Sectarianism

Scores	*Sects*					*Total*
	Roman Catholics	*Protestants*	*Degambars*	*Swetambars*	*Sikhs*	
L	26	24	21	17	65	152
H	24	26	29	33	35	148
Total	50	50	50	50	100	300

Tabulated = 9.49, Calculated = 15.446 d. f. = 4, Level of significance = 5%

Those who have secured high scores on sectarianism form nearly equal frequencies in Roman Catholic and Protestant sects (48% and 52%). Swetambars form higher frequency than Degambars (66% and 58%). Jains form most sectarian religious group. Christians are less sectarian than Jains but more sectarian than Sikhs. Sect and sectarianism are significantly associated. Jains may be treated as least socially developed, Christians form second developed group and Sikhs are most developed (62%, 50% and 35%).

People who have secured high scores on sectarianism form comparatively higher frequencies (i.e., more than half) in the educational categories of matriculates, graduates and postgraduate and higher

Table 5.9: Scores of Different Education Groups on Sectarianism

Education	*Scores*		*Total*
	L	*H*	
Basic or below	20	17	37
Matriculates	30	37	67
Intermediates	36	18	54
Graduates	37	42	79
Higher	30	33	63
Total	153	147	300

Tabulated = 9.49, Calculated = 7.315, d.f. = 4, Level of significance = 5%

(55%, 53% and 52%) as compared to those in basic or below, and intermediate categories. Education and sectarianism are not significantly associated.

Frequencies of those who have secured high scores on sectarianism are comparatively higher in the occupational categories of teaching, business, preaching and private administrative (51%, 58%, 91% and 91%) than in engineering and in other's and in government service (18%, 19% and 35%). Hence, engineering and government

Table 5.10: Scores on Sectarianism of Different Occupations

Occupation	*Scores*		*Total*
	L	*H*	
Business	56	76	132
Government service	47	25	72
Teaching	18	19	37
Engineering	9	2	11
Preaching	1	10	11
Administrative	1	10	11
Others	21	5	26

Tabulated = 12.59, Calculated = 38.703, d.f. = 6. Level of significance = 5%

Table 5.11: Scores of Various Income Groups on Sectarianism

Income Per Month (Rs)	*Scores*		*Total*
	L	*H*	
2,000 & below	42	37	79
2,000–5,000	73	31	104
5,000–10,000	27	52	79
10,000 & above	11	27	38
Total	153	147	300

Tabulated=7.82, Calculated=31.819, d.f.=3. Level of significance = 5%

Table 5.12 : Scores on Religiosity and Sectarianism

	Sectarianism		
Score	*H*	*L*	*Total*
H	103	34	137
L	44	110	163
Total	147	153	300

Tabulated = 3.84, Calculated=69.167, d.f.= 1. Level of significance=5%

Table 5.13 : Scores on Religiosity and Sectarianism

	Sectarianism		
Score	*H*	*L*	*Total*
H	84	28	112
L	63	125	188
Total	147	153	300

Tabulated=3.84, Calculated=48.346, d.f.=1, Level of significance=5%

service occupations may be regarded as more developed whereas preaching, administrative and teaching as less developed. Occupation and sectarianism are not significantly associated.

Ratios of persons securing high scores on sectarianism are comparatively higher in the income groups of Rs 5,000–10,000 per month and Rs 10,000 and above per month (66% and 71%) than in the income groups of Rs 2,000 and below per month and Rs 2,000–5,000 per month (47% and 30%). Income and sectarianism are significantly associated.

There is significant association between religiosity and sectarianism. We may infer that association between ritualism and sectarianism is significant.

On the basis of X^2 values, we may conclude that sectarianism is significantly affected by age ($X^2 = 15.97$ @ 3 d.f.), sect ($X^2 = 15.446$) and income (X^2 between income and sectarianism = 31.819 @ 3 d.f.) whereas education ($X^2 = 7.315$) does not affect but occupation ($X^2 = 38.703$) affects sectarianism. It has been observed that people of different sects largely maintain relations with their sect members especially in the business class and among both the sects of Jains, Christians and Sikhs. Jains generally do not extend their relations with other sects due to reserved food habits and ritualistic differentiation. Christians also remain confined to their own sect members. Sectarianism is significantly associated with religiosity and ritualism (X^2 between sectarianism and religiosity = 69.167 and between sectarianism and ritualism = 48.346).

Finally, we may infer that sect affiliation largely shapes society and vice versa. On the one hand it unites sect members and on the other, separates one sect from another on rituals and ethical basis. We may say that if sect boundaries are made more flexible then there can be more mixing in society within one religious group and among different religious groups.

References

Bellah, R.N. (1968), *Religion and Progress in Modern Asia*, The Free Press, New York.

Bingley, A.H., (1984), *Sikhs: Religio-Political History* and *Origin of Sikhism Sacraments and Rituals, Festivals and Customs*, Sumeet Publications, New Delhi.

Parvathamma, C. (1977), "Religions and Social Change: A Study of Tradition and Change in Virasaivism", in *Dimension of Social Change*, p. 243.

Troeltsch, E. (1931), *The Social Teaching of the Christian Churches*, (Trans.) O. Wyon, George Allen & Unwin.

Weber, Max (1966), *The Theory of Social and Economic Organization* (Trans.) A.M. Handerson & Talcott Parsons, The Free Press, New York.

6 Conflict and Harmony

One of the major obstacles in the social development of society is conflict inherent in it. It can be latent or manifest. Latent is observed when members of a particular religious group or sect interact with the other, whereas manifest is apparent at different times among various social groups, both religious and secular.

Religion binds its members leading to unification and also brings disintegration causing division of society into various segments. This is due to differences in customs and political and economic interests (Kabir, cited in Mathur, 1979). These differences are due to different ethical values preached by different religions. For instance, Jainism stresses upon non-violence and equality; Christianity teaches universal love and brotherhood; and Sikhism insists upon equality and love. Sikhism has reduced communal tensions between Hindus and Muslims (Singh, 1968) On the contrary, Sikh's gurudwaras served as a platform for Sikh agitations (Dhillon, 1989). At the same time, all religious movements are political movements (Narang, 1956). Conflicts within the Sikh sects are on ritualism (Singh, 1990) and on control of important shrines and gurudwaras. Religious leaders are accumulating wealth (Singh, 1986) leading to intense confrontation between rich and poor (Chatterjee, 1981).

Cultural institutions of religion furnish a potential for social integration. Missionaries have worked as a means of social change (Oddie, 1969). Conflict is observed on various grounds within a sect, within different sects of one religious group and between two or more religious groups as religious sects form important components leading to division of society into various segments. In Agra, incidence of inter-religion conflict between Jains, Christians and Sikhs was negligible during the past history. Incidence of inter-sect conflict is also not frequent among the Christian sects (i.e., Roman Catholics and Protestants) rather there is a tendency of reunion of various sects in order to form a majority group, but it has not been a success as yet due to possession of power by either of the two sects.

Among Degambars and Swetambar sects of Jain, inter-sect conflict is apparent on possession of one of the most important temple in Roshan Mohalla at Agra city. Sikhs form a solidarity group due to 1984 riots, but intra-sect conflicts are numerous and distance is maintained on caste basis.

In the present study an attempt has been made to analyse the role of religious sect in bringing harmony within the sect, with other sects or society at large and serving as a causative factor of bringing conflict in the sect, among sects and society. For the analysis of conflict following questions were raised:

1. How much satisfied are you with the standards of honesty and integrity of your religious office's management?
2. How frequent is the incidence of conflict within your sect?
3. What are the major causes of intra-sect conflict?

Following questions have been raised to measure harmony among various sects which in other way also refers to social distance maintained by various sects:

4. How strongly do you favour visiting other's religious places of worship?
5. Other's entrance into your own religious centre.
6. Do you permit your children to visit others' religious place of worship?
7. Do you accept and eat 'prasad' offered by other religious persons? and
8. Do you participate in other sects' ceremonies?

Intra-Sect Conflict

A careful examination of Table 6.1 indicates that percentage of those who feel 'very much satisfied' with the religious organization is highest (32%) among the age group of 56 years and above followed by (45%) of those who feel 'satisfied' among the age group of 46–55 years. Persons who are 'not satisfied' form the highest (47%) proportion in the age group of 35 years or less and those who are not concerned is also maximum (16%) in the age group of 35 years and

Table 6.1: How much satisfied are you with the standards of honesty and integrity of your religious office's management?

Variable	*Categories*	*Very Much Satisfied*		*Satisfied*		*Not at all Satisfied*		*Not Concerned*		*Total*	
		'f'	*%*	*'f'*	*%*	*'f'*	*%*	*'f'*	*%*	*'f'*	*%*
Age	≤–35 years	6	12	12	25	23	47	8	16	49	100
	36 - 45	10	12	32	39	34	42	6	7	82	100
	46 - 55	11	14	35	45	27	35	5	6	78	100
	56 ≥	29	32	28	31	31	34	3	3	91	100
	Total	**56**	**19**	**107**	**36**	**115**	**38**	**22**	**7**	**300**	**100**
Sect	Roman Cath.	8	16	19	38	20	40	3	6	50	100
	Protestant	5	10	12	24	25	50	8	16	50	100
	Degambar	5	10	27	54	15	30	3	6	50	100
	Swetambar	5	19	19	32	22	44	4	8	50	100
	Sikh	30	30	33	33	33	33	4	4	100	100
	Total	**56**	**19**	**107**	**36**	**115**	**38**	**22**	**7**	**300**	**100**
Education	Basic or less	4	54	20	54	13	35	1	1	37	100
	Matriculate	15	22	22	33	25	37	5	7	67	100
	Intermediate	9	17	16	30	25	46	4	7	54	100
	Graduate	16	20	26	33	29	37	5	10	79	100
	P.G. & Higher	12	19	23	37	23	36	5	8	63	100
	Total	**56**	**19**	**107**	**36**	**115**	**38**	**22**	**7**	**300**	**100**
Occupation	Business	18	14	54	41	47	35	13	10	132	100
	Teaching	7	19	10	27	17	46	3	8	37	100
	Govt. Service	13	18	27	38	29	40	3	4	72	100
	Engineering	0	0	5	45	3	27	3	27	11	100
	Preaching	8	75	1	9	2	18	0	0	11	100
	Admn. (pvt.)	3	27	3	27	5	45	0	0	11	100
	Others	7	27	7	27	12	46	0	0	26	100
	Total	**56**	**19**	**107**	**36**	**115**	**38**	**22**	**7**	**300**	**100**
Income	≤ Rs 2000	21	27	19	24	34	43	5	6	79	100
	2000–5000	16	15	40	38	38	37	10	10	104	100
	5000–10000	11	14	28	35	34	43	6	8	79	100
	10000–more	8	21	20	52	9	24	1	3	38	100
	Total	**56**	**19**	**107**	**36**	**115**	**38**	**22**	**7**	**300**	**100**

less. It indicates that, people's dissatisfaction with the management of the religious organization is reported more by the younger generation than the elderly persons.

Regarding sectwise distribution, Table 6.1 shows that among the Christians, Roman Catholics (16%) as compared to Protestants (10%), in Jains, Swetambars (16%) as compared to Degambars (19%) feel very much satisfied. Among the three religious groups, Sikhs form the highest proportion (30%) then the Christians (26%) and Jains (29%) who feel very much satisfied with their religious organization. Whereas, Degambars are in the largest proportion (54%) of those who feel satisfied with the religious organization. Those who are not at all satisfied with the religious organization are maximum (50%) among Protestants and minimum (30%) in Degambars. Frequency of persons who are not at all satisfied with the religious organization shows that Protestants are more prone to conflict than other groups in the present study.

On the basis of education (Table 6.1), it is observed that proportion of those who feel very much satisfied with the standards of honesty and integrity of their religious organization's management is highest (54%) among the basic or below group and the lowest (17%) Among the immediate group forms the maximum proportion (46%) of those who are not at all satisfied with the management of their religious organization's office. Out of a total of 300, 7% persons reported that they are not concerned with the religious organization's management.

Further, it is noted (Table 6.1) that the highest proportion 75% in preaching and 27% in the income group of Rs 2,000 p.m. or less feel 'very much satisfied'; 38% in government service and 52% in Rs 10, 000 p.m. or more income group feel satisfied; 46% in teaching, 40% in government service and 43% in the income group of Rs 2,000 p.m. or less and Rs 5,000–10,000 p.m. do not at all feel satisfied. Those who are involved in the management have shown their satisfaction, whereas those in the highest income group (Rs 10, 000 p.m. or more) have reported that they are maximum (52%) satisfied, and dissatisfaction is shown by 43% in the Rs 2,000 p.m. and Rs 5,000–10,000 p.m. income group with the management of religious organizations. Nevertheless, middle income groups (Rs 2,000–5,000 and Rs 5,000–10,000 p.m.) have shown the highest ratios 10% and 8% of those who are not concerned with the management of religious organization. Hence, on the basis of above Table 6.1, it can be inferred that the type of occupation affects an individual's involvement in matters related to conflict.

Table 6.2 indicates that the highest ratio 20% in the age group of 35 years or less, 22% in Swetambars, 21% in postgraduate and higher qualified group, 27% in administrative services and 21% in the

Table 6.2: How frequent is the incidence of conflict within your sect?

Variable	*Categories*	*Very Frequently*		*Frequently*		*Occasionaly*		*Never*		*Total*	
		'f'	*%*	*'f'*	*%*	*'f'*	*%*	*'f'*	*%*	*'f'*	*%*
Age	≤ 35 years	10	20	10	20	16	33	13	27	49	100
	36–45	10	12	24	29	16	20	32	39	82	100
	46–55	12	15	17	22	27	35	22	28	78	100
	56 ≥	15	17	29	32	12	13	35	38	91	100
	Total	**47**	**16**	**80**	**27**	**71**	**23**	**102**	**34**	**300**	**100**
Sect	Roman Cath.	2	4	17	34	9	18	22	44	50	100
	Protestant	10	20	10	20	15	30	15	30	50	100
	Degambar	7	14	12	24	18	36	13	26	50	100
	Swetambar	11	22	11	22	11	22	17	34	50	100
	Sikh	17	17	30	30	18	18	35	35	100	100
	Total	**47**	**16**	**80**	**27**	**71**	**23**	**102**	**34**	**300**	**100**
Education	Basic or less	4	11	9	24	13	35	11	30	37	100
	Matriculate	8	12	15	22	17	26	27	40	67	100
	Intermediate	8	15	21	39	8	17	16	29	54	100
	Graduate	14	18	17	21	15	19	33	42	79	100
	P.G. & Higher	13	21	18	28	17	27	15	24	63	100
	Total	**47**	**16**	**80**	**27**	**71**	**23**	**102**	**34**	**300**	**100**
Occupation	Business	20	15	33	25	38	29	41	31	132	100
	Teaching	9	24	9	24	7	19	12	33	37	100
	Govt. Service	8	11	22	31	16	22	26	36	72	100
	Engineering	2	18	1	9	1	9	7	64	11	100
	Preaching	2	18	2	18	2	18	5	45	11	100
	Admn. (pvt.)	3	27	2	18	43	27	3	27	11	100
	Others	3	12	11	42	4	15	8	31	26	100
	Total	**47**	**16**	**80**	**27**	**71**	**23**	**102**	**34**	**300**	**100**
Income	≤ Rs 2000	10	13	22	28	16	20	32	39	79	100
	2000–5000	15	14	25	24	25	24	39	38	104	100
	5000–10000	14	18	19	24	22	28	24	30	79	100
	10000–more	8	21	14	37	8	21	8	21	38	100
	Total	**47**	**16**	**80**	**27**	**71**	**23**	**102**	**34**	**300**	**100**

income group of Rs 10,000 p.m. or more have reported intra-sect conflicts as very frequent, whereas 32% in the age group of 56 years or above, 34% in Roman Catholic sect, 39% in intermediate qualified education group, 42% in the occupational group categories as 'others' and 37% in Rs 10,000 p.m. or more income group have reported frequent occurrence of conflict within their sects.

Further, proportion of those who have reported conflicts occasionally is the highest 35% in 46–55 years age group, 36% among Degambars, 35% among the uneducated group, 29% among the business class, and 28% in the income group of Rs 5,000–10,000 p.m., whereas proportion of those who reported never occurrence of conflict is the highest 39% in 36–45 years age group, 44% in Roman Catholics, 42% among graduates, 64% among engineering group and 39% in the income group of Rs 2,000 p.m. or less. It shows that higher the age lesser is the degree of reported conflict. Among Christians, Protestants are more agitating than the Roman Catholics, similarly, Swetambars are more reactionary than the Degambars. Sikhs (17%) are next to Roman Catholics (4%) who form minimum frequencies of persons reporting conflict. Engineering group has shown the least occurrence of conflict to the maximum 64%. Similarly, the lowest income groups that are those who have minimum means of survival are not bothered about extra-familial activities, but the better-off have both time and money to get involved in the management of the religious organization.

Causes of Intra-sect Conflicts

A cursory look at Table 6.3 shows that the maximum percentage (30%) of persons reporting money as the major cause of conflict is in the age groups of 46–55 years and 56 years and above; 5% each in the age group of 36–45 years and 56 years and more reported property as the major cause of conflict. Further, 33% each in the age groups of 35 years and less and 46–55 years reported power/posts as the major cause and 44% in the age group of 36–45 years reported other causes responsible for intra-sect conflicts. On the whole, out of a total of 300, 38% reported other causes of conflict, then 31% as power or posts and 28% said that money is the basic cause of conflict.

Among various sects under present study, causes of intra-sect conflicts differ from sect to sect. In Roman Catholics (34%), Protestants (46%), Degambars (50%), and Swetambars (36%) major causes of intra-sect conflicts are 'others' mentioned in Table 6.3, whereas among Sikhs (39%), the basis of conflict is power and posts.

Proportion of those who have reported 'other' causes of conflicts is the highest (41%, 42%, 37%, 37%, and 34%) in all the educational groups, viz., basic or less, matriculates, intermediates, graduates, and higher (Table 6.3).

Table 6.3: What are the causes of intra-sect conflict?

Categories		*Monetary*		*Property*		*Power/Posts*		*Others*		*Total*	
		'f'	*%*	*'f'*	*%*	*'f'*	*%*	*'f'*	*%*	*'f'*	*%*
Age	≤-35 years	13	26	0	0	16	33	20	41	49	100
	36–45	20	24	4	5	22	27	36	44	82	100
	46–55	23	30	1	1	26	33	28	36	78	100
	56 ≥	27	30	5	5	29	32	30	33	91	100
	Total	**83**	**28**	**10**	**3**	**93**	**31**	**114**	**38**	**300**	**100**
Sect	Roman Cath.	15	30	2	4	16	32	17	34	50	100
	Protestant	13	26	0	0	14	28	23	46	50	100
	Degambar	15	30	3	6	7	14	25	50	50	100
	Swetambar	12	24	3	6	17	34	18	36	50	100
	Sikh	28	28	2	2	39	39	31	31	100	100
	Total	**83**	**28**	**10**	**3**	**93**	**31**	**114**	**38**	**300**	**100**
Education	Basic or less	9	24	3	8	10	27	15	41	37	100
	Matriculate	18	27	3	4	18	27	28	42	67	100
	Intermediate	16	30	2	4	16	30	20	37	54	100
	Graduate	20	25	1	1	29	37	29	37	79	100
	P.G. & Higher	20	32	1	2	20	32	22	34	63	100
	Total	**83**	**28**	**10**	**3**	**93**	**31**	**114**	**38**	**300**	**100**
Occupation	Business	39	30	3	3	44	33	46	35	132	100
	Teaching	5	14	1	3	12	32	19	51	37	100
	Govt. Service	20	28	3	4	23	32	26	36	72	100
	Engineering	1	19	0	0	3	27	7	64	11	100
	Preaching	1	9	0	0	2	18	0	73	11	100
	Admn. (pvt.)	6	54	0	0	3	27	2	18	11	100
	Others	11	29	3	12	6	23	6	23	26	100
	Total	**83**	**28**	**10**	**3**	**93**	**31**	**114**	**38**	**300**	**100**
Income	≤ Rs 2000	21	27	3	4	18	23	37	47	79	100
	2000–5000	23	22	4	4	40	39	37	36	104	100
	5000–10000	24	30	2	3	24	30	29	37	79	100
	10000–more	15	39	1	3	11	29	11	29	38	100
	Total	**83**	**28**	**10**	**3**	**93**	**31**	**114**	**38**	**300**	**100**

Except in administrative and others, rest of the occupational groups have shown higher frequencies (35%) in business, 51% in teaching, 36% in government service, 64% in engineering and 73% in preaching who believe that there are other causes responsible for intra-sectoral conflicts (Table 6.3).

Table 6.3 shows that 47% in the income group of Rs 2,000 p.m. or less, 37% in Rs 5,000–10,000 p.m. have reported other causes of conflicts to the maximum, but 39% in the income group of Rs 2,000–5,000 p.m. have reported power as the major cause and 39% in the income group of Rs 10,000 p.m. or more reported money as the major cause of conflict. Thus, it can be concluded that causes of conflict reported differ in different age groups, religious groups i.e., sects, educational groups, occupational groups and income groups.

Harmony

A careful examination of Table 6.4 shows that inter-sectoral harmony in the form of attitude towards visiting other's religious places very strongly is the highest (12%) in the age group of 35 years and below, 9% in 36–45 years, 6% in 56 years and above, 4% in 46–55 years age group. On the whole, out of a total of 300 only 7% favour very strongly visiting other's religious places. Those who strongly favour visiting other's religious places form the lowest proportion (15%) in the age group of 56 years and above, whereas frequency (40%) of those who less strongly' favour visiting other's religious places is the highest among the age group of 36–45 years. Again proportion of those who do not favour at all visiting other's religious places is the highest (65%) among the age group of 56 years and above. It indicates that among the elderly people harmony, measured in terms of attitude towards visit to other's religious places of worship is less as compared to the younger people.

Table 6.4 shows Protestants (12%) favour very strongly visiting other's places of worship are observed as less conflict-oriented than the Roman Catholics (10%); among the Jains, Degambars (0%) are extremely rigid and feel themselves as separate from the larger society in religious matters than the Swetambars (6%), but Sikhs (7%) fall in between Christians and Jains of those who very strongly favour visit to other's religious places. Percentage of those who strongly favour visit to other religious places is the highest (22%) among Roman Catholics, whereas, those who less strongly favour

Table 6.4: How strongly do you favour visiting other is religious places of worship?

Variable	*Categories*	*Very Strongly*		*Strongly*		*Less Strongly*		*Not at all*		*Total*	
		'f'	%	'f'	%	'f'	%	'f'	%	'f'	%
Age	≤-35 years	6	12	9	18	18	37	16	33	49	100
	36–45	7	9	13	16	33	40	29	35	82	100
	46–55	3	4	14	18	18	23	43	55	78	100
	56 ≥	5	6	14	15	13	14	59	65	91	100
	Total	**21**	**7**	**50**	**17**	**82**	**27**	**147**	**49**	**300**	**100**
Sect	Roman Cath.	5	10	11	22	14	28	20	40	50	100
	Protestant	6	12	8	16	17	34	19	38	50	100
	Degambar	0	0	8	16	16	32	26	52	50	100
	Swetambar	3	6	8	16	17	34	22	44	50	100
	Sikh	7	7	15	15	18	18	60	60	100	100
	Total	**21**	**7**	**50**	**17**	**82**	**27**	**147**	**49**	**300**	**100**
Education	Basic or less	2	6	7	19	9	24	19	51	37	100
	Matriculate	2	3	10	15	19	28	36	54	67	100
	Intermediate	5	9	10	19	17	31	22	41	54	100
	Graduate	8	10	11	14	21	27	39	49	79	100
	P.G. & Higher	4	7	12	19	16	25	31	49	63	100
	Total	**21**	**7**	**50**	**17**	**82**	**27**	**147**	**49**	**300**	**100**
Occupation	Business	11	8	28	21	30	23	63	48	132	100
	Teaching	0	0	2	5	15	41	20	54	37	100
	Govt. Service	6	8	11	15	14	20	41	57	72	100
	Engineering	1	9	4	36	6	55	0	0	11	100
	Preaching	0	0	2	18	5	45	4	37	11	100
	Admn. (Pvt.)	2	18	2	18	4	37	3	27	11	100
	Others	1	4	1	4	8	31	16	61	26	100
	Total	**21**	**7**	**50**	**17**	**82**	**27**	**147**	**49**	**300**	**100**
Income	≤ Rs 2000	4	5	9	11	24	31	42	53	79	100
	2000–5000	6	6	19	18	29	28	50	48	104	100
	5000–10000	5	6	17	21	21	27	36	46	79	100
	10000–more	6	16	5	8	8	21	19	50	38	100
	Total	**21**	**7**	**50**	**17**	**82**	**27**	**147**	**40**	**300**	**100**

visit to other's religious places is the highest (34% each) among Protestants and Swetambars and those who do not at all favour visit to other's places of worship is highest (60%) among Sikhs.

On examining educationwise distribution (Table 6.4) we see that the higher education group forms. 7% and 19% proportion of those who either strongly or very strongly favours visit to other's religious places. On the other hand proportion of those who do not favour at all visiting other religious places of worship is the highest (54%) among the lesser qualified people, i.e., matriculates followed by (51%) uneducated group.

Among various occupational categories it is observed (Table 6.4) that the highest proportion (18%) favouring very strongly is among the administrative group, 36% in engineering favour strongly, further 55% in engineering favour less strongly and maximum (61%) ratio of those who do not at all favour visiting other's religious places is among the occupational group categorized as 'others'. Business class has shown its bilateral attitude towards present issue as they cannot afford to maintain conflict relations with the society in general.

Table 6.4 shows that 16% in the income group of Rs 10,000 p.m. or more, 21% in Rs 5,000–10,000 p.m., 31% in the income group of Rs 2,000 p.m. or less and 53% in the same income group very strongly, strongly, not strongly and not at all favour visit to other's religious places. That is the lowest and the highest income groups (Rs 2,000 p.m. or less and Rs 10,000 p.m. or more) seem to be more conflict oriented on the basis of present statement.

From an overall analysis of Table 6.4 we see that people in all the ages, sects, educational, occupational and income groups do not generally disfavour visiting other religion's people into their own religious place but they do not favour visiting (49% of the total of 300) visiting other religious places. It shows that basically people have feeling of disharmony inherent in themselves that segregates them from the general society, thus, works as an obstruction in social solidarity. With increasing education and income, feeling of conflict and disharmony does not decrease. That is, harmony among various social groups is maintained on religious ground but about 50% (of a total of 300) do not at all favour inter-religion worship.

After interviewing 300 respondents, inter-religion conflicts among Christians, Jains and Sikhs were reported as nil. On asking about people's attitude towards other's entrance into their own religious centre, it is found that out of a total of 300, 78% (Table 6.5) favoured others entrance into their own religious place very strongly, 7% favoured strongly, 11% favoured less strongly and 4% not at all favoured. Those who either very strongly or strongly favoured others

Table 6.5: Are you in favour of other's entrance into your own religious centre

Variable	*Categories*	*Very Strongly*		*Strongly*		*Less Strongly*		*Not at all*		*Total*	
		'f'	*%*	*'f'*	*%*	*'f'*	*%*	*'f'*	*%*	*'f'*	*%*
Age	⩽-35 years	46	94	0	0	3	6	0	0	49	100
	36–45	63	77	8	10	7	8	4	5	82	100
	46–55	53	68	8	10	11	14	6	8	78	100
	56⩾	65	71	6	7	11	12	9	10	91	100
	Total	**233**	**78**	**22**	**7**	**32**	**11**	**13**	**4**	**300**	
Sect	Roman Cath.	37	74	6	12	7	14	0	0	50	100
	Protestant	43	86	1	2	3	6	3	6	50	100
	Degambar	27	54	8	16	10	20	5	10	50	100
	Swetambar	46	92	1	2	1	2	2	4	50	100
	Sikh	80	80	6	6	11	11	3	3	100	100
	Total	**233**	**78**	**22**	**7**	**32**	**11**	**13**	**4**	**300**	
Education	Basic or less	19	51	5	14	6	16	7	19	37	100
	Matriculate	52	78	3	4	10	15	2	3	67	100
	Intermediate	44	82	4	7	4	7	2	4	54	100
	Graduate	59	75	9	11	9	11	2	3	79	100
	P.G. & Higher	59	94	1	1	3	5	0	0	63	100
	Total	**233**	**78**	**22**	**7**	**32**	**11**	**13**	**4**	**300**	
Occupation	Business	82	62	15	11	25	19	10	8	132	100
	Teaching	35	95	0	0	2	5	0	0	37	100
	Govt. Service	61	84	4	6	4	6	3	4	72	100
	Engineering	10	91	1	9	0	0	0	0	11	100
	Preaching	10	91	0	0	1	9	0	0	11	100
	Admn. (pvt.)	9	82	2	18	0	0	0	0	11	100
	Others	26	100	0	0	0	0	0	0	26	100
	Total	**233**	**78**	**22**	**7**	**32**	**11**	**13**	**4**	**300**	
Income	⩽ Rs 2000	75	95	3	4	0	0	1	1	79	100
	2000–5000	84	81	4	4	12	11	4	4	104	100
	5000–10000	45	57	14	18	12	15	8	10	79	100
	10000–more	29	76	1	3	8	21	0	0	38	100
	Total	**233**	**78**	**22**	**7**	**82**	**11**	**13**	**4**	**300**	

entry into their religious places is the highest (94%) in the age groups of 35 years and less and the lowest 78% each in the age groups of 46–55 years and 71% in 56 years and above. Those who not at all favour others entrance into their religious places is the highest 10% in the

Table 6.6: Do you permit your children to visit other's religious places of worship?

Variable	*Categories*	*Very Happily*		*Happily*		*Not Happily*		*Not at all Happily*		*Total*	
		'f'	%	'f'	%	'f'	%	'f'	%	'f'	%
Age	⩽–35 years	4	8	8	16	15	31	22	45	49	100
	36–45	7	8	12	15	22	27	41	50	82	100
	46–55	2	3	12	15	21	27	43	55	78	100
	56⩾	5	6	12	13	21	23	53	58	91	100
	Total	**21**	**7**	**50**	**17**	**82**	**27**	**147**	**49**	**300**	**100**
Sect	Roman Cath.	4	8	10	20	9	18	27	54	50	100
	Protestant	4	8	9	18	13	26	24	48	50	100
	Degambar	0	0	11	22	12	24	27	54	50	100
	Swetambar	4	8	4	8	16	32	26	53	50	100
	Sikh	9	9	16	16	32	32	43	43	100	100
	Total	**21**	**7**	**50**	**17**	**82**	**27**	**147**	**49**	**300**	**100**
Education	Basic or less	2	5	7	19	7	19	21	57	37	100
	Matriculate	3	4	15	23	23	34	26	39	67	100
	Intermediate	4	7	10	19	11	20	29	54	54	100
	Graduate	7	9	10	13	23	29	39	49	79	100
	P.G. & Higher	5	8	8	13	18	28	32	51	63	100
	Total	**21**	**7**	**50**	**17**	**82**	**27**	**147**	**49**	**300**	**100**
Occupation	Business	8	6	30	23	34	26	60	45	132	100
	Teaching	0	0	4	11	6	16	27	73	37	100
	Govt. Service	7	0	11	15	26	36	28	39	72	100
	Engineering	1	9	3	27	3	27	4	37	11	100
	Preaching	1	9	0	0	1	9	9	81	11	100
	Admn. (pvt.)	0	0	2	18	5	45	4	37	11	100
	Others	4	15	0	0	7	27	15	58	26	100
	Total	**21**	**7**	**50**	**17**	**82**	**27**	**147**	**49**	**300**	**100**
Income	⩽ Rs 2000	4	5	9	11	21	27	45	57	79	100
	2000–5000	8	8	16	15	29	28	51	49	104	100
	5000–10000	3	4	19	24	24	30	33	42	79	100
	10000–more	6	16	6	16	8	21	18	47	38	100
	Total	**21**	**7**	**50**	**17**	**82**	**27**	**147**	**49**	**300**	**100**

age group of 56 years and above. The proportion of those who very strongly favour others entry into their religious centre is the highest (92%) in Swetambars followed by Protestants (86%), postgraduate and higher education group (94%), occupational group categorized as 'others' (100%), teaching (95%) and in the income group of Rs 2,000 p.m. or less (95%). Thus, in the higher age group people's attitude towards others entering their religious centre is found as comparatively negative, among various sects. 74% Roman Catholics, 86% Protestants, 54% Degambars, 92% Swetambars and 80% Sikhs favour others entry into their own religious centres 'very strongly'. It indicates that inter-religion harmony is maintained more by Protestants than Roman Catholics, and by Swetambars more than Degambars and more by Christians and Sikhs than Jains. The highest ratio (94%) in the postgraduate and above, 14%, 16% and 19% in basic or below education group favour strongly, less strongly, and not at all others entry into their own religious centre. Those who not at all favour are maximum (19%) among the basic or below education group. Highest frequency of those who favour others entry very strongly is 100% in the others occupational group, of those who strongly favour is maximum '(18%) among the 'administrative' and persons 'less strongly' favouring is highest (19%) among business and 'not at all' favouring is also the highest (8%) among the business class. We may infer that persons belonging to certain occupations (teaching, government service, engineering, preaching and administrative) maintain harmony in society.

In order to study the extent of harmony, people's attitude towards their children's visit to other religious places Table 6.6 are studied. According to our observations (Table 6.6) the highest percentage of those who very happily favour their children to visit other religious centres are 8% in the age groups of 35 years or less, and 36–45 years.

Only 9% among Sikhs, 8% each among the Roman Catholics, Protestants and Swetambars very happily permit their children to visit other's religious places. Degambars are very conservative in this regard.

Nearly 9% among graduates, 15% in others occupational group, and 16% in the income group of Rs 10,000 p.m. or more form the very happily group. Those who happily favour form the highest proportions 16% in the age group of 35 years or less, 22% among Degambars, 23% in matriculates, 27% in engineering and 24% in Rs 5,000–10,000 p.m. income group. Whereas, maximum frequency of those who do not happily favour is the highest (31%) in the age group of 35 years or less, 27% each; in 36–45 years and 46–55 years age group, 32% each among Swetambars and Sikhs. 34% among matriculates, 45% among administrative and 36% among the government servants do not permit your children to visit other's religious places of worship. Teaching (73%) after preaching (81%) constitute the most conservative occupational group, hence less developed socially.

A total of 30% among the income group of Rs 5,000–10,000 p.m. are not happily in favour and further it is indicated that persons who do not at all happily favour their children's visit to other religion's places of worship is the highest (58%) in the age group of 56 years and above, 54% each among Roman Catholics and Degambars and 52% among Swetambars, 57% among basic or less, 81% in preaching and 57% in the income group of Rs 2,000 p.m. or less. Thus harmony is maintained more among the youngest age group Sikhs, matriculates, engineering and administrative group and in the income group of Rs 5,000–10,000 p.m. (Table 6.6).

Our data (Table 6.6) reveals that only 7% of the total sample very happily permit their children to visit other's religious places, 17% favour 'happily' and 27% 'do not happily' favour. Among these, 31% in the age group of 35 years and less, 27% both in 36–45 and 46–55 years age group and 23% in the age group of 56 years and above 'do not happily' favour their children to visit other's religious places. Those who 'do not at all happily' favour their children to visit other's religious places form the highest frequency (58%) among the age group of 56 years and above followed by 55% in 46–55 years, 50% in 36–45 years and the lowest frequency (45%) in the age group of 35 years and less.

Those who 'do not happily' favour form the highest frequency (32% each) among Swetambars and Sikhs, then 26% among Protestants. Ratio of persons 'not at all happily' favouring their children is the highest 54% in Roman Catholics and Degambars and 53% Swetambars, then 48% among Protestants. It is minimum (43%) among the Sikhs. That is, Sikhs then Protestants maintain more harmony with other religious groups whereas, Roman Catholics, Degambars and Swetambars are equally maintaining social harmony with other sects and religious groups. On the whole, harmony and conflict are equally maintained (49% of the total of 300 'not at all happily' favour their children visiting other's religious place) in society. Among the different education groups, 23% (highest frequency) in the matriculates group happily' favour, 34% (highest in the matriculates, not happily favour their children to visit other's religious places and 57% in the basic or below followed by 54% in intermediates and 51% in postgraduate and above, 49% in graduates and 39% (minimum) among the matriculates not at all happily' favour their children to visit other's religious places. We may conclude that uneducated and higher educated (postgraduate and above) persons are less harmonical with other religious groups.

Occupation-based data (Table 6.6) indicates that highest frequencies (15%, 27%, 45% and 81%) of those who very happily, happily, not happily and 'not at all happily' permit their children to visit other's religious places are among-others', engineering, administrative and preaching occupation groups.

Persons in the income group of Rs 10,000 p.m. and above form the highest proportion (16%) of those who 'very happily', 24% in the income group of Rs 5,000–10,000 p.m. 'happily', again the highest ratio 30% in the same income group and 57% in the income group of Rs 2,000 p.m. or less 'not happily' and 'not at all happily' favour their children to visit other religious centres.

We may conclude on the basis of above observations that younger people, Sikhs, matriculates, engineers, and administrators and persons belonging to the income groups of Rs 5,000–1,000 p.m. and Rs 10,000 p.m. and above are more in harmony with the larger society. We also find that there is no change in people's attitude towards visiting other religious places for themselves or for their children. They are equally at conflict and harmony relationship with other religious groups for themselves as well as for their children.

Another indicator of inter-faith harmony is (Table 6.7) 'accepting and eating' of prasad offered by persons of different religions. A cursory look at the Table 6.7 indicates that out of a total of 300, 39% do not at all 'accept and eat' prasad offered by others. Further it is apparent that 18% 'accept and eat' prasad very happily, 25% happily, and 18% not happily. The frequency of those who accept and eat prasad very happily is the highest (27%) in the age group of 35 years and below, 26% in Protestants and Sikhs both, 33% in intermediate qualified group, 27% each among administrative and 'others' and 24% in the income group of Rs 10,000 p.m. or more. The ratio of those who accept and eat prasad 'happily' is minimum (22%) in the age group of 56 years and above, 8% among Degambars 19% in graduates, 0% in preaching and 23% both in the income groups of Rs 2,000–5,000 p.m. and Rs 5,000–10,000 p.m. Persons who do not happily accept and eat prasad are maximum (22%) in the age group of 56 years and above, 22% in Swetambars, 24% in intermediates, 37% in preaching and 20% in the income group of Rs 5,000–10,000

Table 6.7: Do you accept and eat 'prasad' offered by persons of other religions?

Variable	Categories	Very Happily		Happily		Not Happily		Not at all		Total	
		'f'	%	'f'	%	'f'	%	'f'	%	'f'	%
Age	≤ 35 years	13	27	13	27	8	16	15	30	49	100
	36–45	19	23	22	27	12	15	29	35	82	100
	46–55	9	11	20	26	14	18	35	45	78	100
	56 ≥	13	14	20	22	20	22	38	42	91	100
	Total	**54**	**11**	**75**	**25**	**54**	**18**	**117**	**39**	**300**	**100**
Sect	Roman Cath.	5	10	14	28	7	14	24	48	50	100
	Protestant	13	26	13	26	8	16	16	32	50	100
	Degambar	4	8	4	8	10	20	32	64	50	100
	Swetambar	6	12	8	16	11	22	25	50	50	100
	Sikh	26	26	36	36	18	18	20	20	100	100
	Total	**54**	**18**	**75**	**25**	**54**	**18**	**117**	**39**	**300**	**100**
Education	Basic or less	2	6	12	32	7	19	16	43	37	100
	Matriculate	11	16	15	22	13	20	28	42	67	100
	Intermediate	18	33	13	24	13	24	10	19	54	100
	Graduate	15	29	15	19	12	15	37	47	79	100
	P.G. & Higher	8	13	20	32	9	14	26	41	63	100
	Total	**54**	**18**	**75**	**25**	**54**	**18**	**117**	**39**	**300**	**100**
Occupation	Business	21	16	36	27	22	17	53	40	132	100
	Teaching	2	5	6	16	4	11	25	68	37	100
	Govt. Service	18	25	24	33	14	20	16	22	72	100
	Engineering	2	18	4	37	3	27	2	18	11	100
	Preaching	1	9	0	0	4	37	6	54	11	100
	Admn. (pvt.)	3	27	3	27	2	18	3	27	11	100
	Others	7	27	2	8	5	19	12	46	26	100
	Total	**54**	**9**	**75**	**25**	**54**	**18**	**117**	**39**	**300**	**100**
Income	≤ Rs 2000	13	19	21	27	13	16	32	41	79	100
	2000–5000	20	19	24	23	18	17	42	41	104	100
	5000–10000	12	15	18	23	16	20	33	42	79	100
	10000–more	9	24	12	32	7	18	10	26	38	100
	Total	**54**	**18**	**75**	**25**	**54**	**18**	**117**	**39**	**300**	**100**

p.m. Those who 'do not at all' accept and eat prasad form highest proportions (45%) in the age group of 46–55 years followed by 42% in the age group of 56 years and above, 64% (maximum) among Degambars, 50% among Swetambars and 48% among the Roman

Catholics, 47% in graduates, 68% in teaching, followed by 54% in preaching and 41% in the income group of Rs 2,000 p.m. and below and Rs 2,000–5,000 p.m. It shows (Table 6.7) that feeling of harmony is more among the younger people. Jains as compared to Christians and Christians as compared to Sikhs are more rigid. Among Christians Protestants as compared to Roman Catholics and Swetambars as compared to Degambars are less prone to inter-sect and inter-religion conflict and are more harmonical with other sects. On the basis of occupation, it is observed that teaching and preaching are more conservative in this regard. Although teaching class has shown its rationality on other issues, but on this particular issue it has shown reverse results, which may imply that besides occupation other factors also determine harmony of an individual with others. Incomewise data (Table 6.7) shows that higher the income lesser is the tendency towards conflict. Thus age, sect, occupation and income are related with conflict.

Inter-Sect Conflict

As shown in Table 6.8 inter-sect participation is maximum (2%) among the age group 35 years and less, 2% each among Roman Catholics, Protestants and Degambars, 3% among graduates, 5% in teaching and 3% among the income group of Rs 2,000 p.m. and less and is minimum 78% in the age group of 35 years or less, 80% each among Protestants and Degambars, 81% in the lowest educated group (basic or below), 75% in government service and 76% in the income group of Rs 10,000 p.m. or above who do not at all participate in other sect's ceremonies.

Observations on above issue have shown some variations from previous issues pertaining to harmony. The youngest age group (35 years and less) has shown its tendency towards inter-sect distance as compared to the eldest (56 years and more) age group. Protestants in contrast to Roman Catholics are more on the verge of conflict and government servant seems to be more reserve on the present issue. Rest of the categories, education and income, have shown more or less similar results.

On the basis of above observations, we may conclude that in the higher age groups, conflicts have been reported more than the lower age groups, and they have also shown a feeling of discord with the other sects/religious groups. The sectwise observations have shown

Table 6.8: Do you participate in other sects' ceremonies?

Variable	*Categories*	*Very Frequently*		*Frequently*		*Less Frequently*		*Not at all*		*Total*	
		'f'	%	'f'	%	'f'	%	'f'	%	'f'	%
Age	⩽ 35 years	1	2	5	10	5	10	38	78	49	100
	36–45	1	1	7	9	23	28	51	62	82	100
	46–55	1	1	7	9	13	17	57	73	78	100
	56 ⩾	1	1	9	11	15	16	66	72	91	100
	Total	**4**	**1**	**30**	**10**	**56**	**19**	**210**	**70**	**300**	**100**
Sect	Roman Cath.	1	2	6	12	17	34	26	52	50	100
	Protestant	1	2	4	8	5	10	40	80	50	100
	Degambar	1	2	5	10	4	8	40	80	50	100
	Swetambar	0	0	3	6	13	26	34	68	50	100
	Sikh	1	1	12	12	17	17	70	70	100	100
	Total	**4**	**1**	**30**	**10**	**56**	**19**	**210**	**70**	**300**	**100**
Education	Basic or less	0	0	3	8	4	11	30	81	37	100
	Matriculate	0	0	7	10	11	17	49	73	67	100
	Intermediate	1	2	8	15	10	18	35	65	54	100
	Graduate	2	3	10	13	17	22	50	63	79	100
	P.G. & Higher	1	2	2	3	14	22	46	73	63	100
	Total	**4**	**1**	**30**	**10**	**56**	**19**	**210**	**70**	**300**	**100**
Occupation	Business	0	0	18	14	18	14	96	72	132	100
	Teaching	2	5	0	0	11	30	24	65	37	100
	Govt. Service	2	3	3	4	13	18	5	75	72	100
	Engineering	0	0	1	9	2	18	8	73	11	100
	Preaching	0	0	1	9	3	27	7	64	11	100
	Admn. (pvt.)	0	0	3	27	3	27	5	45	11	100
	Others	0	0	4	15	6	23	16	62	26	100
	Total	**4**	**1**	**30**	**10**	**56**	**19**	**210**	**70**	**300**	**100**
Income	⩽ Rs 2000	2	3	5	6	20	25	2	66	79	100
	2000–5000	2	2	9	9	22	21	71	68	104	100
	5000–10000	0	0	12	15	9	11	58	74	79	100
	10000–more	0	0	4	11	5	13	29	76	38	100
	Total	**4**	**1**	**30**	**10**	**56**	**19**	**210**	**70**	**300**	**100**

that Roman Catholics as compared to Protestants, Degambars as compared to Swetambars are more prone to conflict. Among the three religious groups, Jains are found more conservative thus conflict oriented and Sikhs the least. Variations are also observed in relation into various issues pertaining to conflict among different sects. Harmony is observed in the age group of 35 years and less, among Christians and Sikhs, and others, administrative and engineering occupations and in the income groups of Rs 2,000 p.m. or less and Rs 10,000 p.m. or more.

The inter-sect participation as indicated in Table 6.8 is very low among all the age groups. Those who not at all participate in other sect's ceremonies form minimum percentage (62%) in 36–45 year's age group. Those who frequently participate are maximum (12%) both in Roman Catholics and Sikh sects, people participating less frequently are maximum (34%) among the Roman Catholics and those who not at all participate are maximum (80%) each in Protestant and Degambar sects. Only 70% Sikhs do not participate in other sect's ceremonies. Thus, we may infer that Roman Catholics are more harmonical than the Protestants in this particular regard and Swetambars are more at harmony than Degambars. Christians are more harmonical than Sikhs and Sikhs are more harmonical than Jains.

On the basis of education, it is indicated (Table 6.8) that those in the education group of basic or below form maximum concentration (81%) and in the graduate minimum (63%) of those who not at all participate in other sects' activities. Thus, we may say that social distance gets minimized as the level of education increases. Or we may say that education increases harmony in society.

Those in private administrative services are more at harmony with the other sects. Reason behind is that they cannot avoid going to other's ceremonies due to being in top positions.

Persons securing high scores on 'conflict and harmony' scale form more than half ratio in the age group of 56 years and above (56%) and those in the age groups of ⩽35 years, 36–45 years and 46–55 years form lower frequencies (42%, 44% and 36%). Conflict and Harmony is significantly affected by variation in age (Table 6.9).

Table 6.9: Scores According to Age on Conflict and Harmony

Scores	*Age Groups (years)*				
	35 or less	*36–45*	*46–55*	*56 & above*	*Total*
L	28	50	50	40	168
H	21	32	28	51	132
Total	49	72	78	91	300

X^2=8.285, @ 3 d.f., significant at 5% level

Proportions of persons securing high scores on 'conflict and harmony' are in Roman Catholic sect (60%) than in Protestant sect (40%) and it is higher in Swetambar sect (68%) than in Degambar sect (40%). Jains (54%) form highest frequency, Christians (50%) form the second largest group securing high score on 'conflict-harmony' and Sikhs (21%) form minimum frequency in this regard. Thus, Sikhs may be considered as highly developed, Christians as second highly developed and Jains as the least developed. It reflects that sect affiliation significantly affects 'conflict-harmony' thus affecting social development of a sect (Table 6.10).

Table 6.10: Scores According to Sect on Conflict and Harmony

Scores	*Sects*					
	Roman	*Protestant*	*Degambar*	*Swetambar*	*Sikh*	*Total*
L	27	23	30	16	79	168
H	30	20	20	34	21	132
Total	50	50	50	50	50	300

X^2 = 35.41, @ 4 d.f., significant at 5% level

Highest frequency (65%) of those who have secured high score on 'conflict and harmony' scale is in the educational category of basic or low. The second highest frequency (49%) is formed by those in 'postgraduate' and 'higher' educational category. Of these in graduate (46%) and intermediate (41%) categories form comparatively lower proportions and in the matriculate category (28%) form minimum frequency. Education significantly affects 'conflict and harmony' (Table 6.11).

Table 6.11: Scores on Conflict and Harmony According to Education

Scores	*Education Groups*					
	Basic or Below	*Marticulate*	*Intermediate*	*Graduate*	*Post-Graduate & higher*	*Total*
L	13	48	32	43	32	168
H	24	19	22	36	31	132
Total	37	67	54	79	63	300

X^2 = 14.194, @ 4 d.f., significant at 5% level.

In the various occupational category, persons in teaching (57%) and administrative (private) (64%) have secured higher scores on 'conflict and harmony' than in government service (36%), others (35%), engineering (18%) and preaching (18%). Thus, regarding 'conflict-harmony' scale a significant variation is observed in various occupational categories (Table 6.12).

Table 6.12: Scores on Conflict and Harmony According to Occupation

Occupations	*Scores*		*Total*
	L	*H*	
Business	67	65	132
Govt. service	46	26	72
Teaching	16	21	37
Engineering	9	2	11
Preaching	9	2	11
Administrative (private)	4	7	11
Others	17	9	26
Total	168	132	300

X^2 = 14.336, @ 6 d.f., significant at 5% level

Our data (Table 6.13) indicates that no income group forming more than fifty per cent has secured high score on 'conflict and harmony'. Association between income and 'conflict and harmony' is not found statistically significant.

'Conflict and harmony' is significantly affected by religiosity.

'Conflict and harmony' is significantly influenced by ritualism.

Table 6.13: Scores on Conflict and Harmony According to Income

Scores	*Income per month (in Rs)*				
	≤2000	*2000-5000*	*5000-10000*	*10000- & above*	*Total*
L	42	62	41	23	168
H	37	42	38	15	132
Total	79	104	79	38	300

X^2 = 1.716, @ 3 d.f., significant at 5% level

That is conflict and harmony is affected by age, sect, education and occupation but income of an individual does not affect 'conflict-harmony'. On the basis of X^2 calculated, we can conclude that Age and Conflict and Harmony Table 6.9, (X^2 = 8.285 at 3 d.f. and 5% level of significance), Sect and Conflict and Harmony Table 6.10 (X^2 = 35.41), education and conflict and harmony Table 6.10 (X^2 = 14.194 significant at 4 d.f. and 5% level of significance) and Occupation and Conflict and Harmony Table 6.12, (X^2 = 14.336 @ 6 d.f.) are significantly associated whereas Income and Conflict and Harmony Table 6.13 (X^2 = 1.716 at 3 d.f. and 5% level of significance) are not significantly associated. Our data (Tables 6.14, 6.15, and 6.16) indicates that conflict-harmony is significantly associated with religiosity (X^2 = 4.144 at @ 1 d.f. and .05 level of significance), Conflict-harmony and Ritualism Table 6.15 (X^2 = 20.262 @ 1 d.f. and .05 level of significance) and Conflict-harmony and Sectarianism Table 6.16 (X^2 = 34.703 @ 1 d.f. and .05 level of significance) are also significantly associated with each other.

Table 6.14: Scores on Conflict-Harmony and Religiosity

Score	*High*	*Low*	*Total*
H	69	68	137
L	63	100	163
Total	132	168	300

X^2 = 4.144, @ 1 d.f., significant at .05 level

Table 6.15: Scores on Conflict-Harmony and Ritualism

Score	*High*	*Low*	*Total*
H	68	44	112
L	64	124	188
Total	132	168	300

X^2 = 20.262, @ 1 d. f., significant at .05 level

Table 6.16: Scores on Conflict-Harmony and Sectarianism

Score	*High*	*Low*	*Total*
H	90	57	147
L	42	111	153
Total	132	168	300

X^2 =34.703, @ 1 d.f., significant at 0.5 level

References

Chatterjee, S.K. (1981), "A Note on the Study of Religion and Society" in, *Religion and Society*, vol. 28(2), Sept.

Dhillon, G.S. (1989), *Researches in Sikh Religion and History*, Sumeet Prakashan, Chandigarh, pp. 26

Narang, G.C. (1956), *Transformation of Sikhism*, New Book Society, New Delhi (250–255).

Oddie, G.A. (1969), "Protestant Missionary, Caste and Social Change in India, 1850–1914", *Indian Economics and Social History Review*, Vol. 6, pp. 259–61.

Singh, D. (1968), *Indian Bhakti Tradition and Sikh Gurus*, Lyall Book Depot, Bhopal.

Singh, T. (1990), "Ritualism v/s. Reality", *The Sikh Review*, Vol. 38 (441), pp. 16–17.

Singh, T. (1986), "Need of Renewal and Reform in Present Working of Sikh Religious Cultural and Political Institutions", *Sikh Review*, (393), pp. 11–13.

7 Sect and Modernism

Sect as a protest group against established traditional religious forms and the surrounding secular society, forms the bridge between tradition and modernity, and affects an individual's attitudes and values towards various aspects of human life. On one hand, it maintains status quo by sticking to certain religious values and norms while on the other it serves as a dynamic force of social change by accepting and adapting to modern scientific outlook. The cultural prerequisites of a comprehensive modernization process necessitate adaptive changes in the system of values and norms, e.g., secularism, untouchability and non-parochialism, are some demands of modernization in contemporary India, which its traditional value system continues to resist. There is a tendency among the religious sects to organize themselves on rational bureaucratic model. Modernization is understood as growth of uniform set of cultural and role-structural attributes. Huntington (1968) views modernization as "a multifaceted process" involving changes in all areas of human thought and activity. Parsons (1970) defines it as "a process of structural differentiation, functional specialization and adaptive upgrading". Eisenstadt (1966) characterizes modern societies as "highly differentiated and specialized with respect to individual activities and institutional structures". Singh (1978) refers to modernization as "the differentiation and rational organization of roles and its aggregate".

It refers to transition from traditional to industrialized society; from religious to secular ideologies; from particularism, ascriptive diffuseness, self-orientation to universalism, achievement, specificity and collectivity-orientation, from extended to nuclear family etc. (Lerner, 1958; Eisenstadt, 1966; Huntington, 1968).

In the present study, modernization has been conceived as a change in an individual's attitudes towards traditional institutions and their value system and their orientation towards reform. In contrast to conformity to traditional value system as in India, traditionalism is giving way to modernization (Singh, 1973).

The major themes of the present chapter are: (1) to analyse the significance of age, sect, education, occupation, and income of an individual in shaping his modern (rational/modern) or traditional social values and attitudes, and (2) to draw a comparison among different sects in terms of degree of modernization achieved by each sect.

Relationship between sect and modernization will be analysed under two sub-headings, viz., (i) adherence of a sect to traditional institutions and their value systems, and (ii) adapting itself (sect) to modern values. For analysing the first phase, following questions have been raised: (i) do you feel that joint family helps in one's progress? (ii) do you believe in purdah system? (iii) do you favour widow remarriage? and (iv) do you believe that touch of an unclean person will pollute you?

For the study of rational values (modern values) of various religious sects, following indicators have been used: (i) why did you select a particular occupation? (ii) what type of education do you prefer for your children? (iii) do you feel that hard work leads to one's success? (iv) do you feel that honesty is the key to one's success? (v) do you favour woman's participation in job? do you believe that science and technology lead to progress? (vii) do you feel that your daily activities are guided by religious values?

Attitudes Towards Traditional Institutions and Customs

Our data (Table 7.1) shows that only 1% in the age group of 56 years and above strongly disagree with the joint family's contribution in one's life. 8% in the age group of 46–55 years, 26% in 36–45 years and 25% in 35 years or less disagree with the institution of joint family. Proportions of those who strongly agree are 31% in 56 years and above, 21% in 46–55 years, 17% in 36–45 years and 20% in 35 years and below age group. Younger age group is not much in favour of joint family system. On the contrary, older people are mostly in favour of joint family. The rationale behind is that they need support in their old age from their children but younger people do not usually need any support at this age.

Table 7.1 Do you feel that joint family helps in progress of an individual?

Variable	*Categories*	*Strongly Agreed*		*Agree*		*Neutral*		*Disagree*		*Strongly Disagree*		*Total*	
		'f'	*%*	*'f'*	*%*	*'f'*	*%*	*'f'*	*%*	*'f'*	*%*	*'f'*	*%*
Age	⩽ 35 years	10	20	15	31	2	4	10	20	12	25	49	100
	36–45	14	17	24	29	1	1	22	27	21	26	82	100
	46–55	16	21	23	29	4	5	29	37	6	8	78	100
	56 ⩾	28	31	33	36	9	10	20	22	1	1	91	100
	Total	**68**	**23**	**95**	**32**	**16**	**5**	**81**	**27**	**40**	**13**	**300**	**100**
Sect	Roman Cath.	12	24	18	36	1	2	12	24	7	14	50	100
	Protestant	9	18	13	26	6	12	12	24	10	20	50	100
	Degambar	12	24	17	34	4	8	15	30	2	4	50	100
	Swetambar	7	14	16	32	2	4	9	18	16	32	50	100
	Sikh	38	28	31	31	3	3	33	33	5	5	100	100
	Total	**68**	**23**	**95**	**32**	**16**	**5**	**81**	**27**	**40**	**13**	**300**	**100**
Education	Basic or less	16	43	10	27	0	0	9	24	2	6	37	100
	Matriculate	20	30	23	34	10	15	12	18	2	3	67	100
	Intermediate	10	19	17	31	1	2	22	41	4	7	54	100
	Graduate	15	19	26	33	2	3	20	25	16	20	79	100
	P.G. & Higher	7	11	19	30	3	5	18	29	16	25	63	100
	Total	**68**	**23**	**95**	**32**	**16**	**5**	**81**	**27**	**40**	**13**	**300**	**100**
Occupation	Business	42	32	51	39	7	5	26	20	6	4	132	100
	Teaching	6	16	12	33	6	16	9	24	4	11	37	100
	Govt. Service	11	15	18	25	2	3	28	39	13	18	72	100
	Engineering	1	9	2	18	1	9	5	45	2	18	11	100
	Preaching	3	27	0	0	0	0	5	45	3	27	11	100
	Admn. (pvt.)	1	9	2	18	0	0	6	55	2	18	11	100
	Others	4	15	10	38	0	0	2	8	10	39	26	100
	Total	**68**	**23**	**95**	**32**	**16**	**5**	**81**	**27**	**40**	**13**	**300**	**100**
Income	⩽ Rs 2000	14	18	18	23	2	2	41	52	2	5	79	100
	2000–5000	21	20	35	34	5	5	29	28	14	13	104	100
	5000–10000	17	21	34	43	3	4	3	4	22	28	79	100
	10000–more	16	42	8	21	6	16	8	21	0	0	38	100
	Total	**68**	**23**	**95**	**32**	**16**	**5**	**81**	**27**	**40**	**13**	**300**	**100**

Further, it is visible that maximum frequency (28%) among the Sikhs, then in the Roman Catholics (24%) and the Degambars (24%), the Protestants (18%) and minimum (14%) among the Swetambars strongly favour the institution of joint family. Those who disagree or strongly (if we combine the frequencies 9+16) disagree are highest (50%) in the Swetambars 44% in Protestants, 38% both in the Roman Catholics and the Sikhs and 34% among Degambars. On the basis of our data (Table 7.1) we may infer that the Jains are more modern than the Christians and Christians are more modern as compared to the Sikhs. Cause of the Sikhs favouring joint family is that they are suffering with the feeling of insecurity due to Hindu-Sikh riots of 1984. Similarly, Roman Catholics generally form an isolated group. They generally do not mix with the larger society and remain confined to their homes and the Church. They are also Anglo-Indians and feel themselves separated from others. Degambars are most conservative and are mostly tradition bound. But Protestants and Swetambars are most modern on this issue.

Table 7.1 shows educationwise distribution also shows that postgraduate and above educated persons favour least (11%) the joint family system whereas least educated or uneducated persons constitute maximum percentage (43%) of those who strongly favour the joint family system and those who strongly disagree are 25% in postgraduate and higher educated and 20% in graduates, rest of the categories form 7% among intermediates, 3% in matriculates and 6% among basic or below group. Number of persons just favouring joint family is highest (34%) among matriculates followed by graduates (33%) and intermediates (31%) and is minimum (27%) among basic or below group. If we club proportions of strongly agreeing and agreeing persons it is noted that persons in the lowest education group form highest percentage (70%) followed by 64% in matriculates and 50% in intermediates and 52% in graduates; their proportion is minimum (41%) in the postgraduate and higher education group. It is increasing with the decrease in the level of education. Therefore, we may say that modernity increases with the increase in level of education.

Further, it is indicated (Table 7.1) that 71% in business, 53% in other services, 49% in teaching, 40% in government service and 27% each in preaching, engineering and administrative group strongly agree with the institution of joint family. That is preaching, engineering and administrative occupational groups are more modern as compared to other groups because they form lowest frequencies (27% each).

On the basis of income it is found that 41% in Rs 2,000 p.m. or below income group, 54% in Rs 2,000–5,000, 64% in Rs 5,000–10,000 and 63% in Rs 10,000 and above income group agree and strongly agree that joint family helps in progress. We may also say that income and modernism are associated (Table 7.1).

Table 7.2 indicates that frequency of those who very strictly favour purdah system is highest (10%) in the age group of 36–45 years but of those who favour purdah system strictly is highest (9%) in the age group of 46–55 years. Frequency of the less strictly favouring persons is minimum (4%) in 35 years or less age group and 8% (i.e., maximum) in 46–55 years, and of not at all favouring persons is highest (88%) in the age group of 35 years or less.

Sectwise distribution shows that Protestants (92%) than Roman Catholics (78%), and more Swetambars (90%) than Degambars (60%) and Sikhs (82%) do not at all favour purdah system. Thus, we may say that Christians are the most modern sects than Jains and Sikhs. Attitudes towards purdah system show (Table 7.2) that Protestants are more modern than Degambars and Sikhs are equally modern as Jains.

Education has shown significant relationship with modernism. 49% in the basic or below group do not favour purdah system whereas 95% in the higher education group are against purdah system. Rest of the education categories have shown not much variation, i.e., 82% in matriculates, 83% in intermediates and 81% graduates do not favour purdah system at all (Table 7.2).

Among various occupations, business group constitutes 68% and teaching forms 92%, government service constitutes 92%, while others also forms 92%, whereas administrative forms 91%, engineering and preaching 82% are of those who do not at all favour purdah system. Hence, it may be concluded that business class is least modern and teaching, government service and others are most modern. Engineering and preaching fall in between whereas engineering has shown its modernity more than other occupational groups on various issues (Table 7.2).

A change is also observed from lower income group to higher income groups in terms of modernism. 91% in the income group of Rs 2,000 p.m. or less and 72% in the income groups of Rs 5,000–10,000 and 79% in the income group of Rs 2,000–5,000 p.m. and of Rs 10,000 p.m. and above do not favour purdah system at all. That is, modernism has shown varying effects in different groups of income.

Table 7.2: Do you favour purdah system?

Vari-able	*Categories*	*Very Strictly*		*Strictly*		*Less Strictly*		*Not at all*		*Total*	
		'f'	%	'f'	%	'f'	%	'f'	%	'f'	%
Age	⩽–35 years	3	6	1	2	2	4	43	88	49	100
	36–45	8	10	6	7	5	6	63	77	82	100
	46–55	4	5	7	9	6	8	61	78	78	100
	56 ⩾	5	5	6	7	5	5	75	83	91	100
	Total	**20**	**7**	**20**	**7**	**18**	**6**	**242**	**80**	**300**	**100**
Sect	Roman Cath.	4	8	2	4	5	10	39	78	50	100
	Protestant	0	0	1	2	3	6	46	92	50	100
	Degambar	8	6	7	14	5	10	30	60	50	100
	Swetambar	3	6	2	4	0	0	45	90	50	100
	Sikh	5	5	8	8	5	5	82	82	100	100
	Total	**20**	**7**	**20**	**7**	**18**	**6**	**242**	**80**	**300**	**100**
Educa-tion	Basic or less	7	19	7	19	5	13	18	49	37	100
	Matriculate	5	8	3	4	4	6	55	82	67	100
	Intermediate	2	4	4	7	3	6	45	83	54	100
	Graduate	6	8	5	6	4	5	64	81	79	100
	P.G. & Higher	0	0	1	2	2	3	60	95	63	100
	Total	**20**	**7**	**20**	**7**	**18**	**6**	**242**	**80**	**300**	**100**
Occupa-tion	Business	13	10	17	13	12	9	90	68	132	100
	Teaching	2	5	1	3	0	0	34	92	37	100
	Govt. Service	4	5	0	0	2	3	66	92	72	100
	Engineering	0	0	1	9	1	9	9	82	11	100
	Preaching	0	0	0	0	2	18	9	82	11	100
	Admn. (pvt.)	1	9	0	0	0	0	10	91	11	100
	Others	0	0	1	4	1	4	24	92	26	100
	Total	**20**	**7**	**20**	**7**	**18**	**6**	**242**	**80**	**300**	**100**
Income	⩽ Rs 2000	3	4	0	0	4	5	72	91	79	100
	2000–5000	7	7	8	8	6	6	92	79	104	100
	5000–10000	2	10	6	8	8	10	57	72	79	100
	10000–more	2	5	6	16	0	0	30	79	38	100
	Total	**20**	**7**	**20**	**7**	**18**	**6**	**242**	**80**	**300**	**100**

On the basis of our data (Table 7.3) we observe that 34% in the age group of 36–45 years, 31% in 35 years and below age group, 10% in 46–55 years and 18% in 56 years and above favour widow remarriage very strictly, whereas those who favour strictly form highest

Table 7.3: Do you favour widow remarriage?

Variable	Categories	Very Strictly		Strictly		Less Strictly		Not at all		Total	
		'f'	%	'f'	%	'f'	%	'f'	%	'f'	%
Age	≤ 35 years	15	31	16	33	1	16	10	20	49	100
	36–45	28	34	16	20	19	23	19	23	82	100
	46–55	8	10	26	33	26	33	18	23	78	100
	56 ≥	16	18	27	30	35	38	13	14	91	100
	Total	**67**	**23**	**85**	**28**	**88**	**29**	**60**	**20**	**300**	**100**
Sect	Roman Cath.	15	30	8	16	18	28	9	18	50	100
	Protestant	14	28	18	36	10	14	8	16	50	100
	Degambar	3	6	17	34	14	36	16	32	50	100
	Swetambar	18	36	15	30	7	20	10	20	50	100
	Sikh	17	17	27	27	39	39	17	17	100	100
	Total	**67**	**23**	**85**	**28**	**88**	**29**	**60**	**20**	**300**	**100**
Education	Basic or less	3	8	7	19	10	27	17	46	37	100
	Matriculate	14	21	9	13	30	45	14	21	67	100
	Intermediate	14	26	17	31	16	30	7	13	54	100
	Graduate	19	24	23	29	18	23	19	24	79	100
	P.G. & Higher	17	29	29	44	14	22	3	5	63	100
	Total	**67**	**23**	**85**	**28**	**88**	**29**	**60**	**20**	**300**	**100**
Occupation	Business	27	20	33	25	43	33	29	22	132	100
	Teaching	9	24	13	35	4	11	11	30	37	100
	Govt. Service	18	25	19	26	25	35	10	14	72	100
	Engineering	2	18	6	55	1	9	2	18	11	100
	Preaching										
	Admn. (pvt.)	3	27	7	64	0	0	1	9	11	100
	Others	6	23	4	15	10	39	6	23	26	100
	Total	**67**	**23**	**85**	**28**	**88**	**29**	**60**	**20**	**300**	**100**
Income	≤ Rs 2000	17	22	23	29	24	30	15	19	79	100
	2000–5000	24	23	30	29	28	27	22	21	104	100
	5000–10000	15	19	19	24	26	33	19	24	79	100
	10000–more	11	29	13	34	10	26	4	11	38	100
	Total	**67**	**23**	**85**	**28**	**88**	**29**	**60**	**20**	**300**	**100**

proportion (33%) in the age groups of 35 years and below and 46–55 years but those who do not favour widow remarriage at all is lowest (14%) in the age group of 56 years and above. It indicates a change from higher to lower age groups in people's attitude towards various traditions. Persons of younger group are more modern as compared to the older generation.

Among different sects we observe (Table 7.3) that 18% Roman Catholics and 16% Protestants. and 32% Degambars as compared to 20% Swetambars 'not at all' favour widow remarriage. Jains form highest frequency (52%) as compared to Christians (34%) and Sikhs (17%) who 'not at all' favour widow remarriage. Therefore, Christians on this basis may be regarded as more developed as compared to Jains and Sikhs.

On the basis of education it is observed that maximum frequency (29%) is in the postgraduate and higher education group and minimum (8%) in the basic or less education group of those who favour widow remarriage very strictly. That is higher the education more is the level of modernization achieved (Table 7.3).

Occupationwise distribution (Table 7.3) shows that administrative pvt. (27%) and in government service (25%), teaching (24%) and in others (23%) favoured widow remarriage very strictly, thus are more modern and engineering (18%) and preaching (18%) are least. Frequency of those who do not favour at all is highest in teaching (30%) and is minimum in preaching (9%) and administrative Pvt. (9%). On the basis of this it may be concluded that administrative and preaching occupations are more modern. Preaching being the leader of a religious organization is more important in bringing about change.

Income also has shown significant variations. Frequency (11%) of those who do not favour widow remarriage is lowest in the income group of Rs 10,000 p.m. or more, then 19% in Rs 2,000 p.m. or less, 21% in Rs 2,000–5,000 p.m., and 24% in Rs 5,000–10,000 p.m. Thus we may say that modernism is visible in the middle income groups but lower (Rs 2,000 p.m.) and higher (Rs 10,000 p.m.) income groups are bound to traditions.

Associated with the institution of caste is the practice of untouchability. Table 7.4 reveals information on the concept of purity and pollution. A highest frequency (55%) is among the age group of 56 years and above then 51% in 46–55 years and 29% and 25% in the age group of 36–45 years and 35 years and below of those who favour untouchability very strictly. Proportion of those who favour strictly is again highest (26%) in the age group of 56 years and above. A downward trend is seen (Table 7.4) from the younger age group (57%) to older age group (18%) of those who do not at all favour the practice of untouchability.

7.4: Do you believe that touch of an unclean person will pollute you?

Variable	Categories	Very Strictly		Strictly		Less Strictly		Not at all		Total	
		'f'	%	'f'	%	'f'	%	'f'	%	'f'	%
Age	⩽–35 years	12	25	6	12	3	6	28	57	49	100
	36– 45	24	29	5	6	8	10	45	55	82	100
	46–55	40	51	17	22	5	6	16	21	78	100
	56 ⩾	50	55	24	26	1	1	16	18	91	100
	Total	**126**	**42**	**52**	**17**	**17**	**6**	**105**	**35**	**300**	**100**
Sect	Roman Cath.	5	10	3	6	5	10	37	74	50	100
	Protestant	2	4	4	8	3	6	41	82	50	100
	Degambar	25	50	20	40	0	0	5	10	50	100
	Swetambar	31	62	10	20	2	4	7	14	50	100
	Sikh	63	63	15	15	7	7	15	15	100	100
	Total	**126**	**42**	**52**	**17**	**17**	**6**	**105**	**35**	**300**	**100**
Education	Basic or Less	27	73	10	27	0	0	0	0	37	100
	Matriculate	30	45	8	12	9	13	20	30	67	100
	Intermediate	26	48	6	11	4	8	18	33	54	100
	Graduate	28	35	17	22	2	3	32	40	79	100
	P.G. & Higher	15	24	11	17	2	3	35	56	63	100
	Total	**126**	**42**	**52**	**17**	**17**	**6**	**105**	**35**	**300**	**100**
Occupation	Business	78	59	35	26	5	4	14	11	132	100
	Teaching	9	25	4	11	5	13	19	51	37	100
	Govt. Service	18	25	6	8	7	10	41	57	72	100
	Engineering	2	18	1	9	0	0	8	73	11	100
	Preaching	0	0	1	9	0	0	10	91	11	100
	Admn. (pvt.)	4	36	1	9	0	0	6	55	11	100
	Others	15	58	4	15	0	0	7	27	26	100
	Total	**126**	**42**	**52**	**17**	**17**	**6**	**105**	**35**	**300**	**100**
Income	⩽ Rs 2000	40	51	17	21	0	0	22	28	79	100
	2000–5000	35	34	12	11	7	7	50	48	104	100
	5000–10000	27	34	12	15	8	10	32	41	79	100
	10000–more	24	63	11	29	2	5	1	5	38	100

Table 7.4 shows 63% Sikhs have reported that they very strictly believe in the practice of untouchability followed by 62% Swetambars and 50% Degambars. Christians form very low (10% and 4%) percentage of Roman Catholics and Protestants respectively. Propor-

tions of those who do not at all believe in the practice of untouchability is highest (82%) among Protestants and Roman Catholics (74%). It is fairly low 15% among Sikhs, 14% among Swetambars and lowest (10%) among Degambars. That is Jains (24%) believe more in untouchability as compared to Sikhs (15%) and Christians (most of them i.e., 78%) do not believe in the practice of untouchability.

On the basis of observations (Table 7.4) it can be concluded that among Christians, Protestants are more modern than the Roman Catholics, in Jains Swetambars are more modern than Degambars and Sikhs fall in between Swetambars and Roman Catholics. Among the three religious groups Christians form the most modern group, then Sikhs and they are more modern than Jains. A change among Sikhs' attitude is apparent from the above data, whereas untouchability is not permitted among Sikhs to practice. It shows impact of local Hindu culture on Sikhs.

Lowest education groups (i.e., basic or less) form higher ratios (73%) of persons favouring practice of untouchability very strictly. It is still lower (48%) among intermediates and matriculates (45%). Graduates form 35% and postgraduate and higher education group forms minimum (i.e., 24%) proportion of those who very strictly favour untouchability. Those who not at all favour untouchability form highest frequency (56%) in postgraduate and higher education group and minimum (0% and 30%) frequencies in basic or less and in matriculates (Table 7.4).

Among the various occupation groups (Table7.4) preaching (91%) are most modern then engineering (73%) followed by government service (57%) and administrative (55%). The least modern group on this statement is of business (11%) as they do not at all believe in the practice of untouchability. On the whole out of a total of 300 respondents, 42% believe very strictly, 17% believe strictly, 6% believe less strictly and 35% do not believe at all in the practice of untouchability.

Incomewise distribution (Table 7.4) shows that lowest (i.e. Rs 2,000 p.m. or less) and highest (Rs 10,000 p.m. or more) income group form 28% and 5% of those who do not believe in the practice of untouchability, but middle income groups, i.e., Rs 2,000–5,000 p.m. (48%) and Rs 5,000–10,000 p.m. (41%) do not favour untouchability. We may say that there are some other factors which are responsible for modernism than the economic factor.

Rationalism

Our data (Table 7.5) indicates that major cause for the selection of a particular occupation is other (57%) than profit (22%), inheritance (16%) and religion (5%). 53%, 31%, 12%, and 4% in the age groups of 35 years or below

Among Roman Catholics major causes are profit (20%) and inheritance (20%) besides other (50%). In Protestants profit (20%) is the second major cause besides other (60%). Among Degambars profit (22%) and inheritance (26%) constitute the major causes of occupation selection, in Swetambars (24%) and the Sikhs (22%) profit is the second major cause of occupation selection besides other causes (62%).

Among various groups of education basic or below (27%) and matriculates (33%) form the highest ratios of those who selected their occupation because of profit motive. Further, basic or less group form maximum frequency (43%) of those who have inherited the present occupation from their fathers and grandfathers. This group comprises mainly of the business class (especially among the Jain sects). It does not mean that with the increasing education an individual turns towards traditionalism rather, that for the business class profit is the main motive. People in the graduate and post-graduate educational group and above form highest proportions (80% and 76%) of those who have selected a particular occupation due to some 'other' factor.

On the basis of income, we observe that persons belonging to income groups of Rs 5,000–10,000 p.m. and Rs 10,000 p.m. and above constitute maximum frequencies (34% and 40%) of the profit oriented persons, have selected their occupations on the basis of other, profit, inheritance, and religion. 51%, 23%, 20% and 6% in the age group of 36–45 years have selected their occupation on the basis of other, profit, inheritance and religion. In the age group of 46–55 years 59%, 18%, 18% and 5% have selected on other, profit, inheritance and religious basis. 64%, 19%, 14% and 3% in the age group of 56 years and above have selected their occupation on the basic of other, profit, inheritance, and religion.

It is indicated that besides 'other' reasons profit forms the second important factor in determining an individual's occupation. Thus, we may conclude that younger generation is more rational in terms of profit orientation.

7.5: What was the basis of selection of your occupation?

Variable	*Categories*	*Profit*		*Religion*		*Inheritance*		*Other*		*Total*	
		'f'	*%*	*'f'*	*%*	*'f'*	*%*	*'f'*	*%*	*'f'*	*%*
Age	≤-35 years	15	31	2	4	6	12	26	53	49	100
	36–45	19	23	5	6	16	20	42	51	82	100
	46–55	14	18	4	5	14	18	46	59	78	100
	56 ≥	17	19	3	3	13	14	58	64	91	100
	Total	**65**	**22**	**14**	**5**	**49**	**16**	**172**	**57**	**300**	**100**
Sect	Roman Cath.	10	20	5	10	10	20	25	50	50	100
	Protestant	10	20	2	4	5	10	33	66	50	100
	Degambar	11	22	1	2	13	26	25	50	50	100
	Swetambar	12	24	3	6	8	16	27	54	50	100
	Sikh	22	22	3	3	13	13	62	62	100	100
	Total	**65**	**22**	**14**	**5**	**49**	**16**	**172**	**57**	**300**	**100**
Education	Basic or less	10	27	2	5	16	43	9	24	37	100
	Matriculate	22	33	2	3	13	19	30	45	67	100
	Intermediate	10	19	5	9	17	31	22	41	54	100
	Graduate	10	13	5	6	1	1	63	80	79	100
	P.G. & Higher	13	21	0	0	2	3	48	76	63	100
	Total	65	22	14	5	49	16	172	57	300	100
Occupation	Business	57	43	1	1	46	35	28	21	132	100
	Teaching	0	0	2	5	2	5	33	89	37	100
	Govt. Service	4	6	0	0	0	0	68	94	72	100
	Engineering	2	18	0	0	0	0	9	82	11	100
	Preaching	0	0	10	91	0	0	1	9	11	100
	Admn. (pvt.)	0	0	0	0	0	0	11	100	11	100
	Others	2	8	1	4	1	4	22	84	26	100
	Total	**65**	**22**	**14**	**5**	**49**	**16**	**172**	**57**	**300**	**100**
Income	≤ Rs–2000	5	6	2	3	8	10	64	81	79	100
	2000–5000	18	17	7	7	6	6	73	70	104	100
	5000–10000	27	34	4	5	20	25	28	36	79	100
	10000–more	15	40	1	3	15	39	7	18	38	100
	Total	**65**	**22**	**14**	**5**	**49**	**16**	**172**	**57**	**300**	**1000**

Thus, we may infer (Table 7.5) that people belonging to younger age groups are more rational (calculative in terms of profit). In terms of occupation selection both Roman Catholics and Protestants are rational at par. Education indirectly affects choice of one's occupation based on profit. But occupation and income are significantly affected by profit motive (i.e., rational calculation of future).

Responses on people's favourable attitude towards women's participation in jobs have shown (Table 7.6) that maximum frequency (45%) is in the age group of 56 years and above then in 35 years and

Table 7.6: Do you favour women's participation in jobs ?

Variable	*Categories*	*Yes*		*No*		*Total*	
		'f'	%	'f'	%	'f'	%
Age	⩽ 35 years	21	43	28	57	49	100
	36–45	34	42	48	58	82	100
	46–55	32	41	46	59	78	100
	56 ⩾	41	45	50	55	91	100
	Total	**128**	**43**	**172**	**57**	**300**	
Sect	Roman Cath.	28	56	22	44	50	100
	Protestant	21	42	29	58	50	100
	Degambar	11	22	39	78	50	100
	Swetambar	26	52	24	48	50	100
	Sikh	42	42	58	58	100	100
	Total	**128**	**43**	**172**	**57**	**300**	
Education	Basic or less	11	30	26	70	37	100
	Matriculate	18	27	49	73	67	100
	Intermediate	34	63	2	37	54	100
	Graduate	54	68	25	32	79	100
	P.G.& Higher	11	17	52	83	63	100
	Total	**128**	**43**	**172**	**57**	**300**	
Occupation	Business	24	18	108	82	132	100
	Teaching	30	81	7	19	37	100
	Govt. Service	35	49	37	51	72	100
	Engineering	8	73	3	27	11	100
	Preaching	9	82	2	18	11	100
	Admn. (pvt.)	7	64	4	36	11	100
	Others	15	58	11	42	26	100
	Total	**128**	**43**	**172**	**57**	**300**	
Income	⩽ Rs 2000	46	58	33	42	79	100
	2000–5000	57	55	47	45	104	100
	5000–1000	18	23	61	77	79	100
	10000–more	7	18	31	82	38	100
	Total	**128**	**43**	**172**	**57**	300	

below (43%) followed by 42% in 36–45 years and minimum (41%) in 46–55 years age group. Among various sects, frequency (56%) is higher in Roman Catholics than 42% in Protestants; 52% in Swetambars than 22% in Degambars and 42% in Sikhs. Among the three religious groups Christians (49%) are most modern than Sikhs (42%) and as compared to Jains (37%). Further, it is noted that intermediates (63%) and graduates (68%) are the most modern on this issue than the basic or less (30%) and matriculates (27%). Post-graduate and higher qualified persons form only 17% of those who favour women's participation in jobs. That is education has nothing to do with modernism.

Among various occupations, it is found (Table 7.6) that preaching (82%) then teaching (81%) are the most modern occupations whereas, business (18%) is least modern. Similarly, lowest income group (Rs 2,000 p.m. or less) is the most modern (58%) followed by the income group of Rs 2,000–5,000 p.m. (55%) than the upper income groups Rs 5,000–10,000 p.m. being 23% and Rs 10,000 p.m. or more is 18%.

The reason behind business groups' and upper income groups' lower percentage is that these categories are economically well-off and they generally have no need for their women to go for jobs. This was stated by most of the respondents during interview. Therefore, women's non-participation in jobs is also based on economic well being than by any other factor.

Values Towards Hard Work and Honesty

From a careful examination of Table 7.7 we find that social value towards honesty is maximum (79%) in the age group of 56 years and above whereas minimum (43%) in the age group of 35 years or less. Persons belonging to this age group form maximum frequency (12%) of those who feel that honesty is not at all required for success. Thus, we may infer that with the decreasing age, people's attitude towards honesty is changing into negative.

Table 7.7 indicates 72% Protestants, 70% Roman Catholics, 68% Degambars, and 66% Sikhs feel very strongly about honesty as a key to success. Swetambars form the minimum percentage (64%) in this regard. We observe that Protestants have more positive attitude towards honesty than Roman Catholics and Degambars have more as compared to Swetambars, and Sikhs have more than Swetambars. Among the three religious groups Christians have higher positive value towards honesty than Jains and Sikhs.

Unlike hard work, graduates form maximum frequency (79%) of those who feel very strong about honesty as the key to success. Next

7.7: Do you feel that honesty is the key of one's success?

Variable	*Categories*	*Very Strictly*		*Strictly*		*Not Strictly*		*Not at all*		*Total*	
		'f'	%	'f'	%	'f'	%	'f'	%	'f'	%
Age	⩽ 35 years	21	43	13	27	9	18	6	12	49	100
	36– 45	51	62	22	27	5	6	4	5	82	100
	46–55	59	76	12	15	4	5	3	4	78	100
	56 ⩾	72	79	13	14	4	5	2	2	91	100
	Total	**203**	**68**	**60**	**20**	**22**	**7**	**15**	**5**	**300**	**100**
Sect	Roman Cath.	35	70	9	18	4	8	2	4	50	100
	Protestant	36	72	9	18	4	8	1	2	50	100
	Degambar	34	68	10	20	3	6	3	6	50	100
	Swetambar	32	64	9	19	5	10	4	8	50	100
	Sikh	66	66	23	23	3	3	5	5	100	100
	Total	**203**	**68**	**60**	**20**	**22**	**7**	**15**	**5**	**300**	**100**
Education	Basic or less	20	54	8	22	7	19	2	5	37	100
	Matriculate	36	54	18	24	9	13	6	9	67	100
	Intermediate	37	69	9	17	4	7	4	7	54	100
	Graduate	62	79	15	19	1	1	1	1	79	100
	P.G. & Higher	48	76	12	19	1	2	2	3	63	100
	Total	**203**	**68**	**60**	**20**	**22**	**7**	**15**	**5**	**300**	**100**
Occupation	Business	84	64	24	18	16	12	8	6	132	100
	Teaching	30	81	5	13	1	3	1	3	37	100
	Govt. Service	58	81	11	15	1	1	2	3	72	100
	Engineering	7	64	2	18	1	9	1	9	11	100
	Preaching	11	100	0	0	0	0	0	0	11	100
	Admn. (pvt.)	5	46	3	27	2	18	1	9	11	100
	Others	8	31	1	58	1	4	2	7	26	100
	Total	**203**	**68**	**60**	**20**	**22**	**7**	**15**	**5**	**300**	**100**
Income	⩽ Rs 2000	53	67	13	16	7	9	6	8	79	100
	2000–5000	66	63	25	24	7	7	6	6	104	100
	5000–10000	57	73	16	20	5	6	1	1	79	100
	10000–more	27	71	6	16	6	8	2	5	38	100
	Total	**203**	**68**	**60**	**20**	**22**	**7**	**15**	**5**	**300**	**100**

highest frequency (76%) is in the education group of postgraduate and more. It is minimum (54%) each in the basic or less and matriculates.

Preaching occupation forms highest ratio (100%) followed by 81% each in teaching and in government service whereas 46% in administrative services and 31% (minimum) in 'others' feel very strongly that honesty is the key to success.

Table 7.7 indicates that 73% (highest) in the income group of Rs 5,000–10,000 p.m. and 71% (next highest) in the income group of Rs 10,000 p.m. or more feel very strongly about honesty. Those who do not at all feel strongly about honesty form maximum ratios (8% and 6%) in the income groups of Rs 2,000 p.m. or less and Rs 2,000–5,000 p.m. Hence, it may be concluded that honesty is a middle class value.

Values Towards Science and Technology

A positive value towards science and technology indicates a modern outlook. Our observation (Table 7.8) shows that 53% in the age group of 35 years or less, 51% both in the age groups of 36–45 years and 46–55 years and 47% (minimum) in the age group of 56 years and above feel very strongly about science and technology's aid to progress. 32% (highest) in the age group of 56 years and above strongly agree and 23% (maximum) in the age group of 36–45 years less strongly agree and persons in the age group of 56 years and more form highest frequency (7%) who do not at all agree that science and technology lead to progress.

We may infer that with decreasing age people's attitude towards science and technology become positive or modernity increases with the decreasing age.

System

Table 7.8 shows that among the various sects Degambars form minimum frequency (46%) of those who very strongly agree with science and technology's aid to progress. Protestants and Sikhs form highest ratio (30%) of those who strongly agree and Degambars and Sikhs form maximum frequency (6%) who do not at all agree with science's aid to progress.

Further, it is indicated that 84% (maximum) in the postgraduate and above very strongly agree, 39% matriculates strongly agree, 30%

7.8: Do you feel that science and technology lead to progress of society?

Variable	*Categories*	*Very Strongly*		*Strongly*		*Not Strongly*		*Not at all*		*Total*	
		'f'	*%*	*'f'*	*%*	*'f'*	*%*	*'f'*	*%*	*'f'*	*%*
Age	≤ 35 years	26	53	15	31	6	12	2	4	49	100
	36–45	42	51	19	23	19	23	2	3	82	100
	46–55	40	51	18	23	16	21	4	5	78	100
	56 ≥	43	47	29	32	13	14	6	7	91	100
	Total	**151**	**50**	**81**	**27**	**54**	**18**	**14**	**5**	**300**	**100**
Sect	Roman Cath.	26	52	14	28	8	16	2	4	50	100
	Protestant	24	48	15	30	10	20	1	2	50	100
	Degambar	23	46	8	16	16	32	3	6	50	100
	Swetambar	26	52	14	28	8	16	2	4	50	100
	Sikh	52	52	30	30	12	12	6	6	100	100
	Total	**151**	**50**	**81**	**27**	**54**	**18**	**14**	**5**	**300**	**100**
Education	Basic or less	11	30	8	21	11	30	7	19	37	100
	Matriculate	23	34	26	39	15	22	3	5	67	100
	Intermediate	20	37	20	37	12	22	2	4	54	100
	Graduate	44	56	27	27	13	16	1	1	79	100
	P.G. & Higher	53	84	6	10	3	4	1	2	63	100
	Total	**151**	**50**	**81**	**27**	**54**	**18**	**14**	**5**	**300**	**100**
Occupation	Business	57	43	32	24	41	31	2	2	132	100
	Teaching	17	46	11	30	3	8	6	16	37	100
	Govt. Service	47	65	20	28	5	7	0	0	72	100
	Engineering	11	100	0	0	0	0	0	0	11	100
	Preaching	2	18	4	37	2	18	3	27	11	100
	Admn. (pvt.)	3	27	5	45	2	18	1	9	11	100
	Others	14	54	9	34	1	4	2	8	26	100
	Total	**151**	**50**	**81**	**27**	**54**	**18**	**14**	**5**	**300**	**100**
Income	≤ Rs 2000	20	25	37	47	16	20	6	8	79	100
	2000–5000	56	54	25	24	18	17	5	5	104	100
	5000–10000	50	63	14	18	12	15	3	4	79	100
	10000–more	25	66	5	13	8	21	0	0	38	100
	Total	**151**	**50**	**81**	**27**	**54**	**18**	**14**	**5**	**300**	**100**

below basic or less strongly agree and 19% (i.e., maximum) in the same education group do not at all agree with the science and technology's aid to progress (Table 7.8).

On the basis of occupation (Table 7.8) it is observed that 100% in engineering, 65% in government service, 54% in 'others', 46% in teaching and minimum 18% in preaching agree very strongly with science and technology's help to progress. Those who highly disagree constitute maximum frequency (27%) in the preaching occupation. It indicates that most modern occupations are engineering, and government services, whereas preaching is also undergoing a change of value.

Incomewise distribution (Table 7.8) shows that higher income groups i.e. Rs 5,000–10,000 p.m. (63%) and Rs 10,000 p.m. and above (66%) are more modern as they very strongly agree that science and technology are helpful to social development. Thus, on the basis of above observations we may conclude that age, sect, occupation, and income affect modernization of an individual whereas education has indirect affects upon it.

For examining an individual's religious versus secular outlook, domination of his daily activities by religious or logic/scientific outlook has been analysed. We observe (Table 7.9) that only 22% (although constituting the maximum) in the age group of 56 years or more are 'absolutely' governed by religious ethic. 14% (minimum) in the age group of $\leqslant$ 35 years are 'mostly' guided by religious ethics. 18% in the age group of 35 years or below are guided by religion partly (in some of their activities) and 61% in the same age group are not at all guided by religion. It indicates that religion has its dominant effect upon almost all age groups, but eldest age group, i.e. 56 years or more, is governed more by religion than any other age group.

20% Degambars, 18% Swetambars, 13% Sikhs, 12% Protestants, and 10% Catholics are absolutely guided by religious ethics. 32% Roman Catholics, 30% Sikhs, 28% Swetambars, 18% Protestants, and 14% Degambars are 'mostly' guided by religious ethics. 22% Protestants are guided by religious ethics in some of their activities. Whereas 45% Sikhs, 46% Swetambars, 48% Protestants, and 54% both Degambars and Roman Catholics are guided by logic than religion. It indicates that Roman Catholics are more modern than Protestants and Degambars are more modern than Swetambars. Sikhs are least modern; Jains form the bridge between Sikh and Christian sects. Christians are most modern among all the three religious groups.

Highest proportions among different educational groups of those whose all the activities, most of these, some of these, or those who

7.9: Do you think that most of your daily life is governed by religious values/logic?

Variable	*Categories*	*Absolutely*		*Mostly*		*Partly*		*No Not at all*		*Total*	
		'f'	%	'f'	%	'f'	%	'f'	%	'f'	%
Age	≤ 35 years	3	6	7	14	9	18	30	61	49	100
	36– 45	8	10	25	31	6	7	43	52	82	100
	46–55	12	15	21	27	9	12	36	46	78	100
	56 ≥	20	22	23	25	11	12	37	41	91	100
	Total	**43**	**14**	**76**	**25**	**35**	**12**	**146**	**49**	**300**	
Sect	Roman Cath.	5	10	16	32	2	4	27	54	50	100
	Protestant	6	12	9	18	11	22	24	48	50	100
	Degambar	10	20	7	14	6	12	27	54	50	100
	Swetambar	9	18	14	28	4	8	23	46	50	100
	Sikh	13	13	30	30	12	12	45	45	100	100
	Total	**43**	**14**	**76**	**25**	**35**	**12**	**146**	**49**	**300**	
Education	Basic or less	8	22	10	27	7	19	12	32	37	100
	Matriculate	12	18	21	31	9	14	25	37	67	100
	Intermediate	6	11	6	11	8	15	34	63	54	100
	Graduate	9	11	21	27	9	11	40	51	79	100
	P.G. & Higher	8	13	18	28	2	3	35	56	63	100
	Total	**43**	**14**	**76**	**25**	**35**	**12**	**146**	**49**	**300**	
Occupation	Business	20	15	40	30	16	13	56	42	132	100
	Teaching	7	19	10	27	4	11	16	43	37	100
	Govt. Service	8	11	10	14	8	11	46	64	72	100
	Engineering	1	9	3	27	1	9	6	55	11	100
	Preaching	4	37	2	18	1	9	4	36	11	100
	Admn. (pvt.)	0	0	4	37	2	18	5	45	11	100
	Others	3	12	7	26	3	12	13	50	26	100
	Total	**43**	**14**	**76**	**25**	**35**	**12**	**146**	**49**	**300**	
Income	≤ Rs 2000	11	14	20	25	13	17	35	44	79	100
	2000–5000	15	14	20	19	7	7	62	60	104	100
	5000–10000	12	15	21	27	9	11	37	47	79	100
	10000–more	5	13	15	39	6	16	12	32	38	100
	Total	**43**	**14**	**76**	**25**	**35**	**12**	**146**	**49**	**300**	**100**

are guided by logic are 22% in the basic or less, 31% in matriculates, partly (19%) in basic or less and 63% among intermediates. On the basis of our data (Table 7.9) we may say, that, level of education does not affect one's rational outlook. 15%, 30%, 13% and 42% in business are guided absolutely, mostly and sometimes by logic.

About 19%, 27%, 11% and 43% in teaching are guided absolutely, mostly, sometimes and by logic. 9%, 27%, 9% and 55% in engineering, 37%, 18%, 9% and 36% in preaching, 0%, 37%, 18% and 45% in administrative, 12%, 26%, 12% and 50% in others, and 11%, 14%, 11% and 64% in government service are guided absolutely, mostly and sometimes by logic.

Table 7.10 shows that persons who have scored high on modernism (md=18) form comparatively larger frequency (55%) in the age group of ⩽ 35 years. Second highest frequency (49%) is reflected by the age group of 36–45 years. Third highest frequency (47%) is formed by the age group of ⩾ 56 years and persons in the age group of 46–55 years form minimum frequency (40%) of those who have secured above median value (i.e., 18) on modernism. Age does not reflect any significant variation with regard to modernism.

Table 7.10 : Scores on Modernism of Different Age Groups

Age Group / *Score*	*<35 Yrs.*	*36–45 Yrs.*	*46–55 Yrs.*	*56 & more Yrs.*	*Total*
L	22	42	47	48	159
H	27	40	31	43	141
G.Total	49	82	78	91	300

X^2 = 3.047 @ 3 d.f., 5% level of significance

Frequencies of those who have secured high scores on modernism are comparatively higher among the Protestant sect (96%) than in Roman Catholic sect (90%). Further, Swetambar sect reflects higher frequency (36%) than Degambar sect (8%), Christians form maximum frequency (93%) of those who have secured above median score on modernism. Sikhs form second highest ratio (26%) and Jains show minimum frequency (22%) in this regard. Hence, the Christians are most developed, the Sikhs are the second most developed and the Jains are the least developed (Table 7.11).

Table 7.11 : Scores on Modernism of Different Sects

Sectors / *Scores*	*Roman Cath.*	*Protestant*	*Degam bar*	*Swetam bars*	*Sikhs*	*G. Total*
L	5	2	46	32	74	159
H	45	48	4	18	26	141
G.Total	50	50	50	50	100	100

X^2 = 135.969 @ 4 d.f., significant at 5% level of significance

Persons showing higher frequencies in various educational categories are 51% in graduate, 56% in intermediates and 84% in 'post-graduate and higher'. Those who form comparatively lower frequencies are 16% in 'basic or below' and 18% in matriculate education categories. We may say that variation in the level of education significantly affects variation with degree of modernism (Table 7.12).

Table 7.12 : Scores of Various Education Groups on Modernism

Education Score	*Basic or below*	*Matri-culate*	*Interme-diate*	*Gradu-ate*	*P.G.& higher*	*Total*
Low	31	55	24	39	10	159
High	6	12	30	40	53	141
G.Total	37	67	54	79	63	300

X^2 = 73.702 @ 4 d.f. 5% level of significance

In different occupational categories administrative (private) (91%) and teaching (84%) form an overwhelming majority of those who have secured high scores on modernism. Those in engineering (55%), preaching (55%), government service (60%) and in 'others' (62%) (Table 7.13).

Table 7.13 : Scores of Various Occupational Groups on Modernism

Scores Occupation	*L*	*H*	*G. Total*
Business	103	29	132
Govt. Service	29	43	72
Teaching	6	31	37
Engineering	5	6	11
Preaching	5	6	11
Administrative (pvt.)	1	10	11
Others	10	16	26
G.Total	159	141	300

X^2 = 69.198 @ 6 d.f., $P < .005$ Significant

Ratios of those who have secured high on modernism are 63% in ⩽ Rs 2,000 p.m. income group and 59% in the income group of Rs 2,000–5,000 per month. Those in the income groups of Rs 5,000–10,000 and ⩾ Rs 10,000 per month form fairly lower frequencies (24% and 29%) in this regard. Variation in income has significant influence upon modernism (Table 7.14).

Table 7.14 : Scores of Various Income Groups on Modernism

Income Rs Scores	*<2000 P.M.*	*2000–5000 P.M.*	*5000–10,000 P.M.*	*>10,000 P.M.*	*Total*
Low	29	43	60	27	159
High	50	61	19	11	141
G.Total	79	104	79	38	300

X^2 = 35.761 @ 3 d.f., Significant at .005

Modernism is significantly affected by Religiosity (Table 7.15). Modernism is not influenced by ritualism in a significant way.

Table 7.15 : Scores on Modernism and Religiosity

	Modernism			
Religiosity	*Score*	*High*	*Low*	*G. Total*
High	56	81	137	
Low	85	71	163	
G.Total	141	159	300	

X^2 = 5.413 @ 1 d.f., Significant at .005

Modernism is not affected significantly by sectarianism (Table 7.16).

Table 7.16 : Scores on Modernism and Ritualism

	Modernism		
Ritualism Scores	*High*	*Low*	*G. Total*
High	52	60	112
Low	89	99	188
G.Total	141	159	300

X^2 = .0183 @ 1 d.f., Not significant at .005

Table 7.17 : Scores on Modernism and Sectarianism

	Modernism		
Sectarianism Scores	*High*	*Low*	*G..Total*
High	68	79	147
Low	73	80	153
G.Total	141	159	300

X^2 = .0626 @ 1 d.f., Not significant

Modernism and 'conflict-harmony' are significantly affected by each other (Table 7.18). On the basis of X^2 calculated we may infer that age and modernism (Table 7.10) (X^2 calculated = 3.047 at 3 d.f. and 5% level of significance) are not significantly associated whereas sects and modernism, (Table 7.11) (X^2 calculated = 135.969 at 4 d.f. and 5% level of significance), education and modernism (Table 7.12) (X_2 calculated = 73.702 at 4 d.f. and 5% level of significance), occupation and modernism (Table 7.13) (X^2 calculated = 69.198 at 6 d.f. and 5% level of significance) and income and modernism (Table 7.14) (X^2 calculated = 35.761 at 3 d.f. and 5% level of significance) are significantly related. Further, it is indicated (Tables 7.15, 7.16 and 7.17) that modernism is significantly associated with Religiosity Table 7.15 (X^2 = 5.413 @ 1 d.f. significant at .005), Ritualism and Modernism Table 7.16 (X^2 = .0183 @ 1 d.f. N.S.) and Modernism and Sectarianism Table 7.17 (X^2 = .0626 @ 1 d.f. N.S.) but modernism is significantly associated at 5% level of significance with conflict (X^2 = 9.1217 @ 1 d.f.). Thus, we may conclude that conflict is affected by modern outlook of an individual (Table 7.18).

Table 7.18 : Scores on Modernism and Conflict-Harmony

		Conflict-Harmony		
Modernism	*Scores*	*High*	*Low*	*G. Total*
	High	75	66	141
	Low	57	102	151
	G.Total	132	168	300

X^2 = 9.1217 @ 1 d.f., significant at 5%

Remarks

Persons belonging to younger generation are found as more modern than the older generation. Among different sects, the Protestants are more modern than the Roman Catholics and Swetambars are more modern as compared to Degambars. Among the three religious groups under present study Christians are more modern than Sikhs and Jains.

Education has also shown significant variations. Those who are either uneducated or have attained low level of education are traditionalist whereas higher educated persons have shown social modernism. Thus modernism increases with the increase in level of education.

Engineering, preaching, administrative and teaching are more modern than government service, business and occupational group categories as 'others'. Hence, nature of occupation too affects modernism.

Higher income group has shown its conservatism on issues like joint family, untouchability, purdah system and widow remarriage, women's participation in jobs, domination of religion upon daily activities but rational calculation of future on basis of occupation selection, selection of children's education, values towards hard work and honesty, science and technology and change in certain religious practices of their sect. Thus, modernism is also affected by income of an individual.

References

Eisenstadt, S.M. (1966), *Modernization: Protest and Change*, Englewood Cliffs, New Jersey, Prentice Hall..

Huntington, S.P. (1968), *Political Order in Changing Societies* University Press, New Haven.

Lerner (1958), "Modernization: Social Aspects" in *The Passing of Traditional Society: Modernization the Middle East,* The Free Press, New York

Parsons, T. (1970), "Evolutionary Universals in Society", in *Societies: Evolutionary and Comparative Perspectives*, Englewood Cliffs, New Jersey.

Singh, Y. (1973), *Modernization of Indian Tradition: A Systematic Study of Social Change*, Thomson Press, Delhi.

——— (1978), "Facing upto Modernity: Mystification and Contradiction", Paper presented at USICA Seminar, "Towards a Critique of Modernity", India International Centre, Nov. 9, mimeographed.

8 Sect and Development

Social development has gained wider popularity around the world in the present time. Every society has set its own parameters for measuring social development. The concept of social development has wider connotations. Social scientists mainly refer to social development as the move towards better quality of life. It has been defined as the "change towards a social state judged desirable" (Streetan, 1972). To Warner (1971), societal development refers to "an increase in the life chance of people in society". Weber (1963) meant by life chances as "the typical chances for a supply of goods, external living conditions and personal life experience. These include everything from the chance to stay alive during the first year after birth to the chance to view fine arts, the chance to remain healthy and grow tall and if sick to get well again quickly, the chance to avoid becoming a juvenile delinquent and the chance to complete an intermediary or higher educational grade". It refers to the increase in the level of living (i.e., health, education, occupation, income wealth, and assets etc.).

Development mainly refers to achieved rather than ascribed status. It has been observed that some societies as compared to others, some religious groups than the others and one sect within a particular religious group than its counterparts are more developed. Factors responsible for development of a sect, a religious group or of a country have aroused lot of controversies. A larger group of social scientists have established a relationship between religion and economic development. Weber (1930) asserted that the ethics of major oriental religion was not conducive to capitalistic development in Asia. Rao (1969) quoted Rachfahl and Brentano to state, "the spirit of capitalism originated even before the reformation". Tawney (1926) has established a reversible relationship between religion and economic development. Samuelson believes that the size of capitalism can be explained without reference to religion. Some consider other factors as more important. Trevor-Roper (1964) has insisted "the local origin of entrepreneurs as conducive to capitalistic growth than religious affiliation". Bellah (1965) assumes that religion and ideology are important in Asia's success or failure in further progress. Gupta (1974) emphasizing on the role of Ramakrishna Mission in Modernization of India stresses that "it has laid the foundations for India's only possible processes of social change".

The themes of the present chapter are: (1) to analyse the extent of development (social) of a sect and to compare it to its parallel sect; (2) to compare the social development of different religious groups; and (3) to study the factors that are responsible for the development of one sect and hindrance in the development of the other.

For the present purpose, some of the objective indicators are: (1) do you own any property/assets? (2) what is the educational level of yourself? (3) what is your occupation? (4) is your occupation similar to that of your father's occupation? (5) what is your per month income? (6) has anyone in your family suffered or has been suffering from chronic or frequent diseases? (7) do you have membership in any club? (8) have you ever held any office? (9) have you observed progress during the last ten years? (10) how many times have you contested for office in your religious organization? Among the subjective indicators are: (11) do you feel that you should have authority over your religious organization? (12) do you feel like keeping an account of 'the offerings' in your religious organization? and, (13) does your sect render services to the society in general? (14) what type of services are being rendered by your sect to your sect members and to society in general? Apart from the questions raised, those who have secured low on religiosity, ritualism, sectarianism and conflict and harmony and high on modernism scales are regarded as more developed as compared to those who have secured high on religiosity, ritualism, sectarianism and conflict and harmony and low on modernism.

Socio-Economic Background

A cursory look at Table 8.1 reveals that out of a total of 300, 76% possess their own houses, 10% own agricultural land, 16% have their own plots, 15% own shops, 8% have their own factories, 23% have cars and only 10% possess no property of their own.

Table 8.1: Property and Assets Owned by the Head of the Household

Variable	*Categories*	*House*		*Agricultural Land*		*Plot*		*Shop*		*Factory*		*Car*		*Nil*	
		'f'	%	'f'	%	'f'	%	'f'	%	'f'	%	'f'	%	'f'	%
Sect	Roman Cath.	34	68	6	12	9	18	2	4	1	2	5	10	7	14
	Protestant	32	64	5	10	6	12	4	8	2	4	6	12	12	24
	Degambar	46	92	2	4	7	14	13	26	11	22	19	38	1	2
	Swetambar	39	78	5	10	8	16	5	10	6	12	9	18	3	6
	Sikh	77	77	13	13	17	17	13	13	6	6	29	29	6	12
	Total	228	76	31	10	47	16	45	15	25	8	68	23	29	10

Percentage of those who have their own houses is highest (92%) among Degambars (Jains) followed by 78% Swetambars, 77% Sikhs and 68% among Roman Catholics and minimum (64%) among Protestants. Further, it is indicated that 13% Sikhs, 12% Roman Catholics, 10% both among Protestants and Swetambars and 4% Degambars possess agricultural land. 18% Roman Catholics, 17% Sikhs, 16% Swetambars, 14% Degambars and 12% Protestants own plots.

Proportion of those who own their own shops is largest (26%) among Degambars followed by 13% Sikhs, and 10% Swetambars. It is comparatively lower (8%) among Protestants and 4% (minimum) in Roman Catholics. It is further indicated that 22% Degambars and 12% Swetambars own factories followed by Sikhs (6%) and Christians (Roman Catholic, 2% and Protestant, 4%) which form 6% of factory owners. Our data (Table 8.1) also shows that car owners are maximum (38%) among Degambars then in Sikhs (29%) followed by Roman Catholics (10%) and Swetambars 18%. It is lowest (12%) among the Protestants. Those who do not own any property form 24% among Protestants, 14% Roman Catholics, 6% Swetambars, 12% Sikhs and 2% Degambars.

Among three religious groups Jains are found richer in terms of holding of assets than Sikhs, whereas Sikhs are richer than Christians.

Our data (Table 8.2) reveals that 4% among Roman Catholics and 10% among Protestants have (educational qualification) only up to basic or less (i.e., uneducated). Among the Jain sects 22% Swetambars and 20% Degambars are either uneducated or have (qualification) up

Table 8.2 Level of Education of Various Sects

Sects	*Level of Education*											
	Basic or below		*Matri-culate*		*Interme-diate*		*Gradu-ate*		*Higher*		*Total*	
	'f'	%	'f'	%	'f'	%	'f'	%	'f'	%	'f'	%
Roman Cath.	2	4	6	12	14	28	17	34	11	22	50	100
Protestant	5	10	4	8	6	12	9	18	26	52	50	100
Degambar	10	20	8	16	8	16	16	32	7	14	50	100
Swetambar	11	22	14	28	10	20	14	28	1	2	50	100
Sikh	9	9	35	55	16	16	22	22	18	18	100	100
Total	37		67		54		69		63		300	

to basic or below only. Sikhs form the minimum frequency (9%) of those who are qualified up to basic level only.

Ratio of graduates is 18% in the Protestants and 34% among the Roman Catholics forming a total of 52%. In the Jain sects, 32% Degambars and 28% Swetambars, i.e., a total of 60% Jains and 22 Sikhs have (qualification) up to graduation. Frequency of those who have qualified up to postgraduate and higher level of education is 52% Protestants, which is higher than Roman Catholics, (22%) and Degambars have 14% people who have qualified up to higher level of education are greater than Swetambars who have only 2%, while Sikhs have 18% people who have qualification upto postgraduation and higher level of education.

On the basis of our observations (Table 8.2), if we club the number of graduates and higher level, we may say that Protestants with 70% are more educated than the Roman Catholics with 56% people (educated) and Degambars (46%) are more educated than Swetambars (30%). Among the three religious groups, Christians (63%), then Sikhs (40%) followed by Jains (38%) have attained education up to graduation or postgraduation and higher level. Thus, educationwise, Christians are more developed than the Sikhs and Sikhs are more developed than the Jains.

Reasons for Roman Catholics being less educated are due to the fact that most of them have converted from the lowest castes and are engaged in lowly paid occupations. Swetambars form lower percentage due to their expanded businesses. Since they get involved in the business of their fathers at an early age, therefore, they do not get chance to go to college for higher education. Degambars consider themselves superior to Swetambars in terms of education and Swetambars also admit the fact. During the interview, a positive attitude (i.e. the desire to educate their children up to higher level was observed among both the sects of Jains and it was noticed that they feel for the lower percentage of education among their sects.

Table 8.3 shows that highest ratio (88%) of persons engaged in business is among the Swetambars followed by 74% Degambars and 42% Sikhs. The Protestants constitute a lower percentage (12%) and Roman Catholics are the lowest with 6% only. In the government services, Roman Catholics (44%) constitute the highest proportion than Sikhs (34%) followed by 26% Protestants. Jain sects constitute the lowest frequencies, i.e., Degambars 2% and Swetambars 1%

Table 8.3: Occupationwise Distribution of Different Sects

Sects	*Occupation*															
	Business		*Govt. Service*		*Teaching*		*Others*		*Engineering*		*Administration*		*Preaching*		*Total*	
	'f'	%	'f'	%	'f'	%	'f'	%	'f'	%	'f'	%	'f'	%	'f'	%
Protestant	6	12	13	26	15	30	3	6	2	4	7	14	4	8	50	100
Roman Cath.	3	6	22	44	13	26	7	14	1	2	0	0	4	8	50	100
Degambar	37	74	2	4	4	8	4	8	3	6	0	0	0	0	50	100
Swetambar	44	88	1	2	0	0	3	6	2	4	0	0	0	0	50	100
Sikhs	42	42	34	34	5	10	9	9	3	3	4	4	3	3	100	100
Total	132		72		37		26		11		11		11		300	

only. In teaching, Protestants form 30%, Roman Catholics are 26% and 10% among Sikhs. There are 8% Degambars and none (0%) in Swetambars in teaching profession. Total recruitment to engineering and administrative services from the five sects under present study (i.e., Roman Catholic, Protestant, Degambar, Swetambar and Sikh) is very low, i.e., 4% each in both the occupations. In the administrative services, Protestants (14%) form the highest ratio, then Sikhs (4%). There is no representation of other sects in this category. In preaching group, no saints or priests from Jain sects could be included due to their non-availability in the city during the fieldwork. But 8% from both the Roman Catholics and Protestants and 3% from the Sikh could be interviewed.

In the occupational group categorized as others, Roman Catholics form the highest (14%) frequency, then 9% Sikhs and 8% Degambars. Both Protestants and Swetambars form only 6% in this category. Thus, we may say that Jains are the most enterprising. The Sikhs, Christians are the least involved in business. Among them, Protestants (12% in business) are more enterprising than the Roman Catholics (6%) and Swetambars (88%) are more enterprising than Degambars (74%).

Maximum number of Christians in teaching profession is due to the fact that they are highly qualified sects among all the sects under present study. Other reason is that they are controlling the educational institutions in the city, therefore, have better opportunities than other sects. Similarly, due to maximum number in higher education, Protestants (14%) are dominating the administrative services. There is no representation of Roman Catholics, Degambars and Swetambars in this group.

Change in the traditional occupation (Table 8.4) represents occupational mobility implying development of an individual or of a sect. Sikhs (52%) form highly mobile group then 44% Protestants, 32% Swetambars, 30% Degambars, and 18% Roman Catholics whose occupation is different from their father's occupation. It was observed during the interview that Sikhs as compared to other sects form highly mobile sect and most of them are engaged in more than one occupation e.g. engaged in services (mostly government) and simultaneously running the side business as also.

Among the Christian sects, Protestants (44%) are more mobile than Roman Catholics (18%), and Swetambars (32%) are more mobile than Degambars (30%). That is, difference between Degambars and

Table 8.4: Inter-generation Occupational Mobility: Is your occupation similar to that of your father's occupation?

Sects	*Occupation*					
	Similar		*Different*		*Total*	
	f	%	*f*	%	*f*	%
Roman Cath.	41	82	9	18	50	100
Protestant	28	56	22	44	50	100
Degambar	35	70	15	30	50	100
Swetambar	34	68	16	32	50	100
Sikh	48	48	52	52	100	100
Total	186	62	114	38	300	

Swetambars is not much as against Christian sects where there is 44% mobility among the Protestants and only 18% among Roman Catholics. Protestants are striving high in the profit making pursuit.

Our data (Table 8.5) reveals that 50% Roman Catholics, 32% Protestants, 8% Degambars, and 2% Swetambars and 33% Sikhs earn less than or equal to Rs 2,000 p.m. 48% both Roman Catholics and Protestants, 28% Swetambars, 24% Degambars and 30% Sikhs earn between Rs 2,000 – 5,000 p.m. and 2% Roman Catholics, 20% Protestants, 54% Degambars, 30% Swetambars and 26% Sikhs are earning Rs 5,000 – 10,000 p.m. 40% Swetambars and 14% Degambars and 11% Sikhs earn more than Rs 10,000 p.m. There is no representation of either Roman Catholics or Protestants in this income group.

Table 8.5: Monthly Income Distribution Among Various Sects

Sects	*Income per month (in Rs)*									
	≤2000 5000		*2000– 10000*		*5000– & above*		*10000*		*Total*	
	'f'	*%*	*'f'*	*%*	*'f'*	*%*	*'f'*	*%*	*'f'*	*%*
Roman Cath.	25	50	24	48	1	2	0	0	50	100
Protestant	16	32	24	48	10	20	0	0	50	100
Degamber	4	8	12	24	27	54	7	14	50	100
Swetambar	1	2	14	28	15	30	20	40	50	100
Sikh	33	33	30	30	26	26	11	11	100	100
Total	79	26	104	35	79	26	28	13	300	

For the comparative analysis of incomes of different sects, t-test was applied which indicated that (on the basis of mean values of different sects) Protestants (mean income calculated is Rs 3825.66 per month) are richer than Roman Catholics (mean income calculated is Rs 2,266.32 per month) (t-calculated = 3.939 ≥ 1.96 at 5% level of significance), Swetambars (means income is Rs 14316 per month) are richer than Degambars (mean income is Rs 11,130) (t-calculated = 2.88 ≥ 1.96 at 5% level of significance). Jains are the richest group (mean income = Rs 12,723 p.m.), the second richest group is of Sikhs (means income is Rs 7,537 p.m.) and Christians are the least rich group (mean income = Rs 3,045.94 p.m.).

Jains are richer than Sikhs but the difference has not been found significant (t-calculated = ≥ 1.96 at 5% level of significance). Between Sikhs and Christians (t-calculated = 2.85 ≥ 1.96 at 5% level of significance), Sikhs are richer than Christians. Thus, we can say that Jains form the richest section of society than Sikhs. Christians although highest on education scale form the lowest wealthy class.

There are four priest among the Roman Catholics who do not receive any salary for their job unlike the Protestant priests. But have been included in the income group of Rs 5,000–10,000 p.m. on the basis of their expenditure and standard of living. They are maintaining cars, have modern amenities and better quality of food.

Along with education, occupation, income and assets, health forms one of the most important indicators of development, not only in Indian society but all over the world. Measured in terms of number of chronic or frequent occurrence of diseases in a sect, it is observed (Table 8.6) that 20% Roman Catholics and 12% Protestants, 4% Degambars and 0% Swetambars and 3% Sikhs have frequent or chronic occurrence of diseases in their families (including the respondents). It indicates that Protestant sect is more developed than the Roman Catholics, and among Jains, Swetambar sect is more developed than Degambars, and Sikhs are more developed than the Christians and less developed than Jain sects.

Table 8.6 Chronic or Frequent Occurrence of Disease Among Various Sects

Variable	*Categories*	*Roman Catholics*		*Protestant*		*Degambar*		*Swetambar*		*Sikh*		*Total*	
		'f'	*%*	*'f'*	*%*	*'f'*	*%*	*'f'*	*%*	*'f'*	*%*	*'f'*	*%*
Health	Yes	10	20	6	12	2	4	0	0	3	3	21	100
	No	40	80	44	88	48	96	50	100	97	97	79	100
	Total	50		50		50		50		100		100	

General cause of disease was heart trouble and asthma. Among Roman Catholics, some of the households were found in a helpless condition. The poor couple (in one family) was found in a very poor health and there was no one to look after them. Condition of the house was also very bad–no sanitation and no proper light.

Club-membership of an individual indicates both his economic and social development. Generally, upper stratum has membership in clubs. Our Table 8.7, shows that highest frequency of those who have their membership in club is 6% in the age group of 36–45 years, and 5% in the age group of 46–55 years. Roman Catholics, Protestants and Degambars do not have membership in club. Swetambers form 10% ratio whereas Sikhs constitute 4% of persons having membership in club. Thus, Sikhs may be treated as more developed than Jains and Christians as the least developed.

Table 8.7: Do you have membership in any club (international)?

Variable	*Categories*	*Yes*		*No*		*Total*	
		'f'	%	'f'	%	'f'	%
Age	≤35	0	0	49	100	49	100
	36–45	5	6	77	94	82	100
	46–55	4	5	74	95	78	100
	56 & above	0	0	91	100	91	100
	Total	**9**	**3**	**291**	**97**	**300**	
Sect	Roman Cath.	0	0	50	100	50	100
	Protestant	0	0	50	100	50	100
	Degambar	0	0	50	100	50	100
	Swetambar	5	10	45	90	50	100
	Sikh	4	4	96	96	100	100
	Total	**9**	**3**	**29**	**97**	**300**	
Education	Basic or less	0	0	37	100	37	100
	Matriculate	0	0	67	94	67	100
	Intermediate	0	0	54	91	54	100
	Graduate	7	9	72	91	79	100
	P. G. & above	2	3	61	97	63	100
	Total	**9**	**3**	**291**	**97**	**300**	
Occupation	Business	9	7	123	72	93	100
	Teaching	0	0	37	100	37	100
	Govt. Service	0	0	72	100	37	100
	Engineering	0	0	11	100	11	100
	Preaching	0	0	11	100	11	100
	Admn (pvt.)	0	0	11	100	11	100
	Others	0	0	26	100	26	100
	Total		**9**	**3**	**291**	**97**	**300**
Income	≤ 2000	0	0	79	100	79	100
	2000–5000	0	0	104	100	104	100
	5000–10000	0	5	79	100	79	100
	10000 & above	9	24	29	76	38	100
	Total	**9**	**3**	**291**	**97**	**300**	

It is also obvious from our data (Table 8.7) that those in the upper income group and business are more developed than other occupational and income groups.

Authoritarianism

Table 8.8 indicates authoritarianism measured in terms of frequency of office contested by an individual. A cursory glance at the data (Table 8.8) shows that those who have contested once for the office is maximum (8%) in the age group of 56 years and above. Those who have contested twice is maximum (7%) in the 46–55 years age group. Persons who have contested more than twice are maximum (5%) in the 56 years and above age group. Those who have never contested for office form maximum frequency (90%) in the age group of 35 years or below. Thus, it can be inferred that authoritarianism increases with the increasing age. Hence, younger people are less developed than older people. Because in a sect organization, important offices are monopolized by the richest of the sect showing that power (religious, social) is related with economic power.

Sectwise distribution (Table 8.8) reveals that 8% Roman Catholics as compared to 4% Protestants, 8% each among Degambar and Swetambar and 5% Sikhs have contested once for the office. 4% Romans Catholics and 0% Protestants, 4% each among Degambars and Swetambars and 8% Sikhs have contested twice for the office. 2% Roman Catholics and 0% Protestants, 4% Degambars and 6% Swetambars and 3% Sikhs have contested more than twice for the office. Frequency (82%) among the Swetambars is minimum of those who have never contested for office. Authoritarian feeling is maximum among Jains. 83% (minimum) Jains have never contested for office compared to Sikhs (84%). It is minimum among Christians (91% i.e. maximum people have never contested for office). Therefore, we may conclude that Christians are less developed than Sikhs and Sikhs are less developed than Jains. Further, it is indicated (Table 8.8) that those in the intermediate group, constitute highest frequency (90%) of the persons who have, never contested for office and of those who have contested more than twice are maximum (8%) in the basic or below education group. Those who have contested twice are maximum (7%) in the graduates whereas postgraduates and higher form maximum frequency (13%) of persons who have contested only once for the office in their religious organization.

8.8: How many times have you contested for office in your religious organisation

Variable	*Categories*	*More Once*		*Twice*		*More*		*Never*		*Total*	
		'f'	*%*	*'f'*	*%*	*'f'*	*%*	*'f'*	*%*	*'f'*	*%*
Age	⩽ 35 years	3	6	1	2	1	2	44	90	49	100
	36– 45	5	6	3	4	2	2	72	88	82	100
	46–55	4	5	5	7	1	1	68	87	78	100
	56 ⩾	7	8	5	6	5	5	74	81	91	100
	Total	**19**		**14**		**9**		**258**		**300**	
Sect	Roman Cath.	4	8	2	4	1	2	43	86	50	100
	Protestant	2	4	0	0	0	0	48	96	50	100
	Degambar	4	8	2	4	2	4	42	84	50	100
	Swetambar	4	8	2	4	3	6	41	82	50	100
	Sikh	5	5	8	8	3	3	84	84	100	100
	Total	**19**		**14**		**9**		**258**		**300**	
Educa-tion	Basic or less	0	0	1	3	3	8	33	89	37	100
	Matriculate	2	3	3	5	5	7	57	85	67	100
	Intermediate	2	4	2	4	1	2	49	90	54	100
	Graduate	7	9	5	7	0	0	67	84	79	100
	P.G. & Higher	8	13	3	5	0	0	52	82	63	100
	Total	**19**		**14**		**9**		**258**		**300**	
Occupa-tion	Business	7	5	3	2	5	4	117	89	132	100
	Teaching	2	5	1	3	0	0	34	92	37	100
	Govt. Service	3	4	2	3	0	0	67	93	72	100
	Engineering	1	9	0	0	0	0	10	91	11	100
	Preaching	0	0	7	64	4	36	0	0	11	100
	Admn. (pvt.)	3	27	0	0	0	0	8	73	11	100
	Others	3	11	1	4	0	0	22	85	26	100
	Total	**19**		**14**		**9**		**258**		**300**	
Income	⩽ Rs 2000	3	4	2	3	1	1	73	92	79	100
	2000–5000	6	6	5	5	5	5	88	84	104	100
	5000–10000	7	9	4	5	3	4	65	82	79	100
	10000–more	3	8	3	8	0	0	32	84	38	100
	Total	**19**		**14**		**9**		**258**		**300**	**100**

Among various occupations, 27% in private administrative service form maximum proportion who have contested once, in the preaching form maximum ratio (64%) of those who have contested twice, and more than twice (36%). People in the government service (93%), teaching (92%), engineering (91%) and business (89%) form comparatively higher frequencies of those who have never contested for office. None in preaching and 73% in private administration forms minimum ratios of persons who have never contested for office.

It can be concluded that nature of occupation determines authoritarianism. Those in government service, teaching, engineering and business are less authoritarian than private administrative, others and preaching occupations. For obvious reasons, people in preaching have contested maximum times for the office. Income-wise distribution does not indicate significant variation with the increasing income. 92% in the income group of Rs 2,000 p.m., 84% each in Rs 2,000–5,000 p.m. and Rs 10,000 or more income group and 82% in Rs 5,000–10,000 p.m. income group have never contested for office.

Finally, we may conclude that authoritarianism is affected by age, sect, education and occupation of an individual.

The office held by an individual forms one of the important bases for judging his level of development. As mentioned earlier important posts in a sect are usually held by prestigious people of a sect. Therefore, more the posts held, more developed an individual will be.

Our data (Table 8.9) shows that maximum of (79%) persons in the age group of 56 years and above, 53% among Sikhs, 52%, in post-graduate and higher education group, 84% in the income group of Rs 10,000 p.m. or more and 64% in the administrative service have held office.

About 44% Roman Catholics, as compared to 20% Protestants, 44% Degambars and 40% Swetambars and 53% Sikhs, have held any office. Thus, it can be concluded that Sikhs are more developed than Jains and Jains are more developed than Christians. Christians being the least authoritarian are the least developed, whereas, Sikhs are the most authoritarian and the most developed. It can also be inferred that important offices are given to highly qualified and the richest of the society.

Observations

Christians

On the basis of observations during the fieldwork, the researcher found that among the sects of Christians, Protestants as against Roman Catholics own their houses, have better houses in comparatively

Table 8.9: Have you ever held any office?

Variable	*Categories*	*Yes*		*No*		*Total*	
		'f'	*%*	*'f'*	*%*	*'f'*	*%*
Age	≤ 35	9	18	40	82	49	100
	36–45	18	22	64	78	82	100
	46–55	28	36	50	64	78	100
	56 & above	72	79	19	21	91	100
	Total	**127**	**42**	**173**	**58**	**300**	
Sect	Roman Cath.	22	44	28	56	50	100
	Protestant	10	20	40	80	50	100
	Degambar	22	44	28	56	50	100
	Swetambar	20	40	30	60	50	100
	Sikh	53	53	47	47	100	100
	Total	**127**	**42**	**173**	**58**	**300**	
Education	Basic or less	11	30	26	70	37	100
	Matriculate	21	31	46	69	67	100
	Intermediate	24	44	30	56	54	100
	Graduate	38	48	41	52	79	100
	P.G. & above	33	52	30	48	63	100
	Total	**127**	**42**	**173**	**58**	**300**	
Occupation	Business	60	45	72	55	132	100
	Teaching	13	35	24	65	37	100
	Govt. Service	29	40	43	60	72	100
	Engineering	4	36	7	64	11	100
	Preaching	6	55	5	45	11	100
	Admn (pvt.)	7	64	4	36	11	100
	Others	8	31	18	69	26	100
	Total	**127**	**42**	**173**	**58**	**300**	
Income	< 2000	27	34	52	66	79	100
	2000-5000	39	38	65	62	104	100
	5000-10000	29	37	50	63	79	100
	10000 & above	32	84	6	16	38	100
	Total	**127**	**42**	**173**	**58**	**300**	

better localities. They have well furnished houses and are leading a better life. In contrast to them, Roman Catholics are either staying in missionary houses or adjacent to the church or in old houses, mostly with their married children. They are mainly engaged in lowly paid jobs or teaching in schools, whereas Protestants along with school jobs are also engaged in college teaching (because they have their own degree college in the city). Some of them are doing some side businesses.

Jains

Among the Jain sects, Degambars were found leading a comparatively simple life although richer than Christians and Sikhs. They do not mostly have modern houses. Those engaged in business have lot of property but their lifestyle is usually simple. Swetambars have been leading modern life unlike Degambars. As they have been staying in modern houses, have modern amenities etc.

Sikhs

They are also running educational institutions. There is a traditional Gurudwara (along with others) which runs round the clock 'langar', Has large fields where crops are grown. There is a free dispensary open to all sections of society. No specific care is taken by the Sikh sects in terms of welfare institutions.

On the whole it has been observed that all the religious sects (i.e., Roman Catholics and Protestants of Christians, Degambars and Swetambars of Jains and Sikhs religious groups) are mainly engaged in religious activities and are running educational institutions as it serves the economic needs of the respective sect.

Finally, we may say that on the basis of property owned, Jains are found to be more developed than Sikhs and Christians, and Sikhs are more developed than Christians. Similarly, on the basis of family progress during last ten years, Jains are more developed than Sikhs and they are more developed than Christians, Observation on the basis of selection of occupation show that persons belonging to younger age groups are more rational. Similarly, Protestants are more rational than other sects. Among various occupations, it is observed that business class is more rational. Similarly upper income group (Rs 10,000 p.m. or more) is more developed on this statement. In selecting children's education. Younger age group, Swetambars, graduates, business class, engineering occupational group and Rs 5,000–10000 p.m. income group are more developed than their respective categories. On the statement—office held by an individual, Sikhs are more developed than Jains and Jains are more developed than Christians. It is also apparent that highly qualified persons and the richest of the society are monopolizing important offices of the society.

Persons in the age group of 36–45 years constitute highest proportion of those who have membership of clubs. Both Roman Catholic and Protestant sects may be treated as equally developed. Swetambars are more developed than Roman Catholics, among Jains, Swetambars are more developed than Degambars and Sikhs are the most developed because occupational mobility is 52% among them as compared to 31% among both Christians and Jains.

On the basis of chronic or frequent occurrence of diseases. Swetambars are more developed than Sikhs, Degambars and Protestants. Roman Catholics are the developed. On the basis of education, Christians are more developed than Sikhs and Jains.

References

Bellah, R.N. (1965), "Epilogue", *Religion and Progress in Modern Asia*. The Free Press, New York.

Gupta, K.P. (1974a), "Sociology of Indian Tradition and Tradition of Indian Sociology", *Sociological Bulletin*, 23(1) 14–43

Rao, M.S.A. (1969), "Religion and Economic Development", *Sociological Bulletin*, 28(1), 1–5.

Streeten, P. (1972), *The Frontiers of Development Studies*, Halsted, New York.

Tawney, R.H. (1926), *Religion and the Rise of Capitalism*, Harcourt, Brace & Co., New York.

Warner, W.K. (1971), "Structural Matrix of Development" in, G.M. Beal, R.C. Powers and E.C. Cloward Jr. (eds.), *Sociological Perspectives of Domestic Development*, Iowa State University Press, Ames., p. 95.

Weber, M. (1930), *Protestant Sects and the Spirit of Capitalism*, op. cit.

——— (1963), *The Sociology of Religion* (Trans.) by E. Fischoff, Beacon, Boston.

9 Summary and Conclusions

We present here a brief summary of our work in an analytical manner and then, bring out implications of the study.

Summary and Analysis

In the present study, an attempt is made to analyse the role of religious sects in social development in relation to various factors such as age, educations, occupation and income. The sample is drawn from Agra city of Uttar Pradesh, It includes Roman Catholic and Protestant, sects of Christianity, Degambar and Swetambar sects of Jainism and Sikh sect of Sikhism, Those sects have been chosen to see the differential effects of sect affiliation on social development.

Social development is viewed from two perspectives—objectively and subjectively. Objective study examines the educational status of the sect, their involvement in various occupations, occupational mobility, income, property and assets, health, membership in club, office held by member of a sect. The 'subjective' interpretation of social development, examines attitudes, motivations, feelings etc. of various sect members towards diverse aspects of social development.

Religion is one of the sources of values that affect motivation of individuals with regard to their social and economic activities (Rao, 1969:7). Here, we have tried to understand social development by analysing attitudinal differences of different sects regarding preference for children's line of education, attitude towards women's education, women's participation in jobs, regulation of daily activities by religion or by logic, attitude towards sect's help to individual or society, and attitudes towards religion, ritual performance, sect conflict and harmony and modernism. It is observed that sect affiliation and socio-economic background of a person influences social attitudes; sect affiliation helps to shape attitudes of an individual in a varied way and their effects of social development are also multifarious.

Our study shows that the traditional institutions and their value system do not hamper social development as Weber and his followers believe on the bases of both theoretical and empirical grounds. Many Indian scholars also have held that Indian religions and their associated institutions and values do not hinder social development. D.G. Karve (1968), Milton Singer (1956), S.C. Dubey (1965), M.N. Timberg (1978), R.N. Bellah (1965), M.N. Srinivas (1950), Yogendra Singh (1973) etc., have shown that traditional institutions such as caste, joint family, religious affiliation and traditional occupations do not hinder the growth of industrial entrepreneurship, rather these serve as congenial conditions for it.

Religiosity

In our study, we find that feeling about religion is observed more among the elderly people than in the younger people. Among various sects, Roman Catholics as compared to Protestants, Swetambars as compared to Degambars feel more religious. Among the three religious groups Jains feel more religious than Christians and Christians feel more religious than Sikhs. Religious feeling is maximum among preaching, administrative (private) and in business occupational categories and minimum in engineering and 'others' occupational groups.

Visit to religious places has been observed more among the elderly people, but less among the higher educational categories. Preaching class is most regular visitor to place of worship whereas engineering is least. Frequency of church attendance is more in the higher income groups. It is due to the fact that generally as income grows one tends to attach himself with religion (by the respondents during fieldwork). Secondly, economic elites are also assigned various religious duties in the organization. This is also asserted by Saral Kumar Chatterjee that "elites have monopolized development". On the whole, regular attendance to places of worship is decreasing. Shils also supports this fact, Time spent in religious centre is comparatively more, by the elderly people than the younger people, Roman Catholics spend more time than Swetambars—Sikhs spend maximum time in their religious centres. Those in the graduates and postgraduate and higher educational categories spend less time in their religious centres.

Monetary contributions made to religious organization is not affected by age. It is maximum among Jains and Sikh sects and minimum among the Protestants. Lower the level of education higher is the amount contributed. Business class contributes maximum whereas engineering minimum. Higher the income higher the amount contributed to religious organization.

Participation in religious activities increases with the increasing age. Roman Catholics as compared to Protestants and Swetarnbars as compared to Degambars participate more in religious activities. Sikhs are more religious in terms of participation in religious activities than Jains and Jains are more religious than Christians. Participation in religious activities decreases with the increase in the level of education. Nature of occupation and income also affect religious participation of an individual. Religious participation does not obstruct the way to development.

Religiosity measured in terms of religion's role in dividing the society is reported more by the higher age groups. Religious conservatism is less in Protestants, teaching and lower income groups.

Persons in the age groups of 46–55 years and $\geq$ 56 years form higher percentages (50%, 55%) of those who have scored high (median on religiosity = 18) on religiosity, It indicates that higher age groups people have shown more religiosity as compared to the lower age groups. Age and religiosity are significantly associated. Roman Catholics (56%) as compared to Protestants (36%) and Swetambars (64%) than Degambars (42%) form higher frequencies who scored high on religiosity. Protestants are more developed than Swetambars (although on some issues Degambars have reported more on religiosity than Swetambars). Here, Jains form highly religious and Sikhs least religious group (we may regard Sikhs as most developed, Christians as second most developed, and Jains as least socially developed religious groups). Education does not affect religiosity significantly.

Persons in preaching, administrative (private) and in business occupational categories have scored more on religiosity (91%, 55%, 50%) than those in engineering, government service and in teaching (45%, 39%, 38%), Variation in nature of occupation has significant association with regard to religiosity, but income has not shown any significant variation with religiosity.

Ritualism

In our study the higher age group people have been observed as more ritualistic whereas lower age group as less. Ritual performance is higher in the younger and oldest age groups. Change in ritual performance is being observed from older to younger generation. Life cycle rituals are dominantly observed among all age groups. Seasonal rituals are less likely observed among all age groups. Shils also observed that rituals and ceremonials have been simplified. Observance of various sacraments is also decreasing in all age groups. It is slightly higher in the upper age group. Marriage has been made simple in all the age groups, but birth and death rituals are performed strictly. Age and ritualism are significantly associated. (X^2 = 18.253@3d.f.,@5% level of significance). Roman Catholics than Protestants and Degambars than Swetambars are more strict in the performance of seasonal rituals. Rosary is more strictly counted among the Roman Catholics whereas prayer and fasting is strictly observed among the protestants.

Indianization of Christian churches has been taking place. Archbishop of the Archdiocese of Agra reported that Christian brides prefer saree at wedding than the wedding dress. Also, in the church prayers are recited in Hindi so as to reach to the masses. One of the pastor's wife objected on non-Christian's entry in the church with shoes. Similarly, Sikhs practice various Hindu rituals. It is also observed by Bingley that Sikh women prefer Hindu customs and beliefs.

General causes for the decline in ritual observance have been identified as lack of religious training, lack of time and money, materialism Western education, modern rationalistic outlook globalization and terrorism (only reported by Sikhs). Although Sikhism is against ritualism, still ritualism plays a dominant role in Sikh's life. This has also been supported by Singh, Most of the Sikhs and Christians have made altars in their homes to avoid wastage of time in going to place of worship (especially among Christians and Sikhs) and to show their less religious affiliation (especially among Sikhs). Both Roman Catholic and Protestant sects have been observed as equally ritualistic hence may be treated equally developed socially. Swetambars are more ritualistic than Degambars and Sikhs are least ritualistic. Here Christians form the highest frequency (54%) of those scoring high on ritualism. Jains form second largest frequency

(47%) and Sikhs form the minimum frequency (11%) in this regard. Association between sect and ritualism (X^2 = 50.002 @ 4 d.f., 5% level) has been found significant.

On the basis of high scores secured by various educational categories we do not find any significant variation regarding ritualism. Those in preaching (91%), others (77%) and administrative (pvt.) (55%) have scored high on ritualism. Variation in nature of occupation significantly affects ritualism. But income does not reflect any significant variation regarding ritualism.

Religiosity is significantly affected by ritualism (X^2 = 51.171, 1 d.f. @ .05).

Sectarianism

Sectarian feeling is observed more intense among the elderly people. Roman Catholics as compared to Protestants and Swetambars than Degambars feel more strong about their sect. Sectarian feeling is observed more among Jains. Christians feel less strong as compared to Jains and more strong as compared to Sikhs. Persons in preaching, business and in administrative (private) occupations feel more strong about their sect than those in teaching, government service, engineering and in others.

Sectarianism measured in terms of time spent for the sect is observed in varying degrees among different age, sect, education, occupation and income categories. Sectarianism seen in terms of maintaining intra-sect relations showed that Roman Catholics are more sectarian than Protestants, Degambars are more sectarian than Swetambars and Sikhs are most sectarian than Jains and Christians. Hence particularistic attitudes as against universalistic are responsible for lower rate of development.

Belief that 'sect helps in progress' is reported less by the higher educational categories and more by the higher incomes groups. This is because, those who are economically sound do not require any help from their sect—rather they are the managers of the sect therefore, they have shown a positive attitude towards sect's help in progress.

Intra-sect relations have been less intense among the younger age groups. Sect, education, occupation and income also affect intensity of intra-sect relation.

Intra-sect relations are observed less frequent in the lower age groups. Sect, education, occupation and income also affect intensity of intra-sect relations.

Inter-sect visit is more frequent among younger people, higher educational category, Protestants and Swetambars, in 'others' and engineering occupations and in upper income groups. Inter-sect relation is affected by age, income and sect affiliation but not by education and income. Various taboos relating to inter-dining, maintaining purity and pollution have been strictly maintained by sects of Jainism. Endogamy is maintained by all the sects, But it is most strictly followed among Jains than in Sikhs and less strictly among Christian sects.

Sect affiliation shapes society and vice versa is also asserted by E.Troeltsch. Those in the age group of 46–55 years and $\geq$ 56 years (51%, 63%) have secured high scores (median = 18) on sectarianism as compared to those in the age groups of $\leq$ 35 years and 36–45 years (29%, 44%). Association between age and sectarianism ($X^2 = 15.97$ at 3 d.f.) has been found significant.

Those who have scored high on sectarianism are more among Protestants (52%) than in Roman Catholics (48%), and in Swetambars than in Degambars (66%, 58%). Jains form highest frequency (62%) thus may be treated as most sectarian. Christians form second highest frequency (50%) and Sikhs form minimum frequency (35%) in this regard. On Sectarian basis Roman Catholics may be treated as more developed than Protestants and Degambars may be regarded as more developed than Swetambars. Sikhs may be treated as most developed, Christians as second most developed and Jains as least developed socially. Sect and sectarianism ($X^2 = 15.556$ @ 4 d.f.) are significantly related at 5% level of significance.

Education and sectarianism ($X^2 = 7.315$ @ 4 d.f.) are not significantly associated at 5% level of significance.

Frequencies of those who have scored high on sectarianism are comparatively higher in the occupational categories of teaching, business, preaching and in administrative (private) (51%, 58%, "91% and 91%) than in engineering, 'others' and in government service (18%, 19% and 35%). We find a significant variation regarding sectarianism ($X^2 = 38.703$ @ 6 d.f.) significantly at 5% level of significance.

Sectarianism is significantly related with religiosity ($X^2 = 69.167$ at 1 d.f. @ .05) and ritualism ($X^2 = 48.346$ at 1 d.f. @ .05).

Conflict

Reporting of conflict is more by the older age people as compared to the younger ones. Protestants form the most dissatisfied sect with their religious organization. Reporting of conflicts is affected by age, sect, education and type of occupation but not by income. Various causes reported for intra-sectoral conflicts are monetary, or organizational posts and property. Singh (1981) observes that cause of conflict is control of shrines and gurudwaras. He notices Sikh have been harmful. Corruption has increased, Religious leaders are accumulating wealth and assets. Singh finds that conflicts are ritual performance. Kabir observed that unification is on the basis of religion and culture and fragmentation due to differences in customs, political and economic interests. Shils points that priests and pastors and ministers of religion have become more assertive politically. This was also observed by the author during the fieldwork as a general complaint made by the laymen of the congregation both in Roman Catholics and Protestants. Agra does not exhibit significant incidence of inter-sect conflicts. Protestants among Christians and Swetambars among Jains have reported more about inter-sect conflicts.

Harmony

Harmony in terms of visit to other religious places of worship has been observed more in the younger age people. It varies from sect to sect. Protestants are more at harmony than the Roman Catholics and Swetambars are on some issues more harmonical than the Degambars. Christians form the most harmonical group as compared to Sikhs, Jains constitute the least harmonical group. Education and occupation also affect an individual's attitude towards harmony with other religions. Middle income groups are more in harmony than the lowest and highest income groups. On the whole a very low proportion favours visit to others' religious places.

Harmony observed in terms of people's attitudes towards permitting their children to visit other' religious places is affected by age, sect, education occupation and income. Harmony is maintained by the younger people, Sikhs, matriculates, engineering, and administrative groups, and by those in the income groups Rs 5,000–10,000 p.m. and Rs 10,000 p.m. or more.

Inter-faith harmony measured in terms of accepting and eating of Prasad from other than their own religious members is maintained more by youngest people, Protestants, administrative, and others occupational group. Educational group does not effect it. Preaching group maintains no harmony in this regard. Jains as compared to Christians and Christians as compared to Sikhs are more rigid.

Other's entry into one's own religious centre is favoured more by younger persons, Swetambars and Protestant, sects of Jains and Christians respectively, by postgraduate and above education groups, by 'others' and teaching occupational group and by lowest income group. That is harmony is more apparent among the younger age. Business class maintain maximum disharmony with other sects and religious groups.

Inter-sect participation is very low among all the categories. Persons in the lower age groups maintain relations with other sects/ religious groups more as compared to those in the higher age groups. Christians maintain more harmony than Jains and Sikhs. Graduates are more in harmony with other religious sects. Likewise, teaching and administrative occupational categories maintain more harmony, Lowest income group also maintains harmony with the society.

Those scoring high on conflict- harmony (median = 15) scale form higher proportion (56%) in the age group of ≥ 56 years than those in the age groups of ≤ 35 years, 36–45 years and 46–55 years (42%, 44%, 36%). Conflict-harmony is significantly affected by variation in age ($X^2 = 8.285$ @ 3 d.f. 5% level of significance). Roman Catholics (60%) than Protestants (40%), Swetambars (68%) than Degambars (40%) have scored high on conflict-harmony scale. Jains form highest frequency (54%) Christians form second largest frequency (50%) and Sikhs form minimum frequency (21%) in this regard. Protestants than Roman Catholics, and Degambars than Swetambars may be treated as more socially developed. Of the three religious groups, Jains may be treated as least socially developed. Christians as second highly developed and Sikhs as most developed religious groups. It reflects that sect affiliation significantly affects ($X^2 = 35.41$ @ 4 d.f. 5% level of significance) conflict-harmony, hence affecting social development of a sect. Conflict-harmony's significantly affected by variation in the level of education ($X^2 = 14.194$ d.f.). In different occupational categories, those in teaching (57%) and administrative (private) (64%) have scored high on conflict-harmony than those in government service (36%), 'others' (35%), engineering (18%), and in preaching (18%). There is no significant association between conflict-harmony and income (X^2 = 1.716 @ 3 d.f. 5% level of significance).

Conflict-harmony is significantly associated with religiosity (X^2 = 4.144 @ 1 d.f.). Association between conflict-harmony and sectarianism (X^2 = 34.703 @ 1 d.f.) is significant at 5% level of significance.

Modernism

Joint family system is favoured maximum by those in the age group of $\geq$ 56 years. Roman Catholics favoured more than the Protestants and Degambars favoured more than Swetambars. Sikhs favoured most as compared to Jains and Christians. Those in the lower educational categories favoured more than those in graduates and post-graduate and higher. Persons in business and in teaching favoured more than those in others and in engineering. Persons in higher and lower income groups favoured more the institution of joint family.

On 'purdah' systems Protestants are found as most modern than Swetambars and Sikhs. Degambars and Roman Catholics are least moderns on purdah system because they represent culture of U.P. and Rajasthan mainly. Although Christianity does not favour purdah system, Roman Catholics have favoured because they are mostly converts from lower castes of Hindu. Teaching, government service, others, and administrative occupational groups are observed as more modern. Higher income groups are more modern than the lower income groups.

Widow-remarriage is favoured more by the younger people, Swetambars, postgraduate and above other and administrative occupations and higher income groups.

Untouchability is favoured most by upper age group, Sikhs, and Jains, lowest educational group, and by the business class it is favoured more by the upper (middle) income group but less by the highest income group people.

On the issue of women's participation in jobs, age and education do not show significant variation. Christians are more modern than Sikhs and Jains. Preaching, then teaching are more modern than the other groups of occupation. Lower the income more favourable is the attitude towards women's participation in jobs. Positive value towards hard work increases with age. It is still maximum among Swetambers and Sikhs. Protestants and Degambars, are least modern on this issue. Higher the income, favourable is the attitude towards hard work. Honesty has been favoured less by the younger age group and educated persons. Christians favoured honesty more than Jains and Sikhs. Preaching, teaching and government service groups have favoured honestly more than others. People's positive attitude towards science and technology has been reported more favorably among the younger age. Protestants and Sikhs are more modern than other sects. More of higher qualified people have shown a positive attitude towards science and technology. Engineering and government service class are more modern whereas preaching is least modern on 'sciences help in progress'. Those in upper income groups have reported more on modernism.

Younger people are more rational in terms of selection of their occupation. Christians are less rational than Sikhs and they are lesser rational than Jains. Less qualified persons are more rational than the more qualified. Business and engineering classes are more rational than other occupational groups. Rationality increases with income.

Rationality (rational calculation future) has been found more in 46–55 years and least among the upper age group. Protestants and Swetambars preferred technical education more than Degambars. Christians preferred medical educations, Jains preferred commerce as line of education for their children. Postgraduate and above preferred both technical and medical education. Basic and below education group preferred commerce. Line of children's education is also affected by occupation and income.

Religion dominates the life of elderly persons more than the younger people. Swetambars are found as more logical than Degambars and Catholics are more logical than Protestants. Sikhs are guided more by religion than Jains and Christians. Christians are more logical than Jains and they are more logical than Sikhs.

Modernism has been found more in the higher education group. Modernism is significantly related with occupation (Table 7.12, $X^2 = 69.198$). Income of an individual also affects his modern/rational outlook. X^2 between income and modernism (Table 7.13) is 35.761.

A change in attitudinal modernism has been observed from higher to lower age group people, from traditionalism to modernism. Protestants are more modern than Roman Catholics and Swetambars are more modern as compared to Degambars. Christians form most developed and Jains are found as the least modern thus, the least developed. Similarly, teaching and engineering occupations are more modern than others. Business occupational category is the least modern. Income also affects modernism.

Age does not reflect any significant variation with regard to modernism (X^2 = 3.047@ 3 d.f., 5% level of significance).

Protestants form larger frequency (96%) as compared to Roman Catholics (90%) and Swetambars reflect higher frequency (36%) than Degambars (8%) of those who have scored high (median=18) on modernism, Christians form maximum ratio (93%) of those who have scored high on modernism. Sikhs form the second largest ratio (26%) and Jains form minimum frequency (22%) in this regard. Hence Protestants may be regarded as more developed as compared to Roman Catholics and Swetambars can be treated as more developed than Degambars. Christians may be regarded as most developed, Sikhs as second developed, Jains as least developed socially. Sect and modernism is significantly associated with each other (X^2 = 135.969@4 d.f. 5% level of significance).

Persons in lower educational categories form lower frequencies (16%, 18%) of those scoring high on modernism. Education has significant association with modernism (X^2 = 73.702 @ 4 d.f.). Indifferent occupational categories, those in business form minimum frequency (22%) of persons scoring high on modernism. Modernism is significantly affected by nature of occupation (X^2 = 69.198 @ 6 d.f. 5% level).

Those in the lower income groups, i.e., Rs 2,000 per month and Rs 2,000–5,000 per month form higher frequencies (63%, 59%) of those who have scored high on modernism as compared to those in the income groups of Rs 5,000–10,000 per month and Rs 10,000 or more per month (24%, 29%). Variation in level of income indicates significant changes with regards to modernism (X_2 = 35.761 @ 4 d.f. and .05 level).

Modernism is significantly associated with religiosity (X^2 = 5.413 @ 1 d.f.). Modernism and ritualism are not significantly related (X^2 = 0.183 at 1 d.f. @ 05). Modernism is not significantly related with sectarianism (X^2 = .062 at 1 d.f. @ 05). Modernism is significantly associated with conflict-harmony (X^2 = 9.121 at 1 d.f. @ 05%).

Objective Indicators

Several objective indicators of social development have also been examined in case of the different sects under study.

Both Roman Catholics (68%) and Protestants (64%) have their own houses in nearly equal proportions. Degambars (92%) own houses in greater numbers than Swetambars (78%). Jains (85%) own more houses than Sikhs (77%) and Sikhs own more houses than Christians (66%). Agricultural land is owned more by Sikhs (18%) than by Christians (11%) and Jains (7%). Sikhs (17%) own plots in large number than Christians (15%) and Jains own more shops (15%) than (13%) Sikhs (13%) have car nearly equal (29%) to Jains (28%) Christians (17%) own less number or cars (11%). Those who do not own any property are maximum among Christians (19%) then among Sikhs (6%) and Jains (4%). Jains are richer than Sikhs and Sikhs are richer than Christians.

Educationwise, Protestants are more developed than the Roman Catholics and Degambars are more developed than Swetambars and Sikhs are more developed than Jains and less developed than Christians.

Protestants are more in business than Roman Catholics and Swetambars are more than Degambars, and Sikhs are in between two religious groups, i.e., Jains and Christians.

Roman Catholics are more in government services than Protestants and Degambars are more than Swetambars. Sikhs are in between the two. Christians and Sikhs are in larger number in government services than Jains.

Roman Catholics are more in teaching than the Protestants and Degambars and more than the Swetambars, Sikhs constitute the bridge between the Jains and the Christians. Christians are more in teaching than Sikhs and Jains.

Christians are involved more in miscellaneous occupation than Sikhs and Jains. Jains are more in engineering occupation than Christians and Sikhs.

Protestants are more in administrative (private) services than Sikhs. Jains do not contribute to this occupational category.

Jain saints were not available during fieldwork because they do not have a permanent stay at any place unlike Christian and Sikh saints.

Jains are involved more in profit making jobs than Sikhs and Christians.

Occupational mobility is observed more among Protestants than Roman Catholics; Swetambars are more developed than Degambars, Sikhs have shown maximum mobility whereas both Jains and Christians are equally developed. Next to Sikh are Protestants.

Protestants are richer than Roman Catholics; Swetambars are wealthier than Degambars. Sikhs fall in between Jains and Christians.

Healthwise Protestants are more developed than Roman Catholics; Swetambars are more developed than Degambar and Sikhs are more developed than Christians and less developed than Jains.

Club membership indicated that Protestants are as developed as Roman Catholics; and Swetambars are more developed than Degambars and Sikhs are most developed among all. Persons in the higher income groups have more membership in club.

Protestants have observed more progress of the family (material) than Roman Catholics, Swetambars have observed more than Degambars. Sikhs have observed more than Christians and less than Jains.

Protestants have held offices more than the Roman Catholics and Degambars have held more than Swetambars and Sikhs have held more than both Christians and Jains. Sikhs are more developed than Jains and Jains are more developed than Christians. Persons in the higher education and income groups have held offices more than the other educational and income groups. Important offices are held either by the higher educated (especially among Christians). Important decisions of the sect are taken by the economic elites of the sect. They are monopolizing important positions and leading to change in the sect.

Authoritarianism is found more among the elderly people. Sect, education, occupation and income of an individual has shown different degrees of authoritarianism.

Desire to have authority over religious organization is more among Roman Catholics than in Protestants, among Degambars than in Swetambars. Sikhs are least developed, Jains are more developed as compared to Christians and less developed than Sikhs. Higher authoritarianism is shown by Roman Catholics and Degambars show their aspiration to development. Sikhs sect has indicated higher authoritarianism because of material gains are thus more developed.

Protestants are more developed than Roman Catholics; Swetambars are more developed than Degambars and Sikhs are the most dynamic sect.

Roman Catholics are less profit oriented than Protestants, Swetambars are less profit oriented than Degambars and Sikhs basis of occupation selection is other than profit or inheritance.

Roman Catholics are lesser developed than Protestants, Swetambars are lesser developed than Degambars and Sikhs are least developed in profit motive orientation.

Healthwise, Jains are more developed than Sikhs and Christians.

Occupational mobility is maximum among Sikhs compared with Jains and Christians.

Propertywise Jain are more developed than Sikhs and Christians. Incomewise Jains are the wealthwise group in comparison with Sikhs and Christians.

Implications of the Study

Theoretical

The problem related to role of religious sects in social development cannot be understood only in terms of religious ethics causing or hindering economic development, nor is the study of economic development sufficient to understand the process of development. Rather, we have tried to take into account several other factors such as social and psychological, which may have significant effects upon the process of social development. The social-psychological theorists have concentrated on changes in motivations and values of individuals as forces of social change (Pandey, 1985: 264). It seems relevant to talk of the changing attitudes and the factors determining these, vis-à-vis, sect affiliation of an individual and their comparative position in the level of social development. Therefore, a comparative study, here, of Roman Catholic and Protestant, Degambar and Sawatmbar, and Sikh sects provide a wide base for analysis.

Several scholars have touched upon the material aspects of development while ignoring the psychological aspect. In our work we have examined the role of religious sects in its social and psychological aspects. A sects achievement on various indicators would determine their level of development.

We find that the Weberian assumption holding Indian religions not conducive to capitalistic development, does not apply in the actual situation. In our study Protestant, Degambar, Swetambar, and Sikh sects are seen engaged in entrepreneurial activities, though varying in degree. In India it is not the Protestant sect which is most developed economically, but Swetambars and Degambars form the economically most developed sects.

On development scale of different sects have shown a difference as attitudes of different sects on various aspects are different. In our study we have seen how difference of a particular religious group differ from each other and how a specific religious group differs from each other and how a specific religious group differ from the other and the factors responsible for shaping the attitudes.

From this point of view it emerges that development programme should also take into account the psychological factor.

We think that the role or religious sect in the process of social development should, as in our study, be understood against its socio-cultural and historical context. Along with studying the religious groups (sects) as a whole in the process of development, individual attributes and resources should also be analysed as how individual variations account for varying degree of development. Also, how a sect interacts with the society of which it is an integral part and how it functions as a community.

Methodological Implications

There has been two approaches for the study of social development (1) Webarian related to role of religious ethics as conducive to economic development of a particular sect, especially Protestant, and (2) advocating that Hinduism and other Asian religions lack ethics which may cause economic development. Both these approaches have certain limitations as we have seen, and hence the two should be combined in one's study.

Our work suggests that role of religious sects in socio-economic development cannot be understood without proper understanding of factors other than religious ethics. Other factors like materialistic outlook, high prices, worldliness scientific perspective, increasing standards and hereditary occupations are responsible for occupational mobility. Therefore, we think that development of a sect in general and individual in particular has to be analysed contextually.

Moreover, it would be useful to adopt the comparative method of study.

References

Bellah, R.N., (1965), *Religion and Progress in Modern Asia.*, The Free Press, New York.

Dube, S.C., (1965), "Cultural Problems in the Economic Development of India", in *Religions and Progress in Modern Asia*, (Ed.) R.N. Belah, The Free Press, New York.

Eisenstadt, S.M. (1966), *Modernization, Protest, and Change*, Englewood Cliffs, New Jersey, Prentice Halls.

Huntington, S.P. (1968), *Political Order in Changing Societies*, University Press, New Haven.

Karve, D.G., (1968), *Hindu Society an Interpretation.* Ed., Deshmukh, Poona.

Lerner, D. (1958), "Modernization: Social Aspects", in *The Passing of the Traditional Society: Modernization the Middle East*, The Free Press.

Singh, Yogendra. (1973), *Modernization of Indian Tradition: A Systematic Study of Social Change*, Thomson Press, Delhi.

Singer, Milton (1956), "Cultural Values in India's Economic Development", The Annals of the American Academy of Political and Social Science, May, 81–82.

Srinivas, M.N., (1958), "Mobility in the Caste System," in Milton Singer and B.S. Cohen (eds.) *Structure and Change in Indian Society,* Aldine CHICAGO.

Srinivas, M.N., Karve, D.G. and Singer, Milton (1958), "India's Cultural Values and Economic Development: A Discussion", *Economic Development and Cultural Change*, Vol. 7, No.1.

Timberg, M.N., (1978), *The Marwari's: From Traders to Industrialists*, Vikas Pub. House, New Delhi.

Bibliography

Primary Sources

Aukland Paper, British Museum.

Baptismal and Marriage Registers of the Methodist Church of Agra from 1914–1990, Central Methodist Church, Agra.

Baptismal and Marriage Registers of the Cathedral of Agra from 1980–1990. The Cathedral Agra, (unpublished).

Baptismal and Marriage Registers of the Baptist Church of Agra from 1943–1990, Baptist Church, Agra.

Chelmsford Papers, India Office Library.

Political Consultations, Foreign Dept., National Archives of India, New Delhi.

Report by Borghi (1841), Agra Archives, The Cathedral, Agra, 15 December, Report by Joachim of St. Anatolia, Agra Archives, The Cathedral Agra.

Secret Consultations, Foreign Department, National Archives of India, New Delhi.

Books, Articles, Archival Documents and Reports

Adhikari, O. (1945), *Sikhs Homeland Through Hindu-Muslim Sikh Unity*, Popular Prakashan, Bombay.

Agarwal, B.C. (1972), "Diksha Ceremony in Jainism: An Analysis of its Socio-Political Ramifications". *Eastern Anthropologist*, 25 (1) 13–20.

——— (1974) "Changing Patterns of Jati Among the Jains of M.P.", in *Tribe, Caste and Peasantry* (eds), B.C. Agarwal and K.S. Mathur, Ethnographic and Folk Culture Society, Lucknow.

———(1977), *Cultural Contours of Religion and Economics in Hindu Universe*, National Publishing House, New Delhi.

Alice, P.J. (1982), *The Roman Catholic Mission in Agra from 1781–1947*, St. Joseph's Printing School, Agra.

Alport, G.W. (1952), *The Individual and His Religion*, McMillan, New York.

Alzog, Rev. J.D.D. (1882), *Manual of Universal Church History*, Vol IV, Third Period (A.D. 1648–1878), Trans. by the Rev. F.J. Fabisch and The Rev. Thomas, S. Byrne, M.H. Gill and Son, Dublin.

Andreski, S. (ed.) (1983), *Max Weber on Capitalism, Bureaucracy and Religion*, George Allen and Unwin, Boston.

Andreski, S. (1984), *Max Weber's Insights and Errors*, Routledge and Kegan Paul, London.

Annual Guide and Gazetteer (1841), The Bengal and Agra, Vol. I, William Rusthom & Co., Calcutta.

Archer, J.C. (1946), *The Sikhs*, Princeton New Jersey.

Aron, R. (1967), *Industrial Society: Three Essays on Ideology and Development*, Praeger, New York.

Ashby, P. (1963), *History and Future of Religious Thought*, Prentice Hall, New York.

Asiatic Researches XI, pp 197–293.

Badley, Bishop B.T. (1931) *Visions and Victories in Hinduism: Story of the Mission Stations of the Methodist Episcopal Church in Southern Asia*, Diamond Jubilee Edition, Methodist Publishing House, Madras.

Banerjee, I. (1942) "A Short History of the Origin and Rise of the Sikhs" *Indian Historical Quarterly*, Vol., 18, Brown W. Norman.

———(1972), *Evolution of the Khalsa*, Calcutta.

Barth, A. (1969), *The Religions of India* (Trans.) Rev. J. Wood, S. Chand and Co., Delhi.

Bellah, R.N. (1963). "Reflections on the Protestant Ethic Analogy in Asia", *The Journal of Social Issues*, 19: 52–60.

———(1964) "Religious Evolution", *American Sociological Review*, 29 (63): 358–74.

——— (ed.) (1965), *Religion and Progress in Modern Asia*, Free Press, Max Weber, New York.

Benedix, R. (1977), *An Intellectual Portrait of Max Weber*, University of California Press, Berkeley.

Berger, S.D. (1971), "The Sects and the Breakthrough into the Modern World", *Sociological Quarterly* 12: 486–99.

Bharati, A. (1971) "Hinduism and Modernization", in Spencer R.F. (ed.), *Religion and Change in Contemporary Asia*, University of Minnesota Press, Minneapolis, Oxford University Press, Bombay.

Bhardwaj, K. and Kaviraj S. (eds) (1989), *Perspectives on Capitalism: Max Keynes, Schumpeter, and Weber*, Sage Publications, New Delhi.

Bhattacharya, N. and Dutta L. Bela (1973), "A Study of Rituals with Reference to Sex, Age, Segments", *Journal of Social Research*, 16 (1): 72–81

Bhowmick, P.K. (1977) "Cultural Continuity in Social Economic Change: A Study in Religious Complexes in the Rural Setting", *Journal of Social and Economic Studies*, 5(2): 185–99.

Bingley, A.H. (1984), *Sikhs: Religio-Political History and Origin of Sikhism, Sacraments, and Rituals, Festivals and Customs*, Sumeet Publications, New Delhi.

Bose, N.K. (1975), *Structure of Hindu Society*, (Trans.) from Bengali by Andre Beteille, Orient Longman, New Delhi.

Brown, M.J. (1788) *History of the Origin and Progress of the Sikhs in Indian Tracts*, London.

Buhler, G. (1963), *On the Origin of the Indian Brahma Alphabet* (Ed. 3) Book, Chowkhamba Sanskrit Series Office, Varanasi.

Catholic Directory of India (1935, 1956–1980, 1990), St. Paul Publications.

Catholic Encylopaedia, Vol XIII, New York, The Encylopaedia Press, Inc. New York, p. 789.

Catholic Reference Book (1964–65).

Census of India (1861).

——— (1891), Vol XVI, Part-1 1994, Allahabad.

——— (1951), Agra District Census Handbook, (1955).

Census of India Agra City Urban Agglomerate (1971) and (1981).

Chako, Arun (1986) "Change in Church Perspectives", *News Time*, 27 January.

Chandra, Bipan (1964), "The Problems of Poverty and Indian National Leadership" *Enquiry*, 2: 54–106.

Chatterjee, S.K. (1981) "A Note on the Study of Religion and Society" *Religion and Society*, 28 (3) September.

Choudhary, Roy P.C. (1956), *Jainism in Bihar*, Indu Roy Choudhary, Patna.

Cole, W. Owen and Sambhi, P.S. (19), *The Sikhs: Their Religious Beliefs and Practices*, Vikas, New Delhi.

Collins, R. (1980) "Weber's Last Theory of Capitalism: A Systematization", *American Sociological Review*, Dec. 45: 925–42

——— (1985), *Three Sociological Traditions*, Oxford University Press, New York.

——— (1986a), *Max Weber*, Vol. 3, Sage Publications, Beverly Hills, London

Cook, H.T. (1975), *The Sikh Wars: The British Army in the Punjab 1845–1849*, Thompson Press, New Delhi.

Cort, John (1986), "Recent Descriptive Accounts of the Contemporary Jains: A Review Essay", *Man in India*, 66(2): 180–86, June.

Court, M.H. (1985), *History of the Sikhs* (Trans.), Amar Prakashan

Cunningham, J.D. (1915), *History of the Sikhs*, S. Chand, New Delhi.

Daily Telegraph (1986), "Christianity".

Das, S.R. (1962), *Commission Report on Grievances of the Sikhs*, Govt. of India Press, Delhi.

Das. Veena (1976), "The Uses of Liminality: Society and Cosmos in Hinduism", *Contributions to Indian Sociology*, (NS), 10(2).

Datta, B.N. (1954), *Swami Vivekanand: Patriot Prophet*, Nav Bharat Publishers, Calcutta.

Dawson, C. (1949), *Religion and Culture, Clifford Lectures*, Sheed & Ward London.

Demant, V.A. (1952), *Religion and the Decline of Capitalism*, Faber and Faber, London.

Dhami, Sadhu Singh (1943), *The Sikhs and Their Religion: A Struggle for Democracy*, K.D. Society, Vancouver.

Dhillon, G.S. (1989), *Researches in Sikh Religion and History*, Sumeet Prakashan, Chandigarh.

D'Souza, Rev. D. (1982), *The Growth and the Activities of the Catholic Church in North India: 1757–1858*, St. Anne's Friary, Mangalore.

Dube, S.C. (1977), "Oral Traditions and Cultural Development", *East Asian Cultural Studies*, 16 (14): 71–76.

——— (1965a), "Cultural Problems in the Economic Development of India", in *The Economic Religion and Progress in Modern Asia*, (ed.) R.N. Bellah, Free Press, New York.

——— (1988), *Modernization and Development*, Vistaar Publications, New Delhi.

Duncan, J. and Derret, M. (1968), *Religion, Law and the State in India*, Faber and Faber, London.

Eisenstadt, S.M. (ed.) (1968), *Protestant Ethic and Modernization: A Comparative View*, Basic Book New York.

Etzioni, A (1966), *Studies in Social Change*, Holt Rinehart and Winston, New York.

Encyclopedia of Religion and Ethics, (1926), (ed.) James Hastings, T&T Clark, Edinburgh.

Farzuhar, J.N. (1967), *Modern Religious Movements in India*, Munshiram Manoharlal, Delhi.

First & Eighth Five-Year Plans, Planning Commission, Government of India, New Delhi.

Fisch, Jorg (1985), "A Pamphlet War on Christian Mission in India: 1807–1809", *Journal of Asian History*, 19: 24.

Fischer, E. and Jain, J. (1977), *Art and Rituals : 2500 Years of Jainism*, Sterling, Delhi.

Franciscan Annals (1918), April (p. 128)

——— (1918), Vol., IX May, No. 5: 167

——— (1918), No. V., 38, 128, 167

——— (1947), Vol. LXXXXIII (1): 4 Feb., Agra.

Frishby, D., (1987), "The Ambiguity of Modernity : Simmel and Weber" in *Max Weber and His Contemporaries* (eds.) Mommsen, W.J. and Jurgen, O., The German Historical Institute, London.

Gazetteer of the North. West Provinces (1876), IV, Part-I, Agra Division.

Gazetteer, Vol. VII, 1884.

Gazetteer, Agra (1905), VIII (65), 68, 72. (1921): 68, 142.

Gazetteer. U.P. Distt. (1965), Agra.

Gibbs, M.E. (1972), *The Anglican Church in India*, 1600–1970, ISPCK, Delhi.

Giddens, A. (1977), "Marx, Weber and the Development of Capitalism" in A. Giddens, *Studies in Social and Political Theory*, Hutchinson, London.

Gill. P.S. (1973), *Trinity of Sikhism: Philosophy, Religion, State*, New Academic Publishing Co, Jalandhur.

Gisbert, P. (1975), *Fundamentals of Sociology*, Orient Longmans, New Delhi.

Glenn M.V. (1962), *Sociology of Religion*, McGraw Hill, London.

Glenn, N.D. and Hayland, R. (1967), "Religious Preference and Worldly Success: Some Evidence from National Surveys", *American Sociological Review*, Vol. 32 (1): 73–85.

Gopalan (1973), *Outlines of Jainism*, Wiley Eastern Pvt. Ltd., New Delhi

Government Allegations Against the Sikhs (1922), Hyderabad.

Graf, F.W. (1987), "Friendship Between Experts: Notes on Weber and Troeltsch" in *Max Weber and His Contemporaries*.

Gupta, H.R. (1952), *History of the Sikhs*, Vol. 1, Simla.

——— (1973), *History of the Sikh Gurus*. U.C. Kapur & Sons, New Delhi.

——— (1978), *History of the Sikhs, Evolution of Sikh Confederacies*, Munshiram Manoharlal, New Delhi.

——— (1989), *The Sikh Gurus*, Vol., 1, Delhi.

Gupta, K.P. (1971), "A Theoretical Approach to Hinduism and Modernization in India", *Indian Journal of Sociology*, 2 (1): 59–91.

——— (1974a). "Sociology of Indian Tradition and Tradition of Indian Sociology", *Sociological Bulletin*, 23(1): 14–43.

——— (1974b), "Religious Evolution and Social Change in India: A Study of the Rama Krishna Mission Movement", *Contributions to Indian Sociology, (N.S.)*, 8: 25–49.

——— (1978), "Religion and Development: A Non-Sociological Perspective", *Spectra of Anthropological Progress*, Vol. 1.

Guru Nanak Quincentenary Celebrations Society (1969), Sikhism, Punjabi University, Patiala.

Hagen, E. E. (1962), *On the Theory of Social Change: How Economic Growth Begins*, The Dorsey Press Inc, Homewood, Illinois.

Handbook of Diocese of Lucknow (1900). (ed.) G.A. Ford.

Henry, Court (1959), *History of the Sikhs*, Sushil Gupta, Calcutta.

Hole, Rev. C. (1896), "The Early History of the Church Missionary Society for Africa and the East to the end of A.D. 1814", Church Missionary Society, Salisbury Square, London.

Holman, S.C. (1950), *What God Hath Wrougth*, The Book Room, Boston.

Hopkins, E.W. (1895), *The Religions of India*, Ginn & Co., Boston.

Hoselitz, Bert (1960), *The Sociological Aspects of Economic Growth*. Glencoe.

Howe, R.H. (1978), "Max Weber's Elective Affinities", *American Journal of Sociology*, Vol., 84: (366–85).

Hudson, Winthrop's (1949)," Puritainism and the Spirit of Capitalism", *Church History*, No. 1: 89.

Hughes, A.W. (1871), *Outlines of Indian History*, Bell and Daily, London.

Huntington, S.P. (1968), *Political Order in Changing Societies*, University Press, New Haven.

Imperial Gazetteers (1905) United Province, Agra Division, Oxford University Press, Oxford (1908).

Indian Catholic Reference Book (1964), The Catholic Association of Bombay.

India (1991) A Reference Annual, Publication Division, Ministry of Information & Broadcasting, Govt. of India, New Delhi.

Jain, J. (1977), "Jain Ritual and Space" in, *Urban Space and Ritual*, N. Guschow and T. Sieverts (eds), Darmstadt.

——— (1979), "Rathyatra: the Charot Festival of the Jains," *Art and Archaeology Research Papers*, 16: 15–18.

Johnstone, R.L. (1975), *Religion and Society in Interaction*.

John (1986), "Recent Descriptive Accounts of the Jains, a Review Essay", *Man in India*, 66(2): 180–186.

Jones, T.K., Jr. (1963), *Our Mission Today*, World Outlook Press, New York.

Joshi, P.C. (1989), "Religion, Class Conflict and Emancipation Movements", *Social Action*, 39(2): 162.

Kapp, W.K. (1963), *Hindu Culture, Economic Development and Economic Planning in India*, Asia Publishing House, Bombay.

Kapoor, R.A. (1987), *Sikh Separatism*, Vikas Publishing House, New Delhi.

Kariyil, A. (1988), "Religion and Material Development", *Journal of Dharma*, XIII Oct.–Nov. (312–327).

Karve, D.G. (1968), *Hindu Society: A Interpretation* (ed.) Deshmukh, Poona.

Khurana, G. (1985), *British Historiography on the Sikh Power in the Punjab*, Mansell, London.

Kohli, S.S. (1975), *Sikh Ethics*, Munshiram Manoharlal, New Delhi.

Lee, Robert and Marty, M.E. (eds.) (1964), *Religion Social Conflict*, Oxford University Press, New York.

Lerner (1958), "Modernization: Social Aspects", *The Passing of Traditional Society: Modernizing the Middle East*, The Free Press, New York.

Lewis, W.A. (1965), *Theory of Economic Growth*, George Allen and Unwin, London.

Loomis, C.P. and Loomis, Z.K. (1969), "Socio-Economic Change and the Religious Factor in India", *An Indian Symposium of Views on Max Weber*, Affiliated East West Press, New Delhi.

Lowie, R.H. (1936), *Primitive Religion*, Routledge & Sons, London.

Macauliffe, M.A. (1909), *The Sikh Religion*, Oxford University Press.
Madras Catholic Directory, (1863, 1864 and 1909).
Majumdar, R.C. (1965) *Swami Vivekanand: A Historical Review*, General Printers, Calcutta.
Malefitz A.D.W. (1968), *Religion and Culture: An Introduction to Anthropology of Religion*, Mac Millan, New York
Mandelbaum, D.G. (1970a) "Curing and Religion in South Asia", *Journal of the Indian Anthropological Society* 5, (1–2): 171–86.
——— (1970 b), *Society in India: Change an Continuity*, 2 Vols. University of California Press, Berkeley.
Marenco, E.K. (1976), *The Transformation of Sikh Society*, Heritage Publishers, New Delhi.
Marshall, G. (1982), *In Search of the Spirit of Capitalism*, Hutchinson, London (123).
Marx, K. (1967), *Capital*, International Publisher, New York.
Mathur, S.S. (1979) *A Sociological Approach to Indian Education*, Vinod Pustak Mandir, Agra.
Mcleod, W.H. (1968), *Gurunanak and the Sikh Religion*, The Clarendon Press, Oxford.
——— (1975), *The Evolution of the Sikh Community*, Prentice Hall, Delhi.
McNeill, John (1954), *The History and Character of Calvinism*, Oxford University Press, New York.
Menon, N.C. (1976), "Priests Group in Dock for Fund Misuse". *The Hindustan Times*, New Delhi.
Misra, P.K (1973), "Ritual: A Case for Continuity and Change" in K.S. Mathur (ed.). *Studies of Social Change*, Ethnographic and Folk Culture Society, Lucknow.
Misra, R.L. (1972), "The Jains in an Urban Setting: The Ascetics and the Laity and the Jains of Mysore City", *Bulletin of the Anthropological Survey of India*, 21 (1–2) (1–68).
Misra, Vikas (1962), *Hinduism and Economic Growth*, Oxford University Press, Bombay, p. 206.
Momsen, W.J. and Osterhammel, J. (eds.) (1987) *Max Weber and His Contemporaries*, The German Historical Institute, London.
Munch, R. (1988), *Understanding Modernity*, Routledge, London.
Myrdal, G. (1986), *Asian Drama*, (3 vols.), Pantheon Books, New York.
Nag, A.K. (1973) "Christianity and the Role of Church in Mizoram", *The North Eastern Affairs, 2(1)*.
Narang, G.C. (1956), *Transformation of Sikhism*, New Book Society of India, New Delhi.
Narayan, S. (1974a), "Pilgrimage to Kashi", *Journal of Social Research*, 17 (1) (20–22).
National Convention of Catholics 2–5 June, 1989.

Nvaskar B. (1971) *Capitalists without Capitalism: The Jains of India and the Quakers of the West*, Fort C.T. Greenwood.

Oddie, G.A. (1969), "Protestant Missionary, Caste and Social Change in India, 1850–1914", *Indian Economic and Social History Review*, Vol. 6, 259–91.

Pai, D.A. (1928), *Religious Sects in Ancient India*, Eastern Book Linkers, Delhi

Pandey, A. N. (1977), "Modernization and Religious Values" in Romesh Thapar (ed) *Tribe Caste and Religion in India*, Mac Millan, New Delhi,

Pandey, R. (1985), *Sociology of Development*, Mittal Publications, Delhi.

Parsons, T. (1970), "Evolutionary Universals in Society" in *Societies: Evolutionary and Comparative Perspectives*, Englewood Cliffs, New Jersey.

Parvathmma, C. (1977), "Religion and Social Change: A Study of Tradition and Change in Virasavisim", in *Dimensions of Social Change* (eds.) M.N. Srinivas, Allied, Bombay (Reprint 1978).

Patriot (1986), New Delhi, 2 February.

Pimpley, P.N., Singh K.P. and Mahajan, A. (eds.) (1989), *Social Development*, Rawat Publications, Jaipur.

Poggi, G. (1983), *Calvinism and the Capitalistic Spirit, Max Weber's Protestant Ethic*, McMillan.

Polhacumry, T. Archbishop (1961), *The Church of Independent India*. The Examiner Press, Bombay.

Ramachandra, P. (1990), "Profile of Visitors to Place of Worship", *Social Action*, Jan-Mar 40 (1).

Rao, M.S.A. (1969), "Religion and Economic Development", *Sociological Bulletin*, 18(1) (1–15).

Roy, Niranjan (1970), *The Sikh Gurus and the Sikh Society*, Punjabi University, Patiala.

Robert, L. and Marty, M.E. (eds) (1964), *Religion and Social Conflict*, Oxford University Press, New York.

Rudolph, L.L. and Rudolph H.S. (1967), *The Modernity of Tradition: Political Developments in India*, Orient Longmans, Bombay.

Runciman, W.G. (ed.) (1985), *Max Weber*, Cambridge University Press London. Ch-I.

——— (ed.) (1978), *Weber: Selections in Transition* (trans.), E. Mathews, Cambridge University Press, Cambridge (1935).

Saberwal, S. (1971) "Secularism: A Threat to Religion" *Bulletin of the Christian Institute for the Study of Religion and Society*, 13(3).

——— (1977) "Status and Entrepreneurship: the Ramgrahia Case", *Dimensions of Social Change*, op. cit. pp. 155–168.

——— (1976), *Mobile Men: Limits to Social Change in Urban Punjab*, Vikas, New Delhi.

Sahani, R.R. (1922), *The Gurdwara Reform Movement and the Sikh Awakening*, Deshsewak Book Agency, Jalandhar.

——— (1965), "Struggle for Reform in Sikh Shrines", *Sikh Itihas* (ed) Ganda Singh, Amritsar

Saran., A.K. (1963), "Hinduism and Economic Development in India", *Archives de Sociologie des Religious* 15: 87–94.

——— (1969b), "Religion and Society: The Hindu View", *International Yearbook of the Sociology of Religion*, 41–55.

Samuelson, K. (1961), *Religion and Economic Action* (ed.) by D.C. Coleman, Stockholm.

Schluchter, W. (1981) *The Origin and Growth of Religion* (trans) H.J. Rose, Methuen, London.

Schoffeleers, M and Meizers, D. (1978), *Religion, Nationalism and Economic Action*, Van Garum, Assen, The Netherlands.

Schubring, W. (1966), *The Religion of the Jains.* Translated from German by Amulya Chandrasen and T.C. Burke, Sanskrit College, Calcutta.

Schumpeter, J.A. (1949),*The Theory of Economic Development*, Cambridge, Mass.

——— (1987) *Max Weber and His Contemporaries,* (eds) Mommsen, W.J. and Jurgen, O., The German Historical Institute, London.

Selbie, W.B. (1926), *The Psychology of Religion*, Clarendon Press, Oxford.

Shah, G.J. (1932), *Jainism In North India*, Longman Green & Co.

Shils, E. (1987) "Max Weber: The Enduring Contemporary", in *Max Weber and his Contemporaries*, (eds) Mommsen, W.J. and Jurgen, O., The German Historical Institute, London.

Stevensen (1915), *The Heart of Jainism*, Hemphrey, OUP, Bombay.

Sharma, S.L. (1974), "Social Correlates of Gurudwara Participation", *Journal of Social Research*, 17(2).

Singer, Milton. (1968a), *Tradition and Change in India*, (ed.) B. Cohn and M. Singer, New York.

——— (1972), *When a Great Tradition Modernizes: An Anthropological Approach to Indian Civilization*, Preager, New York.

Singh, D. (1968) *Indian Bhakti Tradition and Sikh Gurus*, Lyall Book Depot, Bhopal.

Singh, F., Singh T., Singh, G.B.S., Singh, J.P. and Singh, S. (1969) *Sikhism*, Punjabi University Patiala.

Singh, Gurmukh Nihal (ed.) (1969), *Guru Nanak: His Life, Time and Teachings*, National Publishing House, New Delhi.

Singh, G. (ed.) (1962), *Early European Accounts of the Sikhs*, R.K. Maitra Calcutta.

Singh, Harbans (1964) *The Heritage of the Sikhs*, Asia Publishing House, Bombay.

——— (1969), *Gurunanak and Origins of the Sikh.* Asia Publishing House, Bombay.

Singh, H. (1966) *Guru Gobind Singh*, The Guru Gobind Singh Foundation, Chandigarh.

——— (ed.) (1975), *Perspectives on Guru Nanak*, Punjabi University, Patiala.

——— (1983), *Religions of India*, Clarion Books, New Delhi.

Singh, Jagjit (1981), *The Sikh Revolution*, Bahri Publications, New Delhi.

Singh, Kushwant (1966), *A History of The Sikhs*, 2, Vols., Oxford University Press, Delhi.

Singh, Trilochan (1990), "Ritualism Vs. Reality", *The Sikh Review*, 38 (441) 16–17).

——— (1967), *Guru Teg Bahadur*, Gurudawara Prabandhak Committee. Sis Ganj, Chandni Chowk, Delhi.

———(1986), 'Need of Renewal and Reform in Present Working of Sikh Religious, Cultural and Political Institutions", *Sikh Review*, 34 (393) Sept.

——— (1986) "Crumbling of Sikh Values", *Sikh Review* 34 (394): 21–22 Oct.

Singh, Yogendra (1973), *Modernization of Indian Tradition: A Systematic Study of Social Change*, Thomson Press, Delhi.

——— (1987), "Development in India; Continuities and Contradictions", in K.S. Shukla (ed.), *The Other Side of Development*, Sage, New Delhi.

——— (1989c) "Relevance of Max Weber for the Understanding of Indian Reality" in *Perspectives on Capitalism, Marx, Keynes, Schumpeter and Weber* (eds.), Krishna Bhardwaj and Sudipto Kaviraj, pp. 224–228.

Sinha, S. (1974b), "Sociology of Religion: A Trend Report" in *A Survey of Research in Sociology and Social Anthropology*, Vol, II. Popular Prakashan, Bombay.

——— (ed.) (1977a), *Anthropology in India*, Vol. 1, *Cultural Anthropology*, Anthropological Survey of India, Calcutta.

Smelser, N.J. (1988), *The Sociology of Economic Life*, Prentice Hall of India, New Delhi.

Smith, T. (1980) "Christianity and Christian Institutions in Agra", Souvenir St. John's Church, Agra, Post Centenary Silver Jubilee, p. 33.

Sorenson G. (1988), "Internal and External Interwined: Five Obstacles to Development in India", *Gurunanak Journal of Sociology*, 9(1).

Srinivas, M.N. (1966a), *Social Change in Modern India*, University of California Press, Berkeley.

——— (1976), *The Remembered Village*, Oxford, Delhi.

——— et al. (eds). (1977), *Dimensions of Social Change*, Allied, Bombay.

Streeten, P. (1972), The *Frontiers of Development Studies*, Halsted, New York.

Stevensen, S. (1970), *The Heart of Jainism*, Oxford, London.

Smith, V.W. (1922), Akali Dal and Shriomani Gurudwara Prabandhak Committee. C.I.D. Report. Govt. Printing Press, Simala.

Suda, J.P. (1978), *Religions in India*, Sterling, New Delhi.

Tawney, R.H. (1926), *Religion and the Rise of Capitalism*, The New American Library, New York.

The Christian Missionary Today (ed) (1960), The Joint Section of the Board of Mission of the Methodist Church.

The Examiner (1946), The Examiner Press, Bombay.

The Hindustan Times (1978), August, 28.

——— (1978), "Indian Wind Blowing Through Church", 6th Dec.

Timberg, T.A. (1978), *The Marwaris: From Traders to Industrialists*, Vikas Publishing House, New Delhi.

Tonybee, A. (1947), *A Study of History, 1934–61*, 12 Vols., abridged to 2 vols., by D.C. Domerville, Oxford University Press, London.

Trevor-Roper, H.R. (1964), "Religion the Reformation and Social Change", in *Historical Studies*, (ed) G.A. Hayes Macoy, London.

Troeltsch, E. (1931), *The Social Teaching of the Christian Churches*, (Trans.) O. Wyon, George Allen and Unwin, London.

——— (1958), *Protestantism and Progress*, Beacon Press.

Vannini, F.F. (1981), *Hindustan-Tibet Mission*, OFM Capuchin, New Delhi.

Vidyarthi, L.P.(1970), "Socio-Cultural Implications of Industrialization in India: A Case Study of Tribal Bihar", Planning Commission, New Delhi.

——— (1978), *Sacred Complex in Hindu Gaya*, Concept. Delhi.

Vivekanand, S. (1970), *The Complete Works of Swami Vivekanand, Mayavati Memorial Edition*, Advaita Ashram, Calcutta.

Wand, J.W.C. (1952), *A History of the Modern Church From 1500 to Present Day*, Methuen & Co. Ltd., London.

Warner, W.K. (1971), "Structural Matrix of Development", in G.M. Beal, R.C. Powers and E.C. Cloward Jr. (eds), *Sociological Perspectives of Domestic Development*, Iowa State University Press, Ames.

Weber, M. (1930a), *The Protestant Ethic and the Spirit of Capitalism*, (Trans.), Talcott Parsons, 1958, Charle's Scribner and Sons, New York.

——— (1968b), *The Religions of India: The Sociology of Hinduism and Buddhism*, Trans. and Ed. by H.H. Gerth and Don Martindale, Free Press, London.

——— (1948), *From Max Weber: Essays in Sociology*, Tr. & Ed. By H.H. Gerth and C.W. Mills, Routledge and Kegan Paul, London.

——— (1964), *Theory of Social and Economic Organization*, Tr. by A.M. Henderson and T. Parsons, Free Press, New York.

——— (1963), *Sociology of Religion*, (Trans.) by E. Fischoff, Beacon, Boston.

Wilson, Bryan (1970), *Religious Sects*, McGraw Hill Co., New York.

Wilson, H.H. (1977), *A Sketch of the Religious Sects of the Hindus*, Cosmo Publications, New Delhi.

Yinger, M. (1970), *The Scientific Study of Religion*, McMillan Pub. Co., New York.

Zelliot, E. (1977), "The Psychological Dimension of the Buddhist Movement in India", in G.A. Oddie (ed), *Religion in South Asia: Religious Conversion and Revival Movements in South Asia in Medieval and Modern Times,* Manohar, Delhi.

Hindi Works

Bharilla, H.C. (1981), *Yugpurush Shri Kanj Swami, Kund-Kund Kahan* Degambar Jain Tirtha Suraksha Trust, Jaipur.

Duggad, H. (1979), *Madhya Asia Aur Punjab Main Jain Dharma*, Jain Prachin Sahitya Prakashan Mandir, Delhi.

Jain, J.B., *Itihas Mein Mahavir Ka Sthan*, Shri Mahavir Prakashan, Aligarh, U.P.

Jain, P.R. (1989), *Sri Vijayanad Suri, Mahatara Sadvi*, Sh. Mrigvatiji Foundation, Delhi.

Singh, Achal (1935), *Jail Main Mera Jainabhyas*, Achal Granthamala, Agra.

Singh, Nahar (1956), *Namdhari Itihas*, Eastern Printing Press, Delhi.

Index